LEARN SPANISH FOR BEGINNERS & INTERMEDIATES

4 Books in 1 – 20 Lessons: Spanish Grammar with 1500+ Common Words & Phrases, 500+ Useful Conversations + 20 SHORT and FUNNY STORIES + Questions & Exercises

Copyright © 2022

- Marissa Noble & Juan Mendez -

All rights reserved.

LEARN SPANISH IN YOUR CAR for beginners

The Ultimate Easy Spanish Learning: How to Learn Spanish Language Vocabulary like crazy with over 1500 Common Words & Phrases.

Lesson 1-5
VOL. 1

Contents

Lesson 1-5 VOL.1

FIRST CHAPTER: Let's start from the basics 11
    1.1 Pronunciation in Spanish 11
    1.2 Pronouns 14
    1.3 Articles 15
    1.4 Adjectives 17
    1.5 Adverbs 18
    1.6 To be & to have 23

SECOND CHAPTER: Let's add something new to your Spanish vocabulary 30
    2.1 Numbers, numerals and ordinals 30
    2.2 Colours 33
    2.3 Days and months 35
    2.4 Date and time 38
    2.5 Family and Relatives 44

THIRD CHAPTER: Nature, animals and Geography 46
    3.1 Plants 46
    3.2 Animals (farm, sea, pets etc) 47
    3.3 Geography and Landscapes 50
    3.4 Towns (main towns and capitals around the globe) 53

FOURTH CHAPTER: Sport & Music 56
    4.1 Sports (indoor, outdoor) 56
    4.2 Music (all main types of music) 57
    4.3 Technology & Science 59
    4.4 Schools & Education 60

FIFTH CHAPTER: Food, Drinks & Clothes 62
   5.1 Food (different type of food) 62
   5.2 Drinks (different type of Drinks) 71
   5.3 Meals (different type of meals) 73
   5.4 Clothing 74
BONUS CHAPTER: Tips & Tricks to learn quickly a new language 77
Conclusion..79

Lesson 6-10 VOL.2

INTRODUCTION.. 81
FIRST CHAPTER: We are Travelers (Somos viajeros).......82
   1.1 Directions 82
   1.2 On the street... 85
   1.3 How to book 87
   1.4 How to get informations 89
   1.5 Useful phrases for Hotel accommodation 91
SECOND CHAPTER: Getting to know people (Conociendo a gente) 95
   2.1 Getting to know people... 95
   2.2 Getting to know each other: introducing myself 98
   2.3 Apologise/thank someone 100
   2.4 Complimenting..104
   2.5 Greetings, farewells and courtesy 107
THIRD CHAPTER: Jobs and common situations (Trabajo y situaciones comunes) 110
   3.1 Make an appointment (Pedir una cita) 110
   3.2 Make an Interview (Hacer una entrevsita).................................. 113
   3.3 Different Occupations (Distintos trabajos y oficios) 117

3.4 At the Restaurant (En el restaurante) 121
3.5 At the Hotel (En el hotel) 122
3.6 At the shop floor (En la tienda) 125
FOURTH CHAPTER: Free time & Fun (Tiempo libre y diversión) 127
4.1. Food and drink (Comida y bebida) 127
4.3 Shopping (De compras) 133
4.4 Clothing 136
FIFTH CHAPTER: Expressions, proverbs and sayings 139
CONCLUSIONS 152

Lesson 11-20
VOL.3

INTRODUCTION 155
FIRST CHAPTER: Back to Pronunciation 156
SECOND CHAPTER: Regular verbs in present, past and future 161
THIRD CHAPTER: Vocabulary review 185
FOURTH CHAPTER: Irregular Verbs and how to conjugate 222
FIFTH CHAPTER: Subjunctive, conditional and Imperative 243
BONUS CHAPTER: Tips & Tricks to improve faster our Intermediate Spanish 255
CONCLUSIONS 257

Final Lesson VOL. 4

EN LA FIESTA DE ROSA **262**
    AT ROSA'S PARTY (translation) 263
UNA CENA EN EL RESTAURANTE EL CASTILLO **266**
    DINNER AT EL CASTILLO RESTAURANT (translation) 268
UNA NUEVA MASCOTA **271**
    A NEW PET (translation) 272
PERDIDO EN LA CIUDAD **275**
    LOST IN THE CITY (translation) 276
EL PRIMER DÍA DE CLASE **279**
    FIRST DAY OF CLASSROOM (translation) 280
ENCUENTROS EN EL METRO **283**
    ENCONUNTERS IN THE METRO (translation) 284
UNA CENA CON AMIGOS **287**
    DINNER WITH FRIENDS (translation) 288
VIAJE A ROMA **291**
    TRIP TO ROME (translation) 292
EN LA GRANJA **295**
    AT THE FARM (translation) 296
RESTAURANTE EL VELERO **298**
    EL VELERO RESTAURANT (translation) 299
LA FAMILIA DE PASCUAL **302**
    PASCUAL'S FAMILY (translation) 303
MARC Y GINA **306**
    MARC AND GINA (translation) 307
EN EL AEROPUERTO **310**
    IN THE AIRPORT (translation) 311
RESACA **313**

HANGOVER (translation) 314
EL ULTIMO VERANO **316**
    THE LAST SUMMER (translation) 317
VACACIONES EN ESPAÑA **319**
    HOLIDAYS IN SPAIN (translation) 320
UN LAGO Y MILLONES DE ESTRELLAS **323**
    A LAKE AND MILLIONS OF STARS (translation).................................324
EMPEZAR DE NUEVO **327**
    START AGAIN (translation) 328
UN CACHORRITO LLAMADO KEN................................**331**
    A PUPPY CALLED KEN...332
PADRE E HIJO **335**
    FATHER AND SON (translation)...336

INTRO

Have you been thinking for a while about learning Spanish? Do you need extra motivation? Well, how about knowing that Spanish is spoken by more than 500 million people around the world? So it's useful, great! But, imagine you are travelling or you're going to work or to retire in a Spanish speaking country. Wouldn't be great to be able to communicate with local people and feel integrated? Let's face it, don't expect everybody is going to speak English everywhere and Spanish will let you know your "vecinos" and make new "amigos".

And more good news! Spanish is one of the easiest languages to learn for English speakers: both languages share around 1000 very similar words. But you'll have to work in the pronunciation!
So let's start and enjoy the journey!!

Ah, right!
I promised you the **MP3 AUDIO** files of the whole course as a Bonus right?
I have grouped THE WHOLE COURSE in 4 folders according to the topic covered, in total it is about 10 hours of narration that will take you step by step in your learning path.

IMPORTANT:
The link WORKS and MUST be copied respecting the characters, and written in the search bar (URL) on the Web.
The files are in MP3 format.
So make sure you have a device that supports audio files.
Any problem email me at: simona.lewis82@gmail.com

For MP3 AUDIO click here:
https://mega.nz/folder/sksEmRQL#G8TBEIhlq6zpNlget8ZLNw/folder/ps8iBa4T

Please note: The above course has been compiled to give you the opportunity to jot down any information you find useful, so you will find the text at times heavily spaced, you will find pages with lots of free space for you to practice writing so... take advantage of it and... ¡Feliz estudio!

FIRST CHAPTER: Let's start from the basics

1.1 Pronunciation in Spanish

Pronunciation is something you will have to practice, because that's a key difference between English and Spanish.

In Spanish they speak as they write. This means that words are pronounced exactly as they are written. In general, every letter has only one possible sound, although there are a few exceptions that will see below.

Spanish and English share the alphabet. Let's see the letters and some tips to pronounce them correctly.

We'll start for the vowels:

Letra (letter)	Nombre (name)	Consejos de pronunciación (pronunciation tips)
a	a	This letter sounds like *a* in "*cat*".
e	e	Sounds like the *e* in "*bed*".
i	i	Sounds like *i* in "*him*".
o	o	This letter sounds like *o* in "*song*".
u	u	This letter sounds like *u* in "*flu*".

Consonants in Spanish are same as English but with the addition of "ñ" (that can be typed on an English keyboard when pressing ALT+164)

Letra (letter)	Nombre (name)	Consejos de pronunciación (pronunciation tips)
b	be	This letter sounds like an English *b*.
c	ce	If before *a, o, u* sounds like the English *k in "kite"*. But before *e* or *i*, sounds similar to *th* in "*think*".
d	de	Like English.
f	efe	Like English.

g	ge	Sounds like an English *g* when before *a, o or u*, and similarly to the English *h* when before *e* or *i*.
h	hache	This letter is mute in Spanish, except when follows a *c* that sounds like English *ch*.
j	jota	Similar to English *h* in "hello".
k	ca	Like in English.
l	ele	Like in English.
m	eme	Like in English.
n	ene	Like in English.
ñ	eñe	*There is not any English correspondence but the sound is similar to ny in "canyon", best example can be found in the word "España".*
P	pe	Like in English.
q	cu	Always followed by the letter *u* and sounds like English *k*.
r	erre	Like in English.
s	ese	Like in English.
t	te	Like in English.
v	uve	Sounds like an English *b*.
w	uve doble	This letter has been imported from English to Spanish, hence sounds similar to English *w*.
x	equis	Like in English.

y	ye	Sounds like the *y* in English *"yes"*.
z	zeta	Sounds similar to *th* in *"think"*.

Now is practice time! ¡A practicar!

Say the following words focusing in their pronunciation:

Casa (house), beber (to drink), vivir (to live), gorro (hat), luna (moon), gato (cat), león (lion), jirafa (giraffe), perro (dog), zorro (fox), queso (cheese), tarta (pie), pastel (cake), hospital (hospital), carta (letter), pez (fish), silla (chair), chimenea (chimney), mesa (table), nariz (nose), hombro (shoulder), barriga (belly), vaso (glass), plato (plate), flor (flower), lápiz (pencil), papel (paper), carpeta (folder), maleta (suitcase), chaqueta (jacket), servilleta (napkin), reserva (booking), coche (car), gasolina (petrol), dinero (money), dirección (address), pulsera (bracelet), libro (book), película (film), fotografía (picture), museo (museum), funda (case), rebajas (sales), grande (big), sonreír (smile), ayuda (help), encontrar (to find), buscar (to search), pan (bread)

1.2 Pronouns

A pronoun is a word we use instead of a name, person or thing. We use pronouns when all the people in a conversation are already aware of who or what we are taking about. So, for example in English, when we talk about ourselves, we use the pronoun "I".
In Spanish the pronouns we use to refer to the subject of a sentence are called "pronombres personales".

English	Spanish
I	Yo
You	Tu
He / She / It	El (masculine) / Ella (for feminine) / Ello (undefined)
We	Nosotros (masculine) / Nosotras (femenine)
You	Vosotros (masculine) / Vosotras (femenine)
They	Ellos (masculine) / Ellas (feminine)

As you can see, In Spanish there are different forms for masculine and feminine words, and this happens not only with pronouns. Nouns, articles, adjectives have different gender in Spanish.
Although "it" can be translated into Spanish as "ello", this form is rarely used. Instead it will be used the original noun.

Some examples:
Yo soy arquitecto (I'm an arquitect)
Yo voy a comprar (I'm going to do some shopping)
Tú eres mi hermana (You're my sister)
Tú estás estudiando español (You're studying Spanish)
Él y ella son primos (He and she are cousins)
Él tiene 20 años (He's twenty years old)
Ella tiene veinticinco años (She's twenty five years old)
Nosotros vamos al cine (We're going to the cinema)
Nosotras estudiamos inglés (We study English)
Vosotras vais a llegar tarde (You're going to be late)
Vosotros tenéis que esperar diez minutos (You have to wait for ten minutes)
Ellos se levantan a las siete (They get up at seven)
Ellas están de camino (They are on their way)
Now it's time to practice more sentences:
Yo soy profesora (I'm a teacher)

Tu eres médico (You're a doctor)
Él es entrenador de tenis y ella es entrenadora de natación (He's a tennis coach and she's a swim coach)
Nosotras somos abogadas (We're lawyers)
Nosotros somos veterinarios. (We're vets)
Vosotros sois estudiantes (You're students)
Vosotras sois cantantes. (You're singers)
Ellos son cocineros (They're chefs)
Ellas son actrices (They are actresses)

1.3 Articles

In Spanish articles are used always. Article go always before a noun. In Spanish, articles have different gender and number matching the noun's.
"The" is used in Spanish following these rules:
"El" for masculine singular, "la" for feminine singular; "los" for masculine plural; and "las" for feminine plural.
"A" or "an" follow these rules in Spanish:
"Un" for masculine singular; "una" for feminine singular; and although sometimes "unos" (masculine) and "unas" (feminine) can be used in plural on specific contexts
Note: "Unos" (masculine) / "unas" (feminine) as plural forms of "un / una" usually find their English equivalence in the English determiner "some".
Deciding when using either "el", "la", "los", "las" or "un", "una", "unos", "unas" is same than in English.
The general idea is that "el", "la", "los, "las" are used when we are talking about something specific.
For example: "El libro que estoy leyendo me gusta mucho" (I love the book I'm reading). We are talking about a specific book and people in the conversation know which book is meant.
When we say "Voy a empezar a leer un libro" (I'm going to start reading a book), we refer to any (unspecific) book.

More examples:
La botella de agua es mía (The water bottle is mine)
La mesa está rota (The table is broken)
Las maletas están preparadas (The luggage is ready)
Las naranjas son dulces (The oranges are sweet)
El jersey rojo es de Pedro (The red sweater is Pedro's)
El gato negro esta en el jardín (The black cat is in the garden)
Los zapatos están rotos (The shoes are broken)

Los caballos están comiendo (The horses are eating)
¿Me traes un plato? (Can you bring me a plate?)
Necesito un tenedor (I need a fork)
Quiero unos calcetines nuevos (I want some new socks)
He comprado unos zapatos rojos (I have bought red shoes)
Busco una servilleta (I look for a napkin)
Necesito unas zapatillas nuevas (I need new trainers/sneakers)

Es hora de practicar más (It's time for more practice):

El pasaporte (the passport), los pasaportes (the passports), el billete (the ticket), los billetes (the tickets), el asiento (the seat), los asientos (the seats), el juguete (the toy), los juguetes (the toys).

La ventana (the window), las ventanas (the windows), la maleta (the suitcase), las maletas (the suitcases), la salida (the exit), las salidas (the exits), la escuela (the school), las escuelas (the schools).

Un vaso (a glass), unos vasos (some glasses), un pasajero (a passenger), unos pasajeros (some passengers), un refresco (a soft drink), unos refrescos (some soft drinks), un periódico (a newspaper), unos periódicos (some newspapers).

Una pasajera (a passenger), unas pasajeras (some passengers), una silla (a chair), unas sillas (some chairs), una camisa (a shirt), unas camisas (some shirts), una mujer (a woman), unas mujeres (some women).

1.4 Adjectives

Adjectives in Spanish follow the same rule about gender and number matching the noun's.

Sometimes same form is used for both genders.

To make the plural form from the singular one, you'll have to add an "s" when the adjective ends in vowel, and "es" when ending in consonant.

Examples:
El coche verde (The green car)
Los coches verdes (The green cars)
La mesa grande (The big table)
Las sillas pequeñas (The small chairs)
Note: Watch out! Unlike in English, adjectives in Spanish go after the noun most of times!

Más ejemplos (more examples):
La mujer joven (The young woman)
El hombre viejo (The old man)
Un gato negro (A black cat)
Una silla rota (A broken chair)
Las maletas pesadas (The heavy luggage)
Los pasaportes ingleses (The English passports)
Unos bocadillos calientes (Some hot sandwiches)
Unas bebidas frías (Some cold drinks)

Now practice the following sentences:
El bolso verde es grande (The green handbag is big)
Tengo dos perros blancos (I have two white dogs)
Mi jersey azul es demasiado pequeño para ti (My blue sweater is too little for you).
Mi vestido dorado te ira bien (My golden dress will suit you)
La casa vieja está más cerca (The old house is closer)

1.5 Adverbs

The difference between adjectives and adverb is that the first ones describe nouns whilst adverbs modify adjectives, verbs or another adverb. They tell us when, where or how the action of a verb takes place. Adverbs in Spanish are invariable, they don't change according gender or number because they don't modify nouns.

Here you can find a list of the most used adverbs.

Spanish adverb	*English translation*
Aquí	*Here*
Allí/alllá	*There*
Cerca	*Near*
Delante	*In front*
Encima	*On top*
Dentro/adentro	*In/inside*
Adelante	*Ahead*
Arriba	*Up / above*
Lejos	*Far*
Detrás	*Behind*
Debajo	*Underneath*
Fuera	*Out/outside*
Abajo/bajo	*Down*
Hoy	*Today*
Ayer	*Yesterday*
Mañana	*Tomorrow*
Anoche	*Last night*
Anteanoche	*The night before last*
Recientemente	*Recently*
Brevemente	*Briefly*
Diariamente	*Daily*
Todavía/aun	*Still/yet*
Nunca	*Never*
Ocasionalmente	*Occasionally*
Ahora	*Now*

Anteayer	*The day before yesterday*
Previamente	*Previously*
Actualmente	*Currently*
Permanentemente	*Permanently*
Frecuentemente	*Frequently*
Ya	*Already*
Siempre	*Always*
Semanalmente	*Weekly*
Muy	*Very*
Mucho	*A lot / much*
Menos	*Less*
Demasiado	*Too much*
Poco	*A little*
Más	*More*
Bastante	*Enough*
Nada	*Nothing*
Bien	*Well*
Mejor	*Better*
Rápido	*Fast*
Así	*Like this / this way*
Mal	*Bad*
Peor	*Worse/worst*
Además	*Besides*
Delante/antes	*Before*
Alrededor	*Around*
A menudo	*Often*
En lugar de	*Rather*
Tan pronto como	*As soon as*
Después	*After*
En breve	*Shortly*
Entonces	*Then*
Hacia	*Towards*
Hasta	*Until*
Mientras tanto	*In the meantime*
Pronto	*Soon*

Tal vez	*Perhaps*
Tan	*So*
Tarde	*Late*
Todos los días	*Everyday*
Usualmente	*Usually*
Generalmente	*Generally*
De vez en cuando	*From time to time*
Mensualmente	*Monthly*
Anualmente	*Annually*

Note: Similarly to the English termination of "ly", when adding "mente" to some Spanish adjectives, in its feminine singular form, the word turns into an adverb. E.g. "rápidamente" (quickly)

Ahora practica estas frases (Now practise these sentences):
Puedes dejar las maletas aquí (You can leave the luggage here)
Allí hace mucho calor, por eso no voy en verano (It's too hot there in summer, this is why I'm not going)
Mi casa está cerca, podemos ir andando (My house is nearby, we can go walking)
La farmacia esta delante del banco (The pharmacy is in front of the bank)
Creo que has dejado las llaves encima de la mesa (I think you have left the keys on the table)
¿Puedes poner los libros dentro de la caja? (Can you put the books inside the box?)
Sigue adelante y verás donde están los vinos (Go ahead and you'll see where the wines are)
Tenemos que colgar el cuadro un poco más arriba (We must hang the picture a little bit up)
París está lejos para ir en coche, pero podemos ir en tren (Paris is far to go by car, but we can go by train)
María venía detrás de mí, llegará pronto (Maria was coming behind me, she'll arrive soon)
Se ha escondido debajo de la mesa del comedor (She's hiding under the dining room table)
Ha parado de llover, podéis jugar fuera en el jardín (It stopped raining, you can play outside in the garden)

El restaurante está abajo, en el primer piso (The restaurant is downstairs, in the first floor)
Hoy voy al médico, pero mañana estoy libre (I'm going to the doctor today, but I'll be free tomorrow)
Ayer no fui a trabajar porque me encontraba mal (I didn't go to work yesterday because was feeling unwell)
Mañana iré a comprar el jabón que falta (I'll go to buy the missing soap tomorrow)
Anoche me acosté a las diez, estaba muy cansada (I went to bed at ten last night, was very tired)
Anteanoche salí a cenar con unos amigos y me acosté tarde (The night before last night I went out for dinner with friends and went to sleep late)
He cambiado de trabajo recientemente (I have changed my work recently)
He hablado con mi madre brevemente porque no tenía buena cobertura (I've talked to my mum briefly because she had very bad connection)
Voy al gimnasio diariamente antes de ir a trabajar (I go to the gym daily, before work)
Todavía estoy esperando la comida que he pedido (I'm still waiting the food I have ordered)
Nunca he estado en ningún país asiático (I've never been in any Asian country)
Fumo ocasionalmente, cuando voy a alguna fiesta (I smoke occasionally, when I'm attending a party)
Me ha dicho que viene ahora a arreglar el televisor (He has told me is coming now to fix the TV)
No veo a Carlos desde anteayer, más tarde le llamo (I haven't seen Carlos since the day before yesterday, I'll call him later)
Previamente al despegue, los asistentes de vuelo explican las medidas de seguridad del avión (Previously to take off, flight attendants explain the plane security procedures)
Actualmente estoy estudiando en la universidad (Currently I'm studying at University)
La tienda de helados está cerrada permanentemente (The ice cream shop is closed permanently)
Mi hermana me llama frecuentemente (My sister often calls me)
Ya he acabado, nos podemos ir si quieres (I'm already finished, we can go if you want)
Pedro siempre llega tarde (Pedro is always late)
El boletín de la universidad se publica semanalmente (University newspaper is published weekly)
Aurora es muy agradable, te gustará (Aurora is very nice, you'll like her)
Me gusta mucho la paella de marisco (I like seafood paella very much)
Miguel es menos alto que su hermano Raúl (Miguel is less tall than his brother Raul)
He comido demasiado, me duele la barriga (I've eaten too much, have tummy pain)

Hay poco pan, hay que comprar más para cenar (There's little bread, we must buy more for dinner)
Necesito más tiempo para acabar (I need more time to finish)
Ya tengo bastante vino, no quiero más, gracias (I have enough wine, don't want any more, thanks)
¡Gracias! De nada, ha sido un placer (Thanks! You're welcome, it was my pleasure)
Bien hecho, sigue así (Well done, keep going)
¿Que vino crees que es mejor? (What wine do you think is better?)
Ese coche va demasiado rápido (That car is going too fast)
Hazlo así, es más fácil. (Do it this way, it's easier)
Se siente mal por la discusión (He's feeling bad because of the argument)
Te sentirás peor si sigues bebiendo (You'll feel worse if you keep drinking)
¿Me puedes traer agua además de una servilleta? (Can you bring me some water besides a napkin?)
No te preocupes, le veo porque esta delante de mí (Don't worry, I'm seeing him because he's before me)
Verás el campo alrededor de la casa, es una zona maravillosa (You'll see the countryside all around the house, it's an amazing area)
A menudo me encuentro con la vecina de arriba (I bump into the upstairs neighbour often)
Tienes que ducharte antes de nadar en la piscina (You must take a shower before swim in the swimming pool)
En lugar de enviarle un mensaje, llámale (Rather to send him a message, call him)
Tan pronto como llegues a casa, nos vamos a comer (As soon as you arrive home, we'll go for lunch)
Aun/todavía no he recibido la carta del banco (I haven't received the bank letter yet)
Después de comer, iremos a visitar el museo (After lunch, we'll visit the museum)
En breve sabré si he conseguido el trabajo (I'll know shortly if have got the job)
Entonces fuimos a la habitación a dejar las maletas (Then we went to the room to leave the luggage)
Voy hacia el hospital (I'm going towards the hospital)
Esperaré hasta las dos de la tarde (I'll wait until 2 pm)
Mientras tanto puedes ir preparando tu maleta (In the meantime, you can pack your suitcase)
El paquete llegará pronto (The packet will be here soon)
Tal vez vaya a San Francisco el próximo verano (Perhaps I'm going to San Francisco next sumer)
Has aprendido vocabulario, así que vamos a practicar (You have learnt vocabulary so let's practice)

Hoy saldré tarde, pero podemos quedar para tomar un café (I'll go out late but we can meet to have a coffee)
Trabajo todos los días desde casa (I work from home every day)
Usualmente voy a trabajar en metro (Usually I go to work by tube)
Generalmente no como ternera, solo pollo (Generally I do not eat beef, just chicken)
Voy al cine de vez en cuando (I go to the cinema from time to time)
Mi empresa me paga el sueldo mensualmente (My company pays my salary monthly)
Celebramos una reunión familiar anualmente, desde hace diez años (We celebrate a family meeting yearly, since ten years ago)

1.6 To be & to have

Verb "to be" can be translated into two Spanish verbs: "ser" and "estar".
Using one or another will depend on the following rules:

"SER":
- **for physical descriptions**: Soy alta (I'm tall), soy rubio (I'm blond), ella es joven (She's young)
- **to talk about occupation**: Pablo es profesor (Pablo is a teacher), Marta es doctora (Marta is a doctor), Mi madre es escritora (My mother is a writter)
- **for time and day**: Hoy es lunes (Today is Monday), mañana es Martes (tomorrow is Tuesday), es la una de la tarde (it's one PM)
- **to talk about where someone is from**: Carmen es de Panamá (Carmen is from Panama), Juanma es de España (Juanma is from Spain), Yo soy de Escocia (I'm from Scotland)
- **to talk about family relationship**: Ramon es mi primo (Ramon is my cousin), Rosa es mi hermana (Rosa is my sister), Aina es mi sobrina (Aina is my niece)

"ESTAR":
- **for positions**: Estoy detrás de ti (I'm behind you), Él está delante de mí (He's in front of me), Tú estás a mi lado (You're by my side)
- **for places**: Laura está en el supermercado (Laura is in the supermarket), estoy en el banco (I'm at the bank), estoy en el médico (I'm at the doctor)
- **for actions**: ¿Estás estudiando? (Are you studying?), estoy leyendo el periódico (I'm reading the newspaper), estoy hablando por teléfono (I'm speaking by telephone)

- **for conditions and circumstances**: Miguel está enfermo (Miguel is sick), yo estoy muy cansado (I'm very tired), Sara está aburrida (Sara is bored)
- **for emotions**: Mi madre está contenta (My mother is glad), estoy muy triste (I'm very sad), el bebé está molesto (the baby is upset)

A good help is taking into account that we'll normally use "ser" when talking about something permanent, that it's not going to change. For example: Soy la hermana de Marta (I'm Marta's sister). Being her sister is not going to change!
And oppositely we'll use "estar" when talking about something that is going to (or could) change. For example: "Estoy enfermo" (I'm unwell). It's supposed that the condition is not permanent (i.e. it was different in the past or will be in the future).

Note: When the verb is preceding a noun, only the form "ser" will be used.

More examples:
Juan es bajo (Juan is short)
Juan está enfermo (Juan is sick)
Paula es simpática (Paula is nice)
Paula está durmiendo (Paula is sleeping)

Here you can see the forms for "ser" and "estar" to be used in present tense:

	Ser	**Estar**
Yo	Soy	Estoy
Tú	Eres	Estás
Él/Ella	Es	Están
Nosotros/Nosotras	Somos	Estamos
Vosotros/Vosotras	Sois	Estáis
Ellos/Ellas	Son	Están

Ahora practica tú (now is your turn for practicing):
Yo soy argentina (I'm Argentinian)
Yo estoy sentado (I'm seating)
Tú estás enfermo (You're sick)
Ella es profesora (She's a teacher)
Él está esperando (He's waiting)
Nosotros somos primos (We're cousins)
Nosotras estamos haciendo cola (We're in a queue)

Vosotras sois hermanas (You're sisters)
Vosotros estáis enfadados (You're angry)
Ellos son padres (They are parents)
Ellas están estudiando (They are studying)

"TENER":
When not auxiliary, verb "to have" in Spanish is TENER. We use "tener" for:
- **Age**: Tengo cuarenta años (I'm fourty years old), él tiene dieciocho años (he's eighteen years old), tú tienes treinta y cinco años (you're thirty five years old)
- **To talk about needs**: Tengo que trabajar (I have to work), tengo que ir a la farmacia (I need to go to the pharmacy), tienes que llamar a tu hermano (you have to call your brother)
- **Possession, what someone has**: Tengo un coche azul (I have a blue car), tú tienes un gato marrón (you have a brown cat), ella tiene una casa vieja (she has an old house)
- **Physiological sensations**: Tengo hambre (I'm hungry), tengo sed (I'm thirsty), tengo sueño (I'm sleepy)
- **To express something we wish**: Tengo ganas de irme de vacaciones (I want to go on holidays), tengo ganas de verte (I wish to see you), tengo ganas de ver esa película (I wish to watch that movie)

Note: When "have" is used as auxiliary verb then, in Spanish, the correspondence will be "haber" (instead of "tener").

Let's see how to use "tener" in present tense:

	TENER
Yo	Tengo
Tú	Tienes
Él/Ella	Tiene
Nosotros/Nosotras	Tenemos
Vosotros/Vosotras	Tenéis
Ellos/Ellas	Tienen

¡Vamos a practicar! Let's practice!
Yo tengo tres hermanas (I have tree sisters)
Yo tengo una caravana nueva (I have a new caravan)
Tú tienes sed (You're thirsty)

Tú tienes una moto negra (You have a black motorbike)
Él tiene diecisiete años y ella tiene veinte (He's 17 years old and she's 20)
Él tiene una mochila naranja (He has an orange backpack)
Ella tiene un bolso morado (She has a purple handbag)
Nosotros tenemos que estudiar (We have to study)
Nosotros tenemos un piso compartido (We have a shared flat)
Nosotras tenemos que levantarnos pronto (We have to get up early)
Nosotras tenemos camisetas iguales (We have the same t-shirt)
Vosotros tenéis que llegar pronto (You have to be early)
Vosotros tenéis un armario viejo (You have an old wardrobe)
Vosotras vais a llegar tarde (You're going to be late)
Vosotras tenéis una mesa grande (You have a big table)
Ellos tienen ganas de comer en un restaurante chino (They wish to eat in a Chinese restaurant)
Ellos tienen un perro y un gato (They have a dog and a cat)
Ellas tienen ganas de comer en un restaurante japonés (They want to eat in a Japanese restaurant)
Ellas tienen dos conejos desde que eran pequeñas (They have two rabitts since they were kids)

There are some everyday expressions in which is used "tener" in Spanish, where in English it is common to use "to be". Let's see them:

- tener frío – to be cold

    Tengo frio, necesito una chaqueta (I'm cold, I need a jacket)

- tener calor – to be hot

    Tengo calor, voy a beber agua (I'm hot, I'm going to drink some water)

- tener hambre – to be hungry

    Tengo hambre, voy a comprar comida (I'm hungry, I'm going to buy lunch)

- tener sed – to be thirsty

    Tengo sed, voy a buscar un refresco (I'm thirsty, I'm going to get a soft drink)

- tener sueño – to be sleepy

    Tengo sueño, me voy a dormir (I'm sleepy, I'm going to sleep)

- tener años – to be years old

    Tengo cuarenta años (I'm forty years old)

- tener miedo – to be afraid

    Tengo miedo, no quiero ver esta película (I'm scared, I don't want to watch this film)

- tener prisa – to be in a hurry

    Tengo prisa, te llamo mañana (I'm in a hurry, I'll call you tomorrow)

- tener cuidado – to be careful

    Ten cuidado cuando conduzcas (Be careful when driving)

- tener (la) razón – to be right

    Tienes razón, es major llegar pronto (You're right, it's better to be early)

- tener suerte – to be lucky

    No tengo suerte, no gano nunca nada (I'm not lucky, I never win anything)

- tener celos – to be jealous

    Tiene celos de su exnovio (She's jealous about her exboyfriend)

- tener éxito – to be successful

    Tiene éxito en su carrera profesional (She is successful in her professional career)

- tener (mucho) gusto en – to be (very) glad to

    Hola Emma, tengo mucho gusto en conocerte (Hello Emma, I'm very glad to meet you)

- tener gracia – to be funny

No tengo gracia para contar chistes (I'm not funny to tell jokes)

Now practise these sentences with "ser", "estar" and "tener":
Yo soy veterinaria (I'm veterinary)
Yo soy colombiano (I'm Colombian)

Yo estoy cansada (I'm tired)
Yo estoy dormido (I'm asleep)

Yo tengo un coche negro (I have a black car)
Yo tengo una casa grande (I have a big house)

Tú eres profesora (You're a teacher)
Tú eres ingeniero (You're engineer)

Tú estás enferma (You're sick)
Tú estás despierto (You're awake)

Tú tienes un perro (You have a dog)
Tú tienes una tortuga (You have a turtle)

Él es mi hermano (He's my brother)
Ella es mi hermana (She's my sister)

Él está leyendo (He's reading)
Ella está dibujando (She's drawing)

Él tiene un gato (He has a cat)
Ella tiene una hermana (She has a sister)

Nosotros somos bailarines (We are dancers)
Nosotras somos nadadoras (We are swimmers)

Nosotros estamos esperando (We're waiting)
Nosotras estamos estudiando (We're studying)

Nosotros tenemos un piso compartido (We have a sharing flat)

Nosotras tenemos una barca (We have a boat)

Vosotros sois irlandeses (You are Irish)
Vosotras sois muy habladores (You are very talkative)
Vosotros estáis enfadados (You're angry)
Vosotras estáis sentadas (You're seating)

Vosotros tenéis muchas bicicletas (You have a lot of bikes)
Vosotras tenéis pocas maletas (You have a few suitcases)

Ellos son españoles (They are Spanish)
Ellas son inglesas (They're English)

Ellos están aburridos (They're bored)
Ellas están pensando (They're thinking)

Ellos tienen un caballo gris (They have a grey horse)
Ellas tienen una vaca blanca y negra (They have a black and white cow)

More practice with to have "TENER"
Tengo frío, voy a ir adentro (I'm cold, I'm going inside)
Tengo calor, me gustaria estar en la playa (I'm hot, I would like to be on the beach)
¿Tienes hambre? ¡Vamos a comer! (Are you hungry? Let's go to eat!)
¿Tienes sed? Vamos a tomar algo (Are you thirsty? Let's go to have a drink)
Tengo sueño, necesito dormir mas (I'm sleepy, I need to sleep more)
Tiene más años de los que aparenta (She/he is older than she/he looks)
Mi hermana tiene miedo a las arañas (My sister is afraid of spiders)
Tengo prisa, lo hago luego (I'm in a hurry, I'll do it later)
Ten cuidado cuando conduzcas la moto (Be careful when you drive the motorbike)
Tienes razón, estoy de acuerdo con lo que dices (You're right, I agree what you're saying)
Ella tiene suerte porque tiene un buen trabajo (She's lucky because she has a good job)
Tiene envidia de su prima porque se va a Australia (He/she is jealous from her/his cousin because she's going to Australia)
Es un músico que tiene mucho éxito desde el principio (He's a musician successful since the beginning)
He tenido mucho gusto en conocer a su marido (It's been a pleasure to know her husband)
Emma tiene mucha gracia contando chistes (Emma is very funny telling jokes)

SECOND CHAPTER: Let's add something new to your Spanish vocabulary

2.1 Numbers, numerals and ordinals

Knowing the numbers will be helpful to tell our age, a telephone number or to ask for prices and directions, so let's count in Spanish!
We'll start by cardinal numbers.

1 – uno (one)	**22 – veintidós (twenty two)**
2 – dos (two)	23 - veintitrés (twenty three)
3 – tres (three)	24 - veinticuatro (twenty four)
4 – cuatro (four)	25 - veinticinco (twenty five)
5 – cinco (five)	26 - veintiséis (twenty six)
6 – seis (six)	27 - veintisiete (twenty seven)
7 – siete (seven)	28 - veintiocho (twenty eight)
8 – ocho (eight)	29 - veintinueve (twenty nine)
9 – nueve (nine)	30 - treinta (thirty)
10 – diez (ten)	31 - treinta y uno (thirty one)
11 – once (eleven)	32 - treinta y dos (thirty two)
12 – doce (twelve)	33 - treinta y tres (thirty three)
13 – trece (thirteen)	**40 – cuarenta (fourty)**
14 – catorce (fourteen)	41 - cuarenta y uno (fourty one)
15 – quince (fifteen)	42 - cuarenta y dos (forty two)
16 – dieciséis (sixteen)	50 – cincuenta (fifty)
17 – diecisiete (seventeen)	**60 – sesenta (sixty)**

18 – dieciocho (eighteen)	70 – setenta (seventy)
19 – diecinueve (nineteen)	80 – ochenta (eighty)
20 – veinte (twenty)	90 – noventa (ninety)
21 – veintiuno (twenty one)	100 – cien (a hundred)

Things to consider:
Twenties from 21 to 29 are written and said with "veinti-" and a number from 1-9 (with no space in between).
Forming the numbers from 31 to 99 is easy. You just use a the multiple of 10 adding the conjunction "y" and a number from 1 to 9
So if someone asks us "¿Cuantos años tienes?" We can now answer "Tengo (number) años."
And if someone asks for our telephone number, we can give say it now!

Ahora practica tú:
Try to write down the following telephone numbers:
655487912: seis, cinco, cinco, cuatro, ocho, siete, nueve, uno, dos (six, five, five, four, eight, seven, nine, one, two)
076543217869: cero, siete, seis, cinco, cuatro, tres, dos, uno, siete, ocho, seis, nueve (zero, seven, six, five, four, three, two, one, seven, eight, six, nine)
944320788: nueve cuatro cuatro tres dos zero siete ocho ocho (nine, four, four, three, two, zero, seven, eight, eight)

If we must give an international telephone number with country code, we will say it like that:
+ 34 912345564: más treinta y cuatro (plus thirty-four), nueve, uno, dos, tres, cuatro, cinco, cinco, seis, cuatro (nine, one, two, three, four, five, five, six, four)

Now try to guess the following Spanish numbers:
Cinco (five)
Doce (twelve)
Veintiuno (twenty one)
Treinta y seis (thirty six)
Cuarenta (fourty)
Cincuenta y nueve (fifty nine)

Sesenta y dos (sixty two)
Setenta y ocho (seventy eight)
Ochenta y ocho (eighty eight)
Noventa y uno (ninety one)

Now that we know how to say our telephone number, let's learn the ordinals numbers. These will be helpful when we speak about floors in a building or the order to follow.

1st	**primer, primero /-a**	First
2nd	segundo /-a	Second
3rd	tercer, tercero /-a	Third
4th	cuarto /-a	fourth
5th	quinto /-a	fifth
6th	sexto /-a	sixth
7th	séptimo /-a	seventh
8th	octavo /-a	eighth
9th	noveno /-a	ninth
10th	décimo /-a	tenth
11th	undécimo /-a	eleventh
12th	duodécimo /-a	twelfth
13th	decimotercero /-a	thirteenth
14th	decimocuarto /-a	fourteenth
15th	decimoquinto /-a	fifteenth
16th	decimosexto /-a	sixteenth
17th	decimoséptimo /-a	seventeenth
18th	decimoctavo /-a	eighteenth
19th	decimonoveno /-a	nineteenth
20th	vigésimo /-a	twentieth
21st	vigésimo /-a primero /-a	twenty-fir**st**
30th	trigésimo /-a	thirtieth
31st	trigésimo /-a primero /-a	thirty-first
40th	cuadragésimo /-a	fortieth
50th	quincuagésimo /-a	fiftieth

60th	sexagésimo /-a	sixtieth
70th	septuagésimo /-a	seventieth
80th	octogésimo /-a	eightieth
90th	nonagésimo /-a	ninetieth
100th	centésimo /-a	hundredth

As you can see, ordinal numbers in Spanish has masculine and feminine form, that will be determined by the noun.

Note: Although, in English, ordinal numbers are often used on dates, in Spanish will be used cardinal numbers. E.g. 3 de enero (3rd January)

Some examples:

Yo vivo en el primer piso, cuarta puerta (I live in the first floor, fourth door)
Sigue recto y en la segunda calle, gira a la derecha (Continue straight, and turn right on the second street)
Soy el quinto de la cola (I'm fifth in the queue)
El restaurante está en la tercera planta (The restaurant is in the third floor)
Los lavabos del quinto piso están cerrados (The toilets on the fifth floor are closed)

2.2 Colours

Knowing the colours in Spanish will be helpful and essential on basic conversations so... ¡Vamos a aprender los colores! (Let's learn the colours!)

Amarillo	Yellow
Azul	Blue
Rojo	Red
Rosa	Pink
Naranja	Orange
Verde	Green
Morado	Purple
Negro	Black
Blanco	White
Marrón	Brown
Gris	Grey
Oscuro	Dark

Claro	Light / clear

What colours are you wearing today? Say it in Spanish!

Practice:
La camiseta morada (The purple t-shirt)
Los pantalones azules (The blue trousers)
El abrigo rojo (The red coat)
Las gafas naranjas (The orange glasses)
Los pantalones negros (The black trousers)
Las fresas rojas (The red strawberries)
Las margaritas rosas (The pink daisies)

Note: Have you noticed anything? Yes, colours, when used as adjectives, have gender and number (as any adjective in Spanish!)

More examples:
La silla marrón (The brown chair)
Las mesas verdes (The green tables)
El armario amarillo (The yellow closet)
Los sillones negros (The black armchairs)
Los ojos azules (Blue eyes)
El pelo oscuro (The dark hair)

Now let's practice the following sentences with colours:
Hay tres libros rojos (There are three red books)
Tengo seis sillas amarillas (I have six yellow chairs)
He comprado un plato blanco y una taza negra (I have bought one white plate and one black cup)
El coche es azul oscuro (The car is dark blue)
La bicicleta es verde claro (The bike is light green)
El oso era marrón (The bear was brown)
Mi color favorito es el morado (My favourite colour is purple)
He perdido el bolso naranja (I have lost the orange handbag)
He encontrado un monedero marrón y rojo (I have found a brown and red purse)

2.3 Days and months

It's time now to start learning about days and months to be able to tell dates.

¡Vamos a empezar por los días de la semana! Let's start by the days of the week!
Lunes (Monday)
Martes (Tuesday)
Miércoles (Wednesday)
Jueves (Thursday)
Viernes (Friday)
Sábado (Saturday)
Domingo (Sunday)

Practice: Memorise and tell the days of the week in Spanish
Lunes, martes, miércoles, jueves, viernes, sábado, domingo
(Monday, Tuesday, Wednesday, Thursday, Friday, Saturday, Sunday)

Note: Unlike English, in Spanish, days of the week don't start by capital letter.

Let's practice more sentences:
El lunes voy al gimnasio (I go to the gym on Monday)
Los martes tengo clase de arte (I have art lesson on Tuesdays)
¿Vas a venir el miércoles? (Are you coming on Wednesday?)
No, iré el jueves (No, I'm coming on Thursday)
El viernes empiezo las vacaciones (I'm starting holidays on Friday)
El sábado y el domingo vamos a la playa (We're going to the beach on Saturday and Sunday)
Los lunes trabajo desde casa (I'm working from home on Mondays)
Tengo clase de yoga los viernes (I have yoga class on Fridays)
Los miércoles juego a basket (I play basketball on Wednesdays)
Estoy libre los jueves (I'm free on Thursdays)
Los viernes siempre jugamos a bolos, ¿te apuntas? (We always play bowling on Fridays, do you want to join us?)
El sábado nunca madrugo (I never get up early on Saturdays)
Los domingos viene mi familia a comer a casa (My family comes for lunch to my house every Sunday)

¿Y tú? (And you?) ¿Qué haces cada día de la semana? (What you use to do each day of the week?)

Now that we have seen the days of the week, let's learn the months of the year.
Los meses del año (Months of the year):
Enero (January)
Febrero (February)
Marzo (March)
Abril (April)
Mayo (May)
Junio (June)
Julio (July)
Agosto (August)
Septiembre (September)
Octubre (October)
Noviembre (November)
Diciembre (December)

Note: As on the days of the week, we don't need to use any capital letter on months in Spanish

Practice: memorise and say the months in Spanish, from January to December:
Enero, febrero, marzo, abril, mayo, junio, julio, agosto, septiembre, octubre, noviembre, diciembre.
(January, February, March, April, May, June, July, August, September, October, November, December)

More practice - Now listen randomly months of the year in English and try to say it in Spanish:
 May (mayo)
 December (diciembre)
 February (febrero)
 June (junio)
 October (octubre)
 March (marzo)
 August (agosto)

July (julio)
November (noviembre)
April (abril)
January (enero)
September (septiembre)

Now answer in Spanish:
¿Qué mes es tu cumpleaños? (What month is your birthday?)
¿Qué mes es el cumpleaños de tu padre? (What month is your father's birthday?)
¿Qué mes haces vacaciones? (What month are you going on holiday?)

And now practice the following popular sayings about months of the year. A popular say in Spanish is a "refrán".

En **enero**, se hiela el agua en el puchero (In January, the water is frozen in the pot).

Febrero, siete capas y un sombrero (February, seven layers and a hat).

Marzo varía siete veces en el día (March varies seven times a day).

En **abril**, cada gota vale mil (In April, every drop is worth a thousand).

Truenos por **mayo**, vientos a chorros (Thunder for May, jets winds).

Si en **junio** llueve, en invierno nieva (If it rains in June, it snows in winter).

Julio normal, seca el manantial (Normal July, dry the spring).

En **agosto**, frío al rostro (In August, cold to the face).

Buen tiempo en **septiembre**, mejor en diciembre (Good weather in September, better in December).

El agua de **octubre**, siete lunas cubre (October water, seven moons covers).

Si en **noviembre** oyes que truena, la cosecha siguiente será buena (If in November you hear it thunder, the next harvest will be good).

En **diciembre**, se hielan las cañas y se asan las castañas (In December, the reeds are frozen and the chestnuts are roasted).

2.4 Date and time

Well, we know the numbers, the days of the week and the months of the year, so let's learn how to tell times and dates.
Way to say the date in Spanish:
(the) number of the day of the month + of + month of the year + of + year

Some examples:
25/12/2019: (el) veinticinco de diciembre de dos mil diecinueve (Twenty fifth of December two thousand nineteen)
14/02/2000: (el) catorce de febrero del dos mil (Fourteen of February two thousand)
03/08/1998: (el) tres de agosto de mil novecientos noventa y ocho (Third of August nineteen ninety eight)
15/06/1977 (el) quince de junio de mil novecientos setenta y siete (Fifteen of June nineteen seventy seven)
29/02/1987 (el) veintinueve de febrero de mil novecientos ochenta y siete (Twenty nine of February nineteen eighty seven)

Practice the following dates to see the difference between English and Spanish:

March 5th	(el) cinco de marzo
October 3rd	(el) tres de octubre
July 17th	(el) diecisiete de julio
September 22nd	(el) veintidós de septiembre
January 7th	(el) siete de enero

December 25th   (el) veinte y cinco de diciembre

The years are said in thousands and hundreds, as a cardinal number.
1000: mil (a thousand)
2000: dos mil (two thousand)
3000: tres mil (three thousand)
4000: cuatro mil (four thousand)
5000: cinco mil (five thousand)
6000: seis mil (six thousand)
7000: siete mil (seven thousand)
8000: ocho mil (eight thousand)
9000: nueve mil (nine thousand)
900: novecientos (nine hundred)
800: ochocientos (eight hundred)
700: setecientos (seven hundred)
600: seiscientos (six hundred)
500: quinientos (five hundred)
400: cuatrocientos (four hundred)
300: trescientos (three hundred)
200: doscientos (two hundred)
100: cien (a hundred)

Some examples:
- **2019** dos mil diecinueve (two thousand nineteen)
- **2015** dos mil quince (two thousand fifteen)
- **2010** dos mil diez (two thousand ten)
- **2003** dos mil tres (two thousand tree)
- **1999** mil novecientos noventa y nueve (one thousand nine hundred ninety nine)
- **1980** mil novecientos ochenta (one thousand nine hundred eighty)
- **1975** mil novecientos setenta y cinco (one thousand nine hundred seventy five)
- **1888** mil ochocientos ochenta y ocho (one thousand eight hundred eighty eight)
- **1550** mil quinientos cincuenta (one thousand five hundred fifty)

Note: As in English, most of times years are written as numbers

¿Qué año naciste? (What year were you born?) Say it in Spanish!

Now let's practice telling dates:

25/12/2019 El veinticinco de diciembre de dos mil diecinueve (**twenty fifth of December twenty nineteen**)

01/01/2020 El uno de enero de dos mil veinte (first of January twenty twenty)

15/03/1986 El quince de marzo de mil novecientos ochenta y seis (fifteen of March nineteen eighty six)

23/08/1993 El veintitrés de agosto de mil novecientos noventa y tres (twenty three of August nineteen ninety three)

30/11/1967 El treinta de noviembre de mil novecientos sesenta y siete (thirty of November nineteen sixty seven)

And what about times?
Let's start seeing some useful questions:
¿Qué hora es? (What time is it?)
¿A qué hora es la cita? (What time is the appointment?)
¿A qué hora empieza el embarque? (What time boarding starts?)
¿A qué hora sale el último tren hacia Madrid? (What time is the last train to Madrid?)
¿Puedo cambiar la hora de la cita? (Can I change the time of the appointment?)

We'll need numbers 1 to 12 for hours, and 1 to 60 for minutes, so firstly, let's refresh them!

1	Uno (one)
2	Dos (two)
3	Tres (tree)
4	Cuatro (four)
5	Cinco (five)
6	Seis (six)
7	Siete (seven)
8	Ocho (eight)
9	Nueve (nine)

10	Diez (ten)
11	Once (eleven)
12	Doce (twelve)
13	Trece (thirteen)
14	Catorce (fourteen)
15	Quince (fifteen)
16	Dieciséis (sixteen)
17	Diecisiete (seventeen)
18	Dieciocho (eighteen)
19	Diecinueve (nineteen)
20	Veinte (twenty)
21	Veintiuno (twenty one)
22	Veintidós (twenty two)
23	Veintitres (twenty tree)
24	Veinticuatro (twenty four)
25	Veinticinco (twenty five)
26	Veintiseis (twenty six)
27	Veintisiete (twenty seven)
28	Veintiocho (twenty eight)
29	Veintinueve (twenty nine)
30	Treinta (thirty)
31	treinta y uno (thirty one)
32	treinta y dos (thirty two)
33	treinta y tres (thirty tree)
34	treinta y cuatro (thirty four)
35	treinta y cinco (thirty five)
36	treinta y seis (thirty six)
37	treinta y siete (thirty seven)
38	treinta y ocho (thirty eight)
39	treinta y nueve (thirty nine)
40	cuarenta (fourty)
41	cuarenta y uno (fourty one)
42	cuarenta y dos (fourty two)
43	cuarenta y tres (fourty tree)
44	cuarenta y cuatro (fourty four)
45	cuarenta y cinco (fourty five)
46	cuarenta y seis (fourty six)
47	cuarenta y siete (fourty seven)

48 cuarenta y ocho (fourty eight)
49 cuarenta y nueve (fourty nine)
50 cincuenta (fifty)
51 cincuenta y uno (fifty one)
52 cincuenta y dos (fifty two)
53 cincuenta y tres (fifty tree)
54 cincuenta y cuatro (fifty four)
55 cincuenta y cinco (fifty five)
56 cincuenta y seis (fifty six)
57 cincuenta y siete (fifty seven)
58 cincuenta y ocho (fifty eight)
59 cincuenta y nueve (fifty nine)
60 sesenta (sixty)

"¿Qué hora es?" is the Spanish way to ask "What time is it?"
Let's see how to answer that!
First, we will have to say the hour using the verb "SER" and after that we'll say the minutes.
But let's start with the o'clock hours (las horas en punto).
Es la una (It's one o'clock)
Son las dos (It's two o'clock)
Son las tres (It's three o'clock)
Son las cuatro (It's four o'clock)
Son las cinco (It's five o'clock)
Son las seis (It's six o clock)
Son las siete (It's seven o'clock)
Son las ocho (It's eight o;clock)
Son las nueve (It's nine o'clock)
Son las diez (It's ten o'clock)
Son las once (It's eleven o'clock)
Son las doce (It's twelve o'clock)

Note: If it's AM we'll say "de la mañana"; if it's PM we'll say "de la tarde" when there is still day light (or until 8pm approx.) and "de la noche" when it's dark (from 9pm).

Some examples:

To say 9:00 AM we will say "Son las nueve de la mañana"
10:00 AM - Son las diez de la mañana.
7:00 AM - Son las siete de la mañana.
8:00 AM – Son las ocho de la mañana.

To say it's 4:00 PM we will say "Son las cuatro de la tarde"
2:00 PM - Son las dos de la tarde.
6:00 PM - Son las seis de la tarde.
8:00 PM – Son las ocho de la tarde

To say 10:00 PM we will say "Son las diez de la noche"
9:00 PM - Son las nueve de la noche.
11:00 PM – Son las once de la noche.

Now let's see how to say hour and minutes.
In English we would say "It's five past two" or "It's ten to seven". In Spanish is a little bit different, since the hour is mentioned before the minutes.
"It's five past two" will be translated into Spanish as "Son las dos y cinco". That in English would be literally "It's two and five (minutes)".
"It's ten past seven" In Spanish we will say "Son las siete y diez" ("It's seven and ten").
"It's a quarter past one" In Spanish is "Es la una y cuarto". We use the word "cuarto" to indicate a quarter, 15 minutes.
"It's twenty-two past twelve": "Son las doce y veintidós".
"It's half past eleven": "Son las once y media". "Media" indicates half an hour.
Once minutes are passing half an hour, there are two ways to tell the time:
"It's twenty-five to six": "Son las seis menos veinticinco" That literally translated literally "It's six minus twenty five (minutes)", and we can also say "Son las cinco y treinta y cinco" ("It's five and thirty five").
"It's a quarter to eight" will be said either as "Son las ocho menos cuarto" (literally "It's eight minus a quarter") or as "Son las siete y cuarenta y cinco" (literally "It's seven and forty five").

The secret is to practice telling the time as much as you can!

Let's practise then!
¿Qué hora es? (What time is it?)
10:21 am "Son las diez y veintiuno de la mañana" (It's twenty one past ten)
8:50 am "Son las ocho y cincuenta" o "Son las nueve menos diez" (It's ten to nine)
9:20 am "Son las nueve de la mañana" (It's twenty past nine)
12:35 pm "Son las doce y treinta y cinco" (It's twelve thirty five)
Note: It's not necessary to specify if it's "mañana" (morning) o "tarde" (afternoon) when telling the time.

¿A qué hora sale el tren? (What time does the train leave?)
A las nueve y cuarto (At a quarter past nine)
¿A qué hora llega el avión? (What time does the plane arrive?)
A las 10 de la noche (At 10 pm)
¿A qué hora quedamos? (What time are we going to meet?)
A las cinco y media (At a half past five)
¿A qué hora es la cita? (What time is the appointment?)
A las nueve y veinte (At twenty past nine)

2.5 Family and Relatives

"La familia" (family) is really important in Spanish speaking countries and usually exists a strong bond.
Let's take a look and learn how to talk about our family members and relatives in Spanish.

¡Hola! Me llamo Carmen. Voy a presentarte a mi familia. (Hi! My name is Carmen. I'm going to introduce my family)
Tengo una hermana y un hermano (I have a sister and a brother).
Mi marido se llama Miguel (My husband is called Miguel).
Tenemos un hijo y una hija (We have a son and a daughter).
Mis hijos quieren mucho a sus abuelos (My kids love very much their grandparents).
La hermana de mi marido es mi cuñada (My husband's sister is my sister in law).

Los padres de mi marido son mis suegros (My husband's parents are my parents in law), mi suegra (my mother in law) y mi suegro (my father in law).

Mi hermana es la tía de mis hijos (My sister is my children's aunt) y mi hermano es su tío (and my brother is their uncle).
No tienen primos ni primas porque mis hermanos no tienen hijos (They don't have any cousins because my sister and brother don't have any children).

Now, try to answer the following questions about Carmen's family:

¿Cuántos hijos tiene Carmen? (How many children does Carmen have?)

Answer: Dos, un hijo y una hija. (Two, one son and one daughter)

¿Cómo llamamos a la hermana del marido de Carmen? (How do we say Carmen's husband sister in Spanish?)

Answer: Cuñada (Sister in law)

¿Cuántos hermanos tiene Carmen? (How many siblings does Carmen have?)

Answer: Dos, una hermana y un hermano (Two, one sister and one brother)

¿Como se llama el marido de Carmen? (What's Carmen's husband name?)

Answer: Miguel

Now try to answer the following questions about your family in Spanish using TENER (to have)
Note: Remember that we say "yo tengo" (I have)

¿Tienes tíos y tías? (Do you have any uncle or aunt?)
¿Tus padres tienen hermanos o hermanas? (Do your parents have any brothers or sisters?)
¿Tienes hijos? (Do you have children?)
¿Tienes sobrinos? (Do you have nephews?)

THIRD CHAPTER: Nature, animals and Geography

3.1 Plants

¿Te gusta la jardinería? (Do you like gardening?)
¿Te gusta la naturaleza? (Do you like nature?)
In case you have to buy flowers for someone, or you are going for a nature walk, let's learn some vocabulary to be able to talk about plants.

Flor	Flower
Flores	Flowers
Árbol	Tree
Árboles	Trees
Un ramo de flores	A bouquet of flowers
Rosas	Roses
Margaritas	Daisies
Amapolas	Poppies
Plantas	Plants
Hierba	Grass
Césped	Lawn
Planta de interior	Indoor plant
Planta de exterior	Outdoor plant
Árbol de Navidad	Christmas's tree

Let's put now these words in sentences:
¿Cuál es tu flor favorita? (What is your favourite flower?)
Mi flor favorita es la rosa (My favourite flower is roses)
Quisiera un ramo de flores, por favor (I would like a bouquet of flowers, please)
El jardín de la escuela está lleno de flores amarillas y naranjas (School's garden is plenty of yellow and orange flowers)
El campo está lleno de margaritas y amapolas (Countryside is plenty of daisies and poppies)
Margarita es también un nombre de mujer en español (Margarita is also a women's name in Spanish)
En la Toscana hay muchas amapolas (There are a lot of poppies in Tuscany)

No tengo ninguna planta en casa (I do not have any plant at home)
Mi gato muerde las plantas (My cat bites the plants)
Tengo que cortar la hierba del jardín (I need to cut the garden's grass)
Han cambiado el césped del campo de futbol (They have changed football field grass)
Wimbledon se juega en pista de hierba (Wimbledon is played on lawn's court)
Mi árbol de Navidad es de plástico reciclado (My Christmas's tree is made from recycled plastic)
¿Puedes recomendarme una planta de interior? (Can you advise me any indoor plant?)
Es una planta de interior muy bonita, gracias (It's an indoor plant very beautiful, thanks)

Es una planta de exterior así que la pondré en el jardín (It's an outdoor plant so I'm going to put it in the garden)

¿Me ayudas a decorar el árbol de Navidad? (Can you help me to decorate the Christmas's tree?)

3.2 Animals (farm, sea, pets etc)

¿Te gustan los animales? (Do you like animals?)
¿Cuál es tu animal favorito? (What is your favourite animal?)
¿Tienes mascota? (Do you have pets?)

Vamos a aprender vocabulario sobre animales. (Let's learn some vocabulary about animals!)
Animales de granja (Farm animals)

vaca	Cow
caballo	horse
cerdo	Pig
gallo	Rooster
gallina	Hen
oveja	Sheep
cabra	Goat
conejo	Rabbit
burro	Donkey
pato	Duck

Some sentences:
La vaca es grande (The cow is big)

El caballo es blanco (The horse is white)
El cerdo está gordo (The pig is fat)
El gallo y la gallina están durmiendo (The rooster and the hen are both sleeping)
La oveja está comiendo (The sheep is eating)
La cabra salta la roca (The goat jumps over the rock)
El conejo está escondido (The rabbit is hidden)
El burro está enfadado (The donkey is angry)
El pato está nadando (The duck is swimming)

¿Qué es una mascota? (What is a pet?)
¿Crees que todos los animales pueden ser mascotas? (Do you think all animals can be pets?)

Vamos a ver una lista de las mascotas más típicas (Let's take a look on this list of most typical pets):

perro	dog
gato	cat
tortuga	turtle
Pez	fish
conejillo de Indias	guinea pig
lagarto	lizard
serpiente	snake
hamster	Hamster
conejo	rabbit

Let's practice the following sentences about pets:
Mi perro se llama Bombón (My dog's name is Bombon)
Soy alérgico a los gatos (I'm allergic to cats)
De pequeño tenía una tortuga (When I was a kid, I had a turtle)
El pez de Alfredo es naranja (Alfredo's fish is Orange)
Tengo dos conejillos de indias (I have two guinea pigs)
No me gustan los lagartos (I do not like lizards)
Me dan miedo las serpientes (I'm scared of snakes)
A mi hermana no le gustan los hamsters (My sister doesn't like hamsters)
Hemos adoptado un conejo (We have adopted a rabbit)

¿Y tú? ¿Tienes mascota? (And you? Do you have a pet?)
¿Cuál? (Which one?)

Now practice these tongue-twisters about animals.
"El perro de San Roque no tiene rabo porque Ramon Rodriguez se lo ha robado" (San Roque's dog hasn't got a tail because Ramon Rodriguez stole it)
"Tres tristes tigres comen trigo de un trigal" (Three sad tigers eat wheat from a wheatgrass)
Note: In Spanish a tongue-twister is called "trabalenguas".

Más animals (More animals):

tigre	tiger
león	lion
elefante	elephant
jirafa	giraffe
rinoceronte	rhino
cocodrilo	crocodile
ballena	whale
delfín	dolphin
tiburón	shark
foca	seal
pulpo	octopus
oso	bear
camello	camel
leopardo	leopard

Let's make sentences about animals:

El tigre tiene rayas (Tiger has stripes)

El león vive en la sabana (Lion lives in the savannah)

El elefante africano tiene las orejas muy grandes (African elephant has a very large ears)

La jirafa corre deprisa (Giraffe runs fast)

El rinoceronte tiene dos cuernos (Rhinos have two hornes)

El cocodrilo es un animal muy peligroso (Crocodiles are very dangerous animals)

La ballena azul es el animal más grande de la Tierra (The blue whale is the biggest animal of the Earth)

El delfín es un animal muy inteligente (Dolphin is a very intelligent animal)

El tiburón más pequeño mide unos veinte centímetros (The smallest shark measures around twenty centimetres)

Hay focas en el ártico (There are seals in the Artic)

En España puedes comer pulpo (In Spain you can eat octopus)

No hay muchos osos en el Pirineo (There aren't many bears in the Pyrenees)

Hay camellos en el desierto (There are camels in the desert)

Los leopardos son más pequeños que los tigres (Leopards are smaller than tigers)

3.3 Geography and Landscapes

Now let's learn some useful vocabulary about geography and landscape.

lago	lake
latitud	latitude
llano	plain
longitud	longitude
bosque	forest
cabo	cape
campo	countryside
cascada	waterfall
continente	continent
costa	coast
desierto	desert
mapa	map
estanque	pond
golfo	gulf
hemisferio	hemisphere
isla	island
mar	sea
montaña	mountain
océano	ocean

playa	beach
prado	meadow
puerto	port
río	river
tierra	land
universo	universe
valle	valley
volcán	volcano
norte	North
sur	South
este	East
oeste	West
país	country
ciudad	city
pueblo	village
barrio	borough

Let's see now examples using these words:

El agua del lago está muy fría (Lake's water is very cold)

La latitud especifica si un sitio está en el norte o en el sur (Latitude specifies if a place is North or South)

El paseo es fácil porque es llano (The walk is easy because is plain)

La longitud especifica si un sitio está en el este o en el oeste. (Longitude specifies if a place is east or west)

Gibraltar está en un cabo (Gibraltar is situated in a cape)

Prefiero vivir en el campo que en la ciudad (I prefer living in the countryside than in the city)

Las cascadas del Niágara son muy famosas (Niagara waterfalls are very famous)

Asia es el continente más grande (Asia is the biggest continent)

Este verano viajaremos por la costa (This summer we'll be traveling along the coast)

En el desierto hace mucho calor (It's very hot in the desert)

¿Has encontrado el mapa? (Have you found the map?)

Hay peces en el estanque (There are fishes in the pond)

El golfo de México es el golfo más grande del mundo (Mexico's gulf is the biggest gulf in the world)

Argentina está en el hemisferio sur (Argentina is in the south hemisphere)

Mallorca es una isla (Majorca is an island)

El Mar Muerto tiene mucha sal (The Death Sea has a lot of salt)

Me gusta ir a la montaña a esquiar (I like going to the mountain to sky)

El océano ártico es muy frio (The Arctic Ocean is very cold)

Hay mucha gente en la playa cuando hace buen tiempo (There are a lot of people on the beach when the weather is nice)

La granja está situada en un prado (The farm is placed in a meadow)

Siempre hay muchos barcos en el puerto de Barcelona (There are always a lot of ships in the Barcelona's port)

Este río es muy largo (This is a very long river)

Hay mucha tierra sin ninguna edificación (There is a lot of land without any building)

Es universo es enorme (The universe is huge)

El campamento está en un valle (The camp is in a valley)

En Islandia hay volcanes (There are volcanoes in Iceland)

Canadá está en el hemisferio norte (Canada is in the north hemisphere)

Estados Unidos está al sur de Canadá (USA is at the south of Canada)

China está al oeste de Canadá (China is at the west of Canada)

Inglaterra está al este de Canadá (England is at the East of Canada)

Rusia es el país más grande del mundo (Russia is the largest country in the world)

Vivo en esta ciudad desde que nací (I live in this city since I was born)

Vamos a un pueblo que está cerca de la ciudad (We're going to a village that is near to the city)

Mi barrio es seguro para vivir (My borough is safe for living)

3.4 Towns (main towns and capitals around the globe)

¿Dónde vives? (Where do you live?)
Would you know how to say your city in Spanish? For example, London is Londres in Spanish.
Many sites keep their name unchanged in English and Spanish (or other languages), however there are also a lot in which, names will be translated (generally slightly).
Vamos a ver como se llaman algunas ciudades en español. (Let's see how to tell some cities in Spanish!)

Atenas	Athens
Bucarest	Bucharest
El Cairo	Cairo
Ciudad del Cabo	Cape Town
Copenhague	Copenhagen
Florencia	Florence
Ginebra	Geneve
La Habana	Havana
Estambul	Istambul
Lisboa	Lisbon
Londres	London
Luxemburgo	Luxembourg
La Meca	Mecca
Moscu	Moscow
Nueva Delhi	New Delhi
Nueva Orleans	New Orleans
Nueva York	New York
Filadelfia	Philadelphia
Praga	Prague
Estocolmo	Stockholm
Tokio	Tokyo
Túnez	Tunisia

Varsovia	Warsaw

Note: Although names keep unchanged (or largely similar), pronunciation can be very different.

Let's see some examples:
Atenas fue la capital de la antigua Grecia (Athens was the capital of the Ancient Greece)
Nuestra estancia en Bucarest fue deliciosa (Our stay in Bucharest was lovely)
No dejes de visitar el museo egipcio cuando vayas a El Cairo (Be sure to visit the Egyptian museum when you go to Cairo)
Hacer submarinismo en Ciudad del Cabo fue una experiencia inolvidable (Diving in Cape Town was an unforgetable experience)
Tenías razón, Copenhague es una ciudad muy limpia (You were right, Copenhagen is a very clean city)
Toda la ciudad de Florencia es como un museo (The whole city of Florence is like a museum)
En Ginebra se encuentran las mejores fábricas de relojes (In Geneve can be found the best watches' factories)
La música es parte esencial del alma de La Habana (Music is an essential part of Havana's soul)
Estambul conecta Oriente con Occidente (Istanbul connects East with West)
Las cafeterías en Lisboa son un lugar perfecto para relajarse (Lisbon's cafés are the perfect place to relax)
Londres es la ciudad europea que recibe más turistas (London is the European city that receives more tourists)
Luxemburgo es uno de los estados más pequeños del mundo (Luxembourg is one of the smallest states in the world)
Me dijo que tenía que visitar La Meca al menos una vez en la vida (He told me that I had to visit Mecca at least once in my life)
Moscú es una de las ciudades más caras del mundo (Moscow is one of the most expensive cities in the world)
Si no has estado en Nueva Delhi, no conoces la India (If you haven't been in New Delhi, you don't know India)
Si te gusta la música en vivo, no dejes de visitar los clubes de Nueva Orleans (If you like live music, be sure to visit New Orleans' clubs)
Por muchas razones, Nueva York es una ciudad muy cinematográfica (Due to several reasons, New York is a very cinematographic city)
Tom Hanks ganó el óscar protagonizando "Filadelfia" (Tom Hanks won the Oscar starring in "Philadelphia")

La invasión de turistas en pequeñas ciudades como Praga se está convirtiendo en un gran problema (Tourists invasion in small cities like Prague is becoming a big issue)
Algunas personas consideran Estocolmo como la ciudad más bonita de Europa (Some people consider Stockholm as the most beautiful city in Europe)
La ciudad con más habitantes del planeta es Tokio (The city with more habitants in the planet is Tokyo)
Muchas escenas de 'La guerra de las galaxias' fueron rodadas en Túnez (Many scenes from 'Star Wars' were filmed in Tunisia)
Por su ubicación estratégica, Varsovia ha sufrido mucho en todos los conflictos europeos del siglo XX (Because of its strategic location, Warsaw has suffered a lot during all the European conflicts on the 20th century)

Now is your turn. Try to say the following cities in Spanish:
Cairo (El Cairo)
Florence (Florencia)
Copenhagen (Copenhagen)
Tunis (Túnez)
Geneve (Ginebra)
New York (Nueva York)
Istambul (Estambul)
Moscow (Moscú)

FOURTH CHAPTER: Sport & Music

4.1 Sports (indoor, outdoor)

¿Qué deportes te gustan? (What sports do you like?)
¿Ves algún deporte por televisión? (Do you watch any sport on TV?)
¿Sigues alguna liga de deportes o competición? (Do you follow any sport league or competition?)

Let's see now some examples about main sports:

Baloncesto	Basketball	Cuando iba a la universidad jugaba a baloncesto.	I played basketball when I was at uni.
Fútbol	Football	Me gusta mirar el futbol femenino.	I like watching woman's football.
Tenis	Tennis	Rafa Nadal es un famoso jugador de tenis.	Rafa Nadal is a famous tennis player.
Natación	Swimming	Prefiero nadar en la piscina en vez de en el mar.	I prefer swimming in the swimming pool instead of the sea.
Beisbol	Baseball	Nunca he jugado a beisbol.	I've never been in a baseball match.
Boxeo	Boxing	No me gusta el boxeo.	I don't like boxing.
Criquet	Cricket	Los sábados juego a criquet con mis amigos.	I play cricket on Saturdays with my friends.
gimnasia	Gymnastics	Solía hacer gimnasia en el colegio.	I used to do gymnastics at school.
Balonmano	Handball	En España hay equipos buenos de balonmano.	There are good handball teams in Spain.
Jockey	Hockey	Me gustaría jugar a jockey.	I would like to play hockey.
Tenis de mesa	Ping-pong / table tennis	Nunca he jugado a tenis de mesa.	I've never played ping-pong.
Correr	Running	Salgo a correr todas las tardes.	I go running every evening.

Patinaje	Skating	Voy a ir a patinar sobre hielo.	I'm going to skate on ice.
Buceo	Diving	Estoy estudiando un curso de buceo.	I'm studying a diving course.
Atletismo	Athletics/track & field	¿Quieres venir a ver atletismo?	Do you want to come to watch athletics?
Voleibol	Volleyball	Juego a voleibol cuando voy a la playa.	I play volleyball when I go to the beach.
Esquiar	Skying	Voy a esquiar el próximo fin de semana.	I'm going to sky next weekend.

Practise now answering the following questions in Spanish:

¿Qué deporte se juega sobre hielo y con un stick? (What sport is played in ice with a stick?) (jockey)

¿En qué deporte de equipo tratan de encestar la pelota en un aro? (In what team sport, players try to score shooting to a hoop?) (baloncesto)

¿Qué deporte se practica en la nieve? (What sport is practiced in the snow?) (esquiar)

¿Qué deporte se juega con once jugadores por equipo en un campo? (What sport is played with eleven players by team on the field?) (fútbol)

4.2 Music (all main types of music)

A todo el mundo le gusta la música (Everyone likes music). Pero no a todo el mundo le gusta la misma música (but not everyone likes same music).

¿Qué tipo de música te gusta? (What kind of music do you like?)

Música clásica	classical music
Jazz	Jazz
Blues	Blues
Soul	Soul
Rock	Rock
Salsa	Salsa
Reggaeton	Reggaeton

Country	Country
Disco	Disco
Pop	Pop
Rap	Rap
House	House
Techno	Techno
Heavy	Heavy

Note: As you can see, most types of music are written the same in both languages, but the pronunciation would be different so let's practice it again!

Let's now practice the following sentences about music:
La música clásica me relaja (Classical music relaxes me)
Mi música favorita es el jazz y el blues (My favourite music is jazz and blues)
En este restaurante hacen conciertos de blues (There are blues concerts in this restaurant)
Bruce Springsteen es un cantante de rock (Bruce Springsteen is a rock singer)
Estoy aprendiendo a bailar salsa (I'm learning to dance salsa)
No me gusta el reggaetón (I do not like reggaeton)
La música country proviene de Estados Unidos (Country music comes from the United States)
En los años ochenta había música disco muy buena (In the eighties there was very good disco music)
Hoy en día hay muchos cantantes de música pop (Nowadays there are a lot of pop singers)
La música rap proviene de Nueva York (Rap music comes from New York)
La música house empezó en el año 1977 en Chicago (House music started in nineteen seventy seven in Chicago)
La música techno es un estilo de música electrónica (Techno music is a style from electronic music)
AC/DC es un grupo de música heavy (AC/DC es heavy music band)

Now answer the following questions in Spanish:
¿Qué tipo de música te gusta? (What kind of music do you like?)
¿Cuál es tu estilo de música favorito? (What is your favourite kind of music?)
¿Has estado en algún concierto recientemente? (Have you been in a concert recently?)
¿De qué estilo musical era? (What kind of music was?)

4.3 Technology & Science

Teléfono móvil (or commonly just "móvil") = mobile phone
He perdido el teléfono móvil (I have lost the mobile phone)
Mi móvil no funciona (My mobile phone is not working)
Me han robado el teléfono móvil (My mobile phone has been stolen)
Necesito un cargador para este móvil (I need a charger for this mobile phone)

Tableta = tablet
Llevo en la maleta mi tableta (I'm bringing in the suitcase my tablet)
No leo periodicos, leo las noticias en la tableta (I don't read any newspaper, I read the news on the tablet)
Quiero comprar una funda para esta tableta (I want to buy a case for this tablet)
¿Me prestas tu tableta? (Can I borrow your tablet?)

Ordenador portátil (or commonly just "portátil") = laptop
He traído el ordenador portátil (I have brought my laptop)
Estoy cargando mi portátil (I'm charging my laptop)
Mi ordenador portátil pesa mucho (My laptop is heavy)
Estoy trabajando con mi portátil (I'm working on my laptop)

Auriculares = headphones/earphones
¿Has visto mis auriculares? (Have you seen my headphones?)
He perdido los auriculares (I have lost the earphones)
¿Me pasas los auriculares? (Can you give me the headphones?)
Mis auriculares son inalámbricos (My headphones are wireless)

Operador de telefonía = Mobile network
¿Qué operador de telefonía me recomiendas? (What mobile network do you advise me?)
Tengo problemas con mi operador de telefonía (I'm having issues with my mobile network)
Quiero cambiar de operador de telefonía (I want to switch mobile network)
Las tarifas de este operador móvil son baratas (Rates of this mobile network are cheap)

Cargador = charger
Necesito un cargador para mi teléfono (I need a charger for my phone)
El cargador de mi ordenador portátil servirá para el tuyo (My laptop's charger will work with yours)
He olvidado el cargador (I have forgotten the charger)

Necesito un adaptador para enchufar mi cargador (I need an electric adapter to plug in my charger)

WIFI = WIFI (The same word, different pronunciation)
¿Me puedes dar la contraseña del WIFI, por favor? (Can you give me WIFI's password, please?)
No tengo datos y necesito WIFI (I do not have any data allowance and need WIFI)
Se ha colgado el WIFI (WIFI is frozen)
Estoy conectada en WIFI (I'm on WIFI)

Funda = case
Necesito una funda nueva (I need a new case)
Se me ha roto la funda del teléfono móvil (My mobile's case has broken)
Guarda el ordenador portátil en su funda (Keep the laptop in its case)
La funda de la tableta es negra (The tablet's suitcase is black)

Batería = Battery
Se me está agotando la batería (I'm running out of battery)
No tengo batería (I'm off of battery)
Necesito cargar la batería (I need charging the battery)
Me falla la batería, la tengo que cambiar (The battery is mot working properly, I have to change it)

4.4 Schools & Education

Escuela = School
Los niños van a la escuela (Children go to school)
Hay escuelas de primaria y escuelas de secundaria (There are primary and secondary schools)
Hay escuelas públicas y escuelas privadas (There are public and private schools)

Guarderia = Nursery
Los bebés pueden empezar la guardería con tres meses (Babies can start going to the nursery when are 3 months old)
Hay una guardería al lado de casa (There is a nursery next to home)
Mi hijo está en la guardería porque trabajo (My son attends the nursery because I'm working)

Colegio Universitario (universidad) = college

Estoy estudiando en un colegio universitario (I'm studying in a college)
He empezado este año un curso en la universidad (I've started this year a course at college)
Trabajo como profesora en un colegio universitario (I work as a teacher in a college)

Universidad = University
El año que viene empiezo la universidad (I'm starting university next year)
Mi hermana trabaja en la universidad (My sister works at university)
Este año cambio de universidad (I'm switching university this year)

Residencia de estudiantes = Student's residency
Vivo en una residencia de estudiantes (I live in a student's residency)
La residencia de estudiantes está al lado de la universidad (The student's residency is next to the university)
La residencia de estudiantes está cerrada (The student's residency is closed)

Carrera universitaria (commonly just "carrera") = University degree
Aun no sé qué carrera universitaria voy a elegir (I still don't know what degree I'm going to choose)
Hoy en día hay muchas carreras universitarias para elegir (Nowadays there are a lot of university degrees to choose)
El año que viene tengo que decidir qué carrera universitaria quiero estudiar (Next year I'll have to decide what degree I want to study)

Beca = bursary, scholarship
Ofrecen becas para profesores (They are offering bursaries for teachers)
No tengo ningún gasto porque tengo una beca completa (I do not have any expense because I have a full scholarship)
Ofrecen una beca al mejor deportista (They are offering a scholarship for the best sportsman or women)

Estudiante = Student
Soy estudiante, no trabajo (I'm a student, I'm not working)
He perdido mi carné de estudiante (I have lost my student card)
La tarjeta de estudiante ofrece descuentos (You have some discounts with your student card)

FIFTH CHAPTER: Food, Drinks & Clothes

5.1 Food (different type of food)

Well, it's time to rest and go to grab a snack, to have lunch or to enjoy a special dinner. In Spain is typical to have two different dishes for lunch or dinner. In fact, we can find a lot of restaurants offering menus with a special price offering "primer plato" (meaning first dish or starter) and "segundo plato" (second dish or main). Food quantity can be the same for "primer plato" and "segundo plato". After these two dishes, we can choose a dessert or coffee or both! It's typical to drink coffee after main meals in Spain, but if you think you are drinking too much caffeine, you can always order "café descafeinado" (decaf).

So, let's learn food vocabulary to avoid disappointment with the dish we have chosen. It's also important to be able to communicate clearly if or some of our group suffer some kind of food allergy or is on a special diet.

Some key sentences to order food and drinks:

Tengo hambre	I'm hungry
Tengo sed	I'm thirsty
¿Puedo ver el menú, por favor?	May I have the menu, please?
¿Qué me aconseja?	What do you recommend?
Quisiera…	I'd like…
¿Puede darme…?	May I have some…?
¿Podría darme más…?	Can I have some more…?
Eso es todo, gracias.	That's all, thank you.
¿Dónde está al baño?	Where is the toilette?
Camarero/Camarera	Waiter/Waitress
La cuenta, por favor	The bill, please
Tenemos una reserva	We have a booking/reservation
Soy alérgico/alérgica	I'm allergic

Las comidas durante el día (meals during the day)
- Desayuno = breakfast
  El desayuno se sirve de 8 a 10 de la mañana (Breakfast is served from 8 to 10 am)
- Aperitivo = snack, appetizer

Vamos a tomar un aperitivo antes de comer (Let's go for an appetizer before lunch)
- Comida = lunch
  Comeremos en un restaurant al lado del puerto (We're going to have a lunch in a restaurant next to the port)
- Merienda = snack at tea time
  Tengo hambre, ¿qué tal algo de merienda? (I'm hungry, what about a snack?)
  Note: "merienda" is after lunch and before dinner.
- Cena = dinner
  He reservado mesa para la cena en el restaurant Apolo (I've booked a table for dinner at Apolo restaurant)

Now that we know the meals, let's start with the food.
Trying to make it as easy as possible, let's learn the new vocabulary classified into categories.

Note: consider that in Spanish there are different verbs to say you're going to eat depending of the meal of the day.

"**Desayunar**" means eat or have breakfast.
"**Comer**" means eat or have lunch.
"**Cenar**" means eat or have dinner.

Let's dive into the food vocabulary now!

Desayuno (Breakfast)

Huevo	Egg
Bacon	Bacon
Tostada	Toast
Pan	Bread
Jamón	Ham
Queso	Cheese
Judías	Beans
Mantequilla	Butter
Mermelada	Jam
Sirope	Syrup
Cereales	Cereals

Yogurt	Yogurt
Salchichas	Sausages
Miel	Honey
Fruta	Fruit
Carne	Meat

Now is time to practice these sentences:

Normalmente tomo huevos para desayunar (Usually I get eggs for breakfast)

No suelo comer bacon (I rarely eat bacon)

Prefiero las tostadas con pan integral (I prefer brown bread toasts)

Quisiera un bocadillo de jamón y queso (I would like a ham and cheese sandwich)

Me gustan las judías con tomate (I like beans with tomato)

Voy a desayunar tostadas con mantequilla y mermelada (I'm going to eat for breakfast toast with butter and jam)

¿Tiene sirope para el pancake? (Can I have some syrup for the pancake?)

No tenemos cereales, lo siento (We don't have any cereals, sorry)

¿Me puedes traer un yogurt de fresa, por favor? (Can you bring me a strawberry yogurt, please?)

Me gustan las salchichas muy hechas (I like sausages well done)

Soy alérgico a la miel (I'm allergic to honey)

Me gusta la fruta fresca para desayunar (I like fresh fruit for breakfast)

No como carne, gracias (I do not eat meat, thanks)

Frutas (fruits)

Manzana	**apple**
Pera	pear
Naranja	orange
Plátano	banana
Sandía	watermelon
Melón	melon
Melocotón	peach
Fresas	strawberries
Cerezas	cherries
Arándanos	blueberries
Limón	Lemon
Aguacate	avocado

Example sentences:
¿Quieres un poco de tarta de manzana? (Do you want some apple pie?)
Me gustan las peras amarillas (I like yellow pears)
El plátano es típico de las Islas Canarias (Banana is typical from Canary Island)
Esta sandía es muy grande y pesa demasiado, escoge otra (This watermelon is too big and heavy, choose another one)
En España se come melón con jamón (In Spain you can eat melon with ham)
El melocotón es mi fruta favorita (My favourite fruit is peach)
De postre voy a tomar fresas con nata (For dessert I would like to have strawberries with cream)
¿Te gustan las cerezas? (Do you like cherries?)
Prefiero pastel de queso con arándanos (I prefer blueberries cheesecake)
Quisiera un té con limón, por favor (I would like a tea with lemon, please)
Voy a comprar un aguacate para hacer una ensalada (I'm going to buy an avocado to make a salad)

Vegetales y legumbres	(Vegetables and legumes)
Ensalada	Salad
Tomate	Tomato
Maíz	Corn
Brócoli	Broccoli
Apio	Celery
Calabaza	Pumpkin
Cebolla	Onion
Ajo	Garlic
Pimiento	Pepper
Guisantes	Peas
Lentejas	Lentils
Garbanzos	Chickpeas
Patatas	Potatoes
Puerro	Leek
Pepinillos	Pickles
Pepino	Cucumber
Col	Cabbage
Zanahoria	Carrot

Example sentences:

Quisiera una ensalada de primero (I would like a salad for starter)

Necesito comprar tomates para la ensalada **(I need to buy some tomatoes for the salad)**

¿Quieres maíz en tu ensalada? (Do you want some sweetcorn in your salad?)

No me gusta el brócoli (I do not like broccoli)

¿Cuál es la sopa del día? Sopa de apio y calabaza (What is the soup of the day? **Celery and pumpkin soup)**

La tortilla española lleva patata y cebolla (Spanish omelette is made with potatoes and onions)

El allioli lleva aceite de oliva y ajo (Allioli is made with olive oil and garlic)

Vamos a hacer pimientos a la barbacoa (We are going to cook peppers in the barbecue)

Podemos comer guisantes con jamón, si quieres (We can eat peas with ham, if you want)

¿Qué prefieres, lentejas o garbanzos con chorizo? (What do you prefer, lentils or chickpeas with chorizo?)

¿Te apetece una crema de puerros fresquita? (Fancy a cold leek cream?)

No me gustan los pepinillos (I do not like pickles)

Odio el olor a pepino (I hate cucumber smell)

Me gusta la col con patatas y zanahorias (I like cabbage with potatoes and carrots)

Carne	Meat
Pollo	Chicken
Pavo	Turkey
Ternera	Beef
Cerdo	Pig
Hamburguesa	Hamburger
Salchichas	Sausages
Bistec	Steak
Pastel de carne	Meat pie

Example sentences:

Hoy vamos a comer pollo al horno (Today we are going to eat roasted chicken)

Estas salchichas son de pavo (These sausages are made from turkey)

¿Quieres la hamburguesa de ternera o de cerdo? (Do you want beef or pig hamburger?)

Hoy tenemos barbacoa. Vamos a comer salchichas y hamburguesas (Today we have a barbecue. We are going to eat sausages and hamburgers)

¿Como te gusta el bistec? (How would you like the steak?)

He horneado un pastel de carne. ¿Quieres un poco? (I have baked a meat pie. Do you want some?)

Pescado y marisco	**Fish and seafood**
Almejas	Clams
Anchoas	Anchovies
Atún	Tuna
Bacalao	Cod
Calamares	Squid
Gambas	Shrimps
Cangrejo	Crab
Langosta	Lobster
Langostino	Crayfish
Lenguado	Sole
Mero	Bass
Ostras	Oysters
Pulpo	Octopus
Rape	Monkfish
Róbalo	Haddock
Salmón	Salmon
Sardinas	Sardines
Trucha	Trout

Example sentences:

En este restaurante sirven buen marisco (In this restaurant they serve good seafood)
¿Te gustan las almejas? (Do you like clams?)
No me gustan las anchoas, son demasiadas saladas para mí (I do not like anchovies. They are too salty for me)
Hoy he comido una ensalada de atún (I've had a tuna salad for lunch)
Me gusta el bacalao rebozado (I like battered cod)
En la paella de marisco hay calamares, gambas, almejas y mejillones (In the seafood paella there are squid, shrimps, clams and mussels)
De pequeño solía pescar cangrejos (I used to fish crabs when I was a kid)
La langosta suele ser muy cara (Lobster usually is very expensive)
No me gustan los langostinos, pero sí que me gustan las ostras (I do not like crayfish, but I like oysters)
Para mí, un lenguado con patatas, por favor (For me, a sole with potatoes, please)
Yo prefiero mero con ensalada, gracias (I prefer bass with salad, please)
¿Tiene pulpo a la gallega? (Do you have Galicia style octopus?)
Hoy tenemos rape y róbalo con guisantes y salsa (Today we are serving monkfish or haddock with peas and sauce)
Me gusta el sushi de salmón (I like salmon sushi)

En la costa brava puedes comer sardinas en una tostada (You can eat sardines in a toast in the Costa Brava)

En este río puedes pescar truchas (You can fish trout in this river)

Postres	Desserts
Arroz con leche	Rice pudding
Flan	Custard
Galletas	Cookies
Helado	Ice cream
Pastel	Cake
Tarta	Pie
Fruta fresca	Fresh fruit

Example sentences:

¿Queréis tomar postre? (Do you want anything for dessert?)

Yo sí, quiero un arroz con leche (I do, I want a rice pudding)

Para mí un flan (A custard for me)

Yo estoy llena, pero me comeré un helado (I'm full but I'll eat ice cream)

¿Quieres un trozo de pastel de chocolate? (Do you want a piece of chocolate cake?)

Prefiero un trozo de tarta de limón (I prefer a piece of lemon pie)

Hoy de fruta fresca tenemos melón y manzana (Today for fresh fruit we have melon and apple)

Estilos de cocina	Cooking styles
Al horno	Baked
A la barbacoa	Barbequed
Frito	Fried
A la parrilla	Grilled
En escabeche	Marinated
Hervido	Boiled
Crudo	Raw
Ahumado	Smoked
Estofado	Stewed
Pollo al horno	Baked roasted chicken
Bistec a la barbacoa	Barbecue steak
Pescado frito	Fried fish
Verduras a la parilla	Grilled vegetables

Atún en escabeche	Marinated tuna
Huevo duro	Boiled egg
Pescado crudo	Raw fish
Salmón ahumado	Smoked salmon
Carne estofada	Stewed meat
Pedir carne	**Steak ordering**
Crudo	Raw
Poco hecho	Rare
En su punto	Medium
Bien hecho	Well done

Now, let's listen more sentences about food and meals:
Yo desayuno fruta y cereales (I eat for breakfast fruit and cereals).
El hotel sirve la comida de 12 a 3 de la tarde (The hotel serves lunch from 12 to 3 pm).
Quisiera pollo al horno (I'd like roast chicken).
Vamos a cenar paella (We're going to eat paella for dinner).
Me gustaría cenar un buen bistec (I would like to have a good steak for dinner).
¿Qué quieres comer? (What would you like for eating?)
¿Tiene la carta en inglés, por favor? (Can we have the menu in English, please?)
Soy alérgico al gluten (I have gluten allergy).
Tengo alergia a los cacahuetes (I have peanut allergy).
¿Queréis tomar postre? (Do you want something for dessert?)
¿Os apetece un café después de la comida? (Fancy a coffee after the meal?)
¿Has hecho la reserva? (Have you made the booking?)
Hemos quedado a las 8 para cenar (We're going to meet at 8 for dinner).
El restaurante del hotel sirve desayunos, comidas y cenas (Hotel's restaurant offers breakfast, lunch and dinner).
¿Cuál es tu comida favorita? (What is your favourite food?)
¿Hay algún restaurante abierto cerca? (Is any open restaurant nearby?)
Este es un restaurante mejicano (This is a Mexican restaurant).
No me gusta el pescado crudo (I do not like raw fish).
Me gusta la comida tailandesa (I like Thailand meals).
Prefiero la carne al punto (I prefer meat cooked medium).
A mí me gusta la carne muy hecha (I like my meat well done).

Now, imagine you are in a restaurant and try to answer in Spanish the following questions:
¿Qué quieres de primer plato? (What do you want for starter?)

¿Qué quieres de segundo plato? (What do you want for main?)
¿Quieres postre o café? (Do you want dessert or coffee?)

How many foods can you remember in Spanish? Let's try it!

5.2 Drinks (different type of Drinks)

Now we are experts in food, so let's learn about drinks!
Let's start with these useful sentences:

¿Qué vais a tomar?	What do you want for drink?
Para mí una coca cola, por favor	A coke for me, please
Para mí un vino tinto, por favor	A red wine for me, please
Yo quiero un café	I want a coffee
Quisiera un agua con gas	I'd like a sparkling water
¿Algo más?	Anything else?
No, gracias	No, thanks
La cuenta, por favor	The bill, please

Let's listen this short dialog in a bar:
Buenos días, ¿qué vais a tomar? (Good morning, what are you going to drink?)
Yo quiero un café solo, por favor (I want an espresso, please)
Y para mí un café con leche (A latte for me, please)
¿Algo más? (Anything else?)
No, gracias. Es todo. (No, thanks. That's all)

Once we know the sentences, let's learn vocabulary to understand and be able to order different drinks in Spanish.

Café con leche	Latte
Cappuccino	Cappuccino
Café solo	Ristretto / espresso
Cortado	Macchiato
Té	Tea

Leche	Milk
Zumo	Juice
Refresco	Soft drink
Agua	Water
Agua con gas	Sparkling water
Vino	Wine
Vino negro	Red wine
Vino rosado	Rosé wine
Vino blanco	White wine
Cerveza	Beer
Combinado	Mixed spirit
Ron	Rum
Ginebra	Gin
Vodka	Vodka
Cóctel	Cocktail
Sin alcohol	Alcohol free

Now listen the following short texts:

En esta cafetería sirven distintos tipos de café: café con leche, capuccino, café solo, cortado, pero, si lo prefieres, tienen también té. (In this coffee shop are serving different types of coffee: latte, cappuccino, ristretto, machiatto, but, if you prefer, they have also tea.

¿Quieres tomar algo? Yo quiero una ginebra con tónica, ¿y tú? Yo quiero un combinado de ron con coca cola. (Do you want something to drink? I want a gin tonic, and you? I want a rum and cola mixed)

¿Nos puedes traer una botella de vino tinto, por favor? (Can you bring a bottle of red wine, please?)

Now that we know how to order food and drinks, let's put everything together!

¿Buenas tardes, qué vais a tomar? (Good afternoon, do you want something to drink or eat?)

Yo quiero un zumo de naranja (I want an orange juice)

Para mí un té con leche (A tea with milk for me)

¿Queréis algo para comer? (Do you want something to eat?)

Una bolsa de patatas, por favor (A packet of chips, please)

¡Enseguida! (Right away!)

How many drinks can you remember in Spanish? Let's say it!

5.3 Meals (different type of meals)

As you have seen when we were talking about food, we saw different types of meals during the day.
Can you remember? Let's try to say what is...
Desayuno? Breakfast.
Comida? Lunch.
Cena? Dinner.
Aperitivo? Appetizer or snack.
Merienda? Food we eat between lunch and dinner.

Let's make a quick refresh of types of the meal depending on the time of the day:
- Desayuno = breakfast
  El desayuno se sirve en el restaurante del primer piso (The breakfast is served at the first floor restaurant)
- Aperitivo = snack, appetizer
  ¿Os apetece tomar algo de aperitivo? (Fancy a snack?)
- Comida = lunch
  La comida se sirve de 12 a 2 de la tarde (Lunch is served from 12 to 2pm)
- Merienda = snack around tea time
  ¿Por qué no hacemos una merienda con chocolate caliente y churros? (Why don't we eat hot chocolate and churros at tea time?) **Reminder**: "merienda" is after lunch and before dinner.
- Cena = dinner
  Vamos a ir a cenar al restaurante del hotel. Me han dicho que la comida es estupenda (We're going to have dinner at the hotel's restaurant. They have told me the food is amazing)

But let's take a look now on different meals depending on the occasion:

Comida de negocios	Business lunch
Cena de negocios	Business dinner
Comida con amigos	Friends lunch
Cena con amigos	Friends dinner
Comida de Navidad	Christmas lunch

Cena de Navidad	Christmas dinner
Cena de despedida	Farewell dinner
Comida de despedida	farewell lunch
Cena de cumpleaños	Birthday dinner
Comida de cumpleaños	Birthday lunch

"Un banquete" is a banquet.
"Una celebración" is a celebration.
"Un festín" is a feast.
"Una fiesta" is a party.

¡Siempre hay una buena razón para una buena comida! (There's always a good reason for a good meal!)

More sentences:
Hoy tengo una comida de negocios (I have a business lunch today).
Mañana ceno con amigos (I'm having a friend's dinner tomorrow).
Este año la comida de navidad es en mi casa (This year Christmas lunch is at my house).
Laura se va de la empresa. La semana que viene es su comida de despedida (Laura is leaving the company. Next week we'll have the goodbye lunch).
Estoy preparando la cena de cumpleaños (I'm making the Birthday dinner).
Están preparando un gran banquete (They are preparing a big banquet)
¡Vamos a celebrar una fiesta! (Let's make a party!)

5.4 Clothing

Knowing vocabulary about clothes can be useful in some situations as shopping, packing or even if we must describe what someone was wearing.
Let's see the following list of clothes and related elements:

Cinturón	Belt
Blusa	Blouse
Botas	Boots
Botón	Button
Gorro	Cap
Abrigo	Coat
Algodón	Cotton
Franela	Flannel
Guantes	Gloves

Bata	Gown
Sombrero	Hat
Chaqueta	Jacket
Cuero	Leather
Chándal	Tracksuit
Corbata	Tie
Camisón	Nightdress
Pijama	Pyjamas
Bolsillo	Pocket
Impermeable	Raincoat
Bufanda	Scarf
Camisa	Shirt
Zapatos	Shoes
Bermudas	Shorts
Seda	Silk
Falda	Skirt
Zapatillas	Slippers
Calcetín	Socks
Traje	Suit
Gafas de sol	Sunglasses
Suéter	Sweater
Pantalón	Trousers
Esmoquin	Tuxedo
Ropa interior	Underwear
Chaleco	Vest
Lana	Wool
Cremallera	Zipper

Now let's put the new vocabulary in some sentences:
Necesito comprar un cinturón (I need to buy a belt)
Llevo una blusa de color rosa (I'm wearing a pink blouse)
Si vas a la montaña, mejor lleva las botas (If you're going to the mountain, better you wear boots)
He perdido un botón (I have lost a button)
Hace frio, coge un gorro (It's cold, take a hat)
He visto a Eva, llevaba un abrigo rojo (I have seen Eva, she was wearing a red coat)
Esta camiseta es de algodón y este jersey es de franela (This t-shirt is made of cotton and this sweater is made of flannel)
¿Has visto mis guantes marrones? (Have you seen my brown gloves?)

En el hospital hace frio, llévate una bata (It's going to be cold in the hospital, take a gown)
Hace mucho viento. Mi sombrero se ha ido volando (It's very windy. My hat has gone flying)
Me he encontrado una chaqueta de piel en el metro (I have found a leather jacket in the tube)
Tengo que comprar un chándal nuevo (I have to buy a new tracksuit)
No es obligatorio llevar corbata (Wearing tie is not mandatory)
¿Crees que le gustara este camisón? (Do you think she's going to like this nightdress?)
Quiero comprar un pijama de inverno (I want to buy a winter pyjama)
Pon las monedas en el bolsillo (Putt he coins in the pocket)
Llueve, coge el impermeable (It rains, take the raincoat)
María tiene una bufanda rallada (María has a striped scarf)
Tienes que llevar una camisa blanca (You must wear a white shirt)
¿Te gustan mis nuevos zapatos? (Do you like my new shoes?)
Juan tiene calor y lleva bermudas (Juan is hot and is wearing shorts)
No me gusta la seda (I do not like silk)
¿Tienes esta falda en una talla más grande? (Do you have this skirt in one size bigger?)
Quisiera estas zapatillas en el número cuarenta (I would like these slippers in a number seven)
Quiero unos calcetines negros de lana, por favor (I want a black wool socks, please)
Nunca llevo traje (I never wear suit)
He perdido las gafas de sol (I have lost my sunglasses)
Tengo un suéter amarill. (I have a yellow sweater)
¿Dónde has comprado estos pantalones? (Where have you bought these trousers?)
Está muy guapo con esmoquin (He looks very handsome wearing tuxedo)
Necesito comprar ropa interior (I need to buy underwear)
¿Quieres la chaqueta o el chaleco? (Do you want the vest or the jacket?)
Necesito cambiar la cremallera porque está rota (I need to change the zipper because is broken)

Now try to guess what clothes is:
Una camisa (shirt)
Un pantalón (trouser)
Una camiseta (t-shirt)
Unos zapatos (shoes)
Unos calcetines (socks)

¿Qué ropa llevas hoy tu? (What clothes are you wearing today?)

BONUS CHAPTER: Tips & Tricks to learn quickly a new language

¡Enhorabuena! (Congratulations!) You have started your Spanish learning journey and you have finished the first stage!

It can be overwhelming to learn a lot of new vocabulary and you can think"how am I going to remember everything I have learnt?".
No, it's not easy. The secret is that there is not any secret, you have to keep practising. Use it as much as you can is best advise you can get! But there are some tips and tricks to make the process less complicated.

Let's make a list of things we can't forget when we speak Spanish:

In Spanish we write like we speak; **every letter has an only sound** (most of times).

We always use articles before each noun, and noun has gender and number, that means that **articles, nouns (and also adjectives) must match gender and number**.

Unlike English, in Spanish **adjectives, most of times, go after the noun** (El libro rojo = the red book)

And tricks to keep practicing Spanish and enjoy doing it:

Make Spanish be part of your life.
Why not switch your mobile phone language into Spanish? You're likely using your mobile phone daily and if you have its menus in Spanish you will be learning same time you keep using it as usual, so no extra time needed. It will be tricky for the first days, but you'll get used shortly. You can also practice your Spanish and pronunciation with your mobile virtual assistant!

Learning a foreigner language takes effort and you can give up if you're feeling bored. **It will be easier if you read something you are really interested in, in Spanish**. Why not read about cooking in Spanish if you enjoy baking pies? Do you like sports? Try to read sports news in Spanish. Interested in music? The same!

You can also start watching some TV shows in Spanish, with English subtitles at the beginning, but switching to Spanish subtitles when you feel ready.

Listen Spanish podcasts or radios will also help.

You can read newspapers in Spanish as well. If you are interested into traveling to a Spanish speaking country, you can get informed about how things are there, reading the local newspapers.

Finding a pal to exchange language would be really good. There's always some Spanish speaker who would like to improve English, so meeting up for a café and practice both languages will be very helpful. Not just for learning the language, but for understanding better the culture and, of course, to make friends!

Fancy a **Spanish karaoke?** Why not! Is a funny way to practice the language.

If you are a board games lover, playing in Spanish is a good option to practice and keep learning Spanish. You can try to get the Spanish version of the game or **create your own Spanish board game.**

If you are more an old school learner, you can **create Spanish vocabulary flashcards**. Writing is also a good method to learn and memorize vocabulary. You can create different flashcards classified in different topics and you can then practice a topic per day.

> You have started the journey, and it's going to be a long journey, but starting is the most difficult stage and you have already done a lot so… **don't stop and keep going**!

Conclusion

Thank you for making it through to the end of "Learn Spanish in your car – Level 1", let's hope it was informative and able to provide you with all of the tools you need to achieve your goals whatever they may be.

We really hope you enjoyed this guide, customer satisfaction for us is very important.
If you found this book useful in any way, a review on Amazon is always appreciated! ☺

LEARN SPANISH IN YOUR CAR
for beginners

The Ultimate Easy Spanish Learning Guide: How to Learn Spanish Language Vocabulary like crazy with over 500 Useful Phrases.

Lesson 6-10
level 2

INTRODUCTION

¡Hola de nuevo! Hi again! Have you started your Spanish learning journey, or you are starting just now? Either way you are *bienvenido* (welcome) to this new book!

As you know Spanish is a useful language to know. Why? Well, it's spoken in twenty countries around the world as an official language and it's the second language with more native speakers. In United States is spoken by more than 40 million people!

But if you like travelling or you are considering moving for a while or permanently to a Spanish speaking country, knowing the language will do things easier. It's important to be able to communicate with local people for everyday situations. You can find people who speaks English in big cities (but it's not required to speak English everywhere, don't forget that), but if you like to visit and discover small villages, you'll need to know how to say things in Spanish.

We're going to learn Spanish vocabulary and sentences to get along in everyday situations such as bookings, ask and get directions, jobs and interviews, questions and answers to know people and some expressions very useful when we speak Spanish. Spanish is not a difficult language to learn. We can say that the most complicated competence about Spanish is the pronunciation, and the secret to achieve confidence on that is repeat, repeat and repeat again. You don't have to feel shame to make a mistake or to sound like an English speaker speaking Spanish. It's same in the other way! We all have our mother tongue, and this will influence when we speak other languages! So, try to relax and enjoy this Spanish learning adventure. Confidence is what you will need to achieve your goal, and confidence comes with practice!

Imagine a situation where you have a room booked but you must change the booking. It's a small rural hotel in the mountain, where there's no internet, so no email, and you have to give them a call. They don't speak English. Don't panic! You will learn how to tell in Spanish all the important things in Spanish to be successful with that call!

This book will cover several useful topics to make you feel you are not wasting time because you are learning useful Spanish. This book is not based in grammar rules, it's based in words and sentences. These will help you to learn vocabulary, and without being aware, to be used to the Spanish speaking way to make sentences.

Hoping you enjoy your journey, let's start to learn some Español! ¡Relájate y diviértete! (Relax and have fun!)

FIRST CHAPTER: We are Travelers (Somos viajeros)

1.1 Directions

Starting a journey is very ex   e are in a country and we have no clue of the language they are speaking. Even without knowing Spanish, if we can read Spanish words, we can guess what those means, because English and Spanish share more than a thousand words that are written the same way even having different pronunciation. But more than a thousand aren't all the words, so it's convenient to learn basic vocabulary when we are travelling through a Spanish speaking country.
So, let's think about travelling. What words are coming to our minds?

Tren	train
Autobús	bus
Autocar	coach
Entrada	entrance
Salida	exit
Mostrador	counter
Equipaje	luggage
Baño	toilet
Billete	ticket
Pasaporte	passport
Cola	queue
Asiento	seat
Abierto	open
Cerrado	closed
Avión	aeroplane
Pasajero	passenger
Reclamación	claim
Vuelo	flight
Despegue	take off

Aterrizaje	landing
Ayuda	help

Now let's put these words into sentences:

El tren hacia Sevilla sale a las 10 (The train to Sevilla departs at ten)

El autobús número treinta cuatro llega hasta la catedral (The bus number thirty four go through the cathedral)

Este autocar va desde Santiago de Chile hasta Valparaíso (This coach goes from Santiago de Chile to Valparaiso)

Espérame al lado de la entrada, llegaré en cinco minutos (Wait for me next to the entrance. I'll be there in ten minutes)

¿Dónde está la salida? No la encuentro (Where is the exit? I can't find it)

Puedes pedir información en el mostrador de la aerolínea (You can ask for information at the airline counter)

No llevo mucho equipaje, solo una maleta de cabina (I'm not bringing a lot of luggage, only a cabin size suitcase)

Necesito ir al baño (I need to go to the toilet)

No te olvides los billetes (Don't forget the tickets)

Necesitas el pasaporte para visitar ese país (You need the passport to visit that country)

Hay mucha cola para dejar las maletas (There's a long queue to drop off the luggage)

Mi asiento es el siete B (My seat is seven B)

El bar del tren está abierto de ocho a diez (The train bar is open from eight to ten)

El restaurante está cerrado hasta mañana (The restaurant is closed since tomorrow)

El avión viene con retraso (The plane is coming delayed)

Hay muchos pasajeros esperando el equipaje (There are a lot of passengers waiting for luggage)

Quiero hacer una reclamación porque han perdido mi maleta (I want to make a claim because they have lost my suitcase)

El vuelo con destino a Londres sale ahora (The flight to London is now departing)

Tenemos que abrocharnos los cinturones para el despegue (We have to fasten the seatbelts for taking off)

Vuelvan a sus asientos para el aterrizaje (Return to your seats for landing)

Necesito ayuda, no me encuentro bien (I need help, I'm not feeling well)

Let's practice more some handy words. Let's take a look at the following conversations.

En el aeropuerto (At the airport):
- Hola, buenos días. ¿Me ensenan los pasaportes, por favor? (Hello, Good morning. Can you show me your passports, please?)
- Aquí están (Here they are)
- Gracias. ¿Tienen alguna maleta para facturar? (Thanks. Do you have any suitcase to check?)
- No, solo llevamos equipaje de cabina (No, we only have cabin size luggage)
- Perfecto, aquí tienen sus tarjetas de embarque (Perfect, here you have your boarding passes)
- Gracias. Vamos hacia el control de seguridad pues (Thanks. Let's go the security control, then)

En la estación de tren (At the train station):
- Buenas tardes. Estoy buscando el tren que va a París (Good afternoon. I'm looking for the train to Paris)
- Saldrá en una hora desde el andén cuatro (It Will depart in one hour from the platform four)
- Genial, gracias (Great, thanks)
- ¿Hay bar en esta estación para hacer tiempo? (Is there a bar in this station to spare time?)
- Si, junto al andén uno (Yes, next to platform one)

Comprando un billete (Buying a ticket):
- Hola, quiero comprar un billete de avión de Málaga a Ibiza (Hello, I want to buy a ticket from Málaga to Ibiza). ¿Cuándo es el siguiente vuelo? (When is it the next flight?)
- Mañana por la mañana, a las diez y media (Tomorrow morning, at thirty past ten)
- ¿Hay asientos disponibles? (Are there any available seats?)
- Si, todavía quedan unos pocos asientos (Yes, there are still a few seats)
- Genial. ¿Cuánto cuesta el billete? (Great. How much is the ticket?)
- Son ciento diez euros (It's one hundred ten euros)
- Perfecto (Perfect)

1.2 On the street

We all know the importance to know how to ask for directions and to be able to understand the directions someone have given us when being a tourist. You can think we have google maps nowadays but even with that, you must have seen someone lost with the mobile phone in the hand asking a direction.

Let's start to learn the following useful sentences to ask for directions and indications:
¿Dónde está…? (Where is…?)
¿Dónde hay…? (Where there is…)

These two sentences are used in different context. When we ask "Dónde está" (where is) we are asking for a specific place. For example: "¿Dónde está la catedral?" (Where is the cathedral?). But when we ask "Dónde hay" we are not asking for any specific place. For example "¿Dónde hay una farmacia?" (Where is a pharmacy? The meaning of the Spanish questions is pretty similar to if we are asking in English "Is there any pharmacy close?".

Now, we continue with the sentences:
¿Me puedes decir dónde está…? (Can you tell me where is…?)
Estoy perdido o perdida (I'm lost) (**Note**: remember in Spanish we use different gender. In this case "perdido" is for male and "perdida" for female)
¿Está muy lejos? (Is it far?)
¿Cuánto tardo en llegar? (How long it takes to get there?)
¿Cómo puedo llegar? (How can I get there?)
¿Puedo llegar andando? (Can I get there walking?)
¿Debo coger algún transporte? (Should I get any transport?)

Now let's learn the basic verbs to understand the indications:
Girar (to turn around)
Atravesar (to cross)
Seguir (to continue)
Caminar (to walk)
Tomar (to take)

Examples with these verbs:

Sigue recto y en la tercera calle gira a la derecha (Continue straight and turn right at the third street)

What new vocabulary we can learn from this sentence?

Straight means "recto"

Rights is "derecha" in Spanish

Street is "calle" in Spanish

Atraviesa el parque y entonces gira a la izquierda (Cross the park and then turn left)

Left is "izquierda" in Spanish.

Park is "parque"

Camina tres bloques y el banco estará en la esquina (Walk for three blocks and the bank will be in the corner)

Blocks is "bloques" in Spanish.

Corner is "esquina" in Spanish.

Toma la primera calle a la derecha y sigue recto (Take the first Street right and then continue straight)

Now let's learn some locations and prepositions to understand the indications given:

- ✓ En frente de (In front of)
  La iglesia está en frente de la estación de autobuses (The church is in front of the bus station)
- ✓ Al lado de (next to)
  Hay un parking al lado de la gasolinera (There is a parking next to the petrol station)
- ✓ Detrás (behind)
  El teatro está detrás del cine (The theatre is behind the cinema)
- ✓ Entre (between)
  Yo vivo entre el colegio y la cafetería (I live between the school and the coffee shop)
- ✓ En la esquina (on the corner)
  Tengo el coche aparcado en la esquina (I have the car parked on the corner)
- ✓ Próxima (next)
  Es la próxima estación (It's the next station)
- ✓ Lejos (far)
  No está lejos, puedes ir andando (It's not far, you can go walking)
- ✓ Cerca (near, close)
  Está cerca, a cinco minutos en coche (It's close, five minutes by car)

1.3 How to book

When booking a flight, train, transport, etc... there are some facts that we need to know and that we have to specified before booking such us:

El origen (departing place)
El destino (destination)
La hora (time)
El número de pasajeros (Number of passengers)
El coste (The cost)
Si hay costes extras (If there are any extra costs)

Let's take a look at the following situations:

Quisiera reservar un taxi (I would like to book a taxi)
Para ir del Hotel Juan Carlos al aeropuerto (To go from Hotel Juan Carlos to the airport)
El lunes quince de agosto (Monday fifteen of August)
Necesito estar en el aeropuerto a las 12 (I need to be at the airport at twelve)
Tendrá que ser un coche grande porque llevo tres maletas grandes (It must be a big car because I'm bringing three big suitcases)
Gracias (Thanks)

Quisiera reservar un billete de avión para ir a Nueva York desde Madrid (I would like to book a flight from Madrid to New York)
No me importa el día o la hora (I don't mind any day or time)
Quiero la tarifa más barata (I want the cheapest fare)
Somos dos adultos y un niño de dos años (We are two adults and a two years old kid)
¿Cuánto cuestan los billetes? (How much are the tickets?)
¿Hay algún coste extra? (Is there any extra cost?)
Gracias (Thanks)

Quisiera saber los horarios del tren que va a Buenos Aires para reservar un billete (I would like to know the timetable for the train to Buenos Aires to book a ticket)
¿Cuál es el primer tren de la mañana? (Which is the first train in the morning?)
Quisiera un billete en primera clase (I would like a first class ticket)

¿A qué hora sale el autocar hacia el aeropuerto? (At what time departs the coach to the airport?)

¿Puedo comprar el billete el mismo día o es necesario reservar? (Can I buy the ticket the same day or I must book it in advance?)

Trick: It can be useful before making a call, to write down all the information and to have it translated into Spanish. As you are learning Spanish, you know vocabulary, but you can feel stressed by phone so to be prepared will do the process less stressful.

1.4 How to get informations

Now let's imagine the situation that we are at the airport, or at the train or bus station without a ticket, and we want to know the timetable before buying our ticket.

El horario (The timetable)
El primero de la mañana (The first in the morning)
El último de la noche (The last one in the night)
Directo (Direct)
Tarifa (Fare)

Querría saber el horario de trenes hacia Miami, por favor (I would like to know the timetable for trains to Miami, please)
¿Me puedes informar de los horarios de los próximos vuelos a Valencia? (Can you inform me about the timetable for flights to Valencia, please?)
Ya sé el horario de autocares hacia el aeropuerto (I already know the timetable for coaches to the airport)

El primer tren de la mañana sale a las seis y cuarto (The first train in the morning departs at a quarter past six)
El primer avión de la mañana sale a las siete y diez (The first plane in the morning departs at ten past seven)
El primer autocar de la mañana sale a las ocho y cinco desde el centro de la ciudad (The first coach in the morning departs at five past eight from city centre)

El último tren de la noche saldrá a las once y cincuenta (The last train in the night will depart at ten to twelve)
El último vuelo de la noche hacia Barcelona sale a las doce en punto (The last flight in the night to Barcelona departs at twelve o clock)
El ultimo autocar hacia el aeropuerto ya ha salido, lo siento (The last coach to the airport has already departed, I'm sorry)

¿Este vuelo a Nueva York es directo o hace escalas? (This flight to New York is a direct flight or has stops?)
Voy a ir en el tren directo porque tarda menos (I'm going with the direct train because it takes less time)

Este vuelo a Shanghái no es directo. Vuela vía Ámsterdam. Tendrás que esperar en el aeropuerto de Ámsterdam dos horas (This flight to Shanghai is not a direct flight. It flies via Amsterdam. You will have to wait in Amsterdam airport two hours)

¿Cuál es la tarifa más barata? (Which is the cheapest fare?)
¿Que está incluido en esta tarifa? (What is it included with this fare?)
Quiero una mejora (I want an upgrade) ¿Cuánto más tengo que pagar para incluir el equipaje? (How much I have to pay to include luggage?)

1.5 Useful phrases for Hotel accommodation

Once we are able to book a ticket, let's learn now some vocabulary and sentences to book accommodation and everything we will need to make our stay comfortable.

Hotel	Hotel
Albergue	Hostel
Pensión	Pension
Habitación individual	Single room
Habitación doble	Double room
Habitación triple	Triple room
Habitación familiar	Family room
Cama individual	Single bed
Cama doble	Double bed
Literas	Bunk bed
Cuna	cot
Habitación compartida	Shared room
Baño	Bathroom
Baño compartido	Shared bathroom
Desayuno	Breakfast
Comida	Lunch
Cena	Dinner
Servicio de habitaciones	Room service
Recepción	Reception
Gimnasio	Gym
Piscina	Swimming pool
Oferta	Offer
Reserva	Booking
Casa rural	Rural house

- El hotel está situado cerca de la Sagrada Familia

(The hotel is situated close to the Sagrada Familia)

- Hay un albergue muy bien valorado cerca del centro y no es caro

(There is a hostel very good rated close to the centre and it's not expensive)

- Solo hay habitaciones libres en la pensión de al lado de la estación de tren

(There are only available rooms at the pension next to the train station)

- Necesitaría una habitación individual para una semana

(I would need a single room for a week)

- ¿Tienes disponible una habitación doble para este fin de semana?

(Do you have available a double room for this weekend?)

- Somos dos adultos y un niño, necesitamos una habitación triple

(We are two adults and a kid, we need a triple room)

- Somos dos adultos y dos niños. ¿Disponen de habitaciones familiares?

(We are two adults and two children. Do you have available family rooms?)

- Prefiero dos camas individuales, gracias

(I prefer two single beds, thanks)

- ¿Podemos disponer de una cama doble, por favor?

(Can we have a double bed, please?)

- Las habitaciones familiares tienen una cama doble y unas literas

(Family rooms have a double bed and bunk beds)

- Podemos poner una cuna para un bebé si lo necesitas

(We can put a cot for the baby, if you need it)

- Nos queda una habitación compartida de chicas para esta semana

(We only have a girl shared room for this week)

- La habitación doble tiene baño completo

(The double bedroom has a complete bathroom)

- Podemos poner una cuna para un bebé si lo necesitas

(We can put a cot for the baby, if you need it)

- Nos queda una habitación compartida de chicas para esta semana

(We only have a girls shared room for this week)

- La habitación doble tiene baño completo

(The double bedroom has a complete bathroom)

- Hay un baño compartido en cada piso

(There is a shared bathroom in each floor)

- El desayuno está incluido y se sirve de siete y media a diez de la mañana

(The breakfast is included and is served form half past seven to ten in the morning)

- La comida se sirve en el restaurante de la planta baja de doce y media a cuatro de la tarde

(The lunch is served in the ground floor restaurant from half past twelve to four in the afternoon)
- La cena se sirve en el restaurante del último piso de siete de la tarde a diez de la noche

(The dinner is served in the last floor restaurant from seven in the evening to ten in the night)
- ¿Quieres pedir algo al servicio de habitaciones?

(Do you want to ask for something to the room service?)
- La recepción está abierta veinticuatro horas

(Reception is open twenty-four hours)
- Este hotel tiene un gimnasio en el segundo piso

(This hotel has a gym in the second floor)
- Lo siento, pero este hotel no tiene piscina

(I'm sorry but we don't have a swimming pool in this hotel)
- ¿Quieres la oferta con desayuno incluido?

(Do you want the breakfast included offer?)
- Tengo una reserva a nombre de Aurora Gutiérrez

(I have a booking. My name is Aurora Gutierrez)
- Este pueblo no tiene ningún hotel. Pero puedes reservar una habitación en una casa rural

(There no hotels in this village, but you can book a room in a rural house

There are some hotels that offer different types of accommodations including meals. For example:
Habitación con desayuno incluido (room with breakfast included)
Media pensión (room with breakfast and other meal, lunch or dinner)
Pensión completa (room and three meals included, breakfast, lunch and dinner)
Todo incluido (everything included, room, food and drinks all day long)

So take a look at this conversation:
- Buenos días. Hotel Playa Grande. ¿En qué puedo ayudarle?
  Good morning. Playa Grande Hotel. How can I help you?
- ¿Tenéis habitaciones libres para la semana que viene?
  Do you have available rooms for next week?
- ¿Qué tipo de habitación?
  What kind of room?
- Una habitación doble con cama doble, por favor.

A double room with double bed, please.
- Sí, tenemos habitaciones con la tarifa de media pensión, por cien euros la noche.
  Yes, we have rooms with the "media pension" fare for one hundred euros per night.
- Genial. Me gustaría hacer una reserva, pues.
  Great. I would like to make a reservation, then.
- Perfecto. ¿A qué nombre, por favor?
  Perfect. Your name, please?
- ¿Qué días necesitan la habitación?
  What days you need the room?
- Del lunes 3 (tres) al viernes 7 (siete).
  From Monday 3rd to Friday 7th.
- Perfecto. Reservada.
  Perfect. Booked.
- ¿Algo más?
  Anything else?
- No, gracias. Eso es todo. Hasta entonces.
  No, thanks. That's all. See you then.

SECOND CHAPTER: Getting to know people (Conociendo a gente)

2.1 Getting to know people

It's time to socialize and start knowing new people. And to do that we are going to learn some basics questions and how to answer these questions.

Let's start from the beginning:
- ¿Cómo te llamas? (What is your name?)
- ¿Cuántos años tienes? (How old are you?)
- ¿De dónde eres? (Where are you from?)
- ¿Dónde vives? (Where do you live?)
- ¿A qué te dedicas? (This is a typical Spanish question to ask about the profession. If we translate literally the question would be more or less "What you spend time on?")
- ¿Dónde trabajas? (Where do you work?)
- ¿Qué te gusta hacer en tu tiempo libre? (What do you like to do in your free time?)

Let's put the questions in a conversation and then learn how to answer.
- Hola. ¿Como te llamas? (Hi. What's your name?)
- Me llamo Carla. ¿Y tú? (My name is Carla. And you?)
- Yo me llamo Susana (My name is Susana)
- ¿Cuántos años tienes? (How old are you?)
- Tengo veintiséis años, ¿y tú? (I'm twenty-six years old, and you?)
- Yo tengo veintisiete (I'm twenty seven)
- ¿De dónde eres? (Where are you from?)
- Soy de Colombia. ¿Y tú? (I'm from Colombia. And you?)
- Soy de Argentina. (I'm from Argentina)
- ¿Dónde vives? (Where do you live?)
- Vivo en España. ¿Y tú? (I live in Spain. And you?)
- Vivo en París (I live in Paris)
- ¿A qué te dedicas? (What is your profession?)

- Soy profesora de música. ¿Y tú? (I'm a music teacher. And you?)
- No trabajo actualmente. Estoy estudiando (I'm not currently working. I'm studying)
- ¿Y qué estudias? (And what are you studying?)
- Estudio psicología (I'm studying psicology) ¿Dónde trabajas, Carla? (Where do you work, Carla?)
- Trabajo en una escuela de primaria en el centro de la ciudad (I work in a primary school next to the city centre)
- ¿Qué te gusta hacer en tu tiempo libre? (What do you like to do during your free time?)
- Me gusta ir al cine. Y a ti? (I like going to the cinema. And you?)
- Me gusta dar paseos con mi perro (I like going for a walk with my dog)

Now is your turn. Try to answer the following questions:

- ¿Cómo te llamas? (What is your name)
  Me llamo … (My name is…)
- ¿Cuántos años tienes? (How old are you)
  Tengo … años (I'm … years old)
- ¿De dónde eres? (Where are you from?)
  Soy de … (I'm from …)
- ¿Dónde vives? (Where do you live?)
  Vivo en … (I live in …)
- ¿A qué te dedicas? (What is your profession?)
  Soy … (I'm a …)
- ¿Dónde trabajas? (Where do you work?)
  Trabajo en … (I work in a …)
- ¿Qué te gusta hacer en tu tiempo libre? (What do you like to do in your free time?)
  Me gusta … (I like …)

We have learnt how to ask and answer in face to face conversation. But now let's imagine that we want to ask questions about a third person (he or she). The questions will be the same, but we will have to change the pronouns and the verbs.

Let's practice!

- ¿Cómo se llama? (What's her or his name?)
  Se llama Carlos o se llama Laura (His name is Carlos or her name is Laura)

- ¿Cuántos años tiene? (How old is he or she?)
  Tiene treinta y tres años (He or she is thirty-three years old)
- ¿De dónde es? (Where he or she is from?)
  Es de Paraguay (He or she is from Paraguay)

NOTE: As you can see, in Spanish it's not mandatory to use the personal pronoun as a subject in each sentence. We can avoid it when all the people involved in the conversation already know who the subject is. If you want to use it to have clearer what verb use, you can, don't hesitate to use any tricks you find helpful to make you feel more confident.

- ¿Dónde vive? (Where does he or she live?)
  Vive en Nueva York (He or she lives in New York)
- ¿A qué se dedica? (What is his or her profession?)
  Es bailarín (If he's a male dancer) Es bailarina (If she's a fenale dancer)
- ¿Dónde trabaja? (Where does he or she work?)
  Trabaja en el ballet de Nueva York. (He or she Works in the New York ballet)

Fancy to try to answer now the questions about a friend of yours? Why not? Let's do that!

- ¿Cómo se llama? (What's her or his name?)
  Se llama ... (His or her name is ...)
- ¿Cuántos años tiene? (How old is he or she?)
- Tiene ... años (He or she is ... years old)
- ¿De dónde es? (Where he or she is from?)
- Es de .... (He or she is from ...)
- ¿Dónde vive? (Where does he or she live?)
- Vive en .... (He or she lives in ...)
- ¿A qué se dedica? (What is his or her profession?)
- Es ... (He or she is ...)
- ¿Dónde trabaja? (Where does he or she work?)
- Trabaja en .... (He or she works in ...)

2.2 Getting to know each other: introducing myself

Now we know how to make questions to know people and how to answer if someone asks us about ourselves. Now we are going to practice how to introduce our selves without answering questions. Imagine that you are making a presentation, you just have known someone while doing tourism or you have a learning Spanish partner and you want to practice how to introduce yourselves.

¡Vamos a practicar! Let's practice!

- ¡Hola! Me llamo Carlos y tengo cincuenta y dos años
  Hello! My name is Carlos and I'm fifty-two years old
- Soy de España, pero ahora vivo en Londres
  I'm from Spain but I'm living in London
- Soy administrativo y trabajo en una empresa de muebles
  I'm an administrative and work in a furniture company
- Llevo estudiando español dos meses
  I've been learning Spanish for two months
- Me gusta jugar a básquet y escuchar música
  I like playing basketball and listening to music
- Estaré en Sevilla por una semana
  I'll stay in Seville for a week

Now let's practice another introduction!

- Hola Carlos, encantada de conocerte
  Hello Carlos, it's nice to meet you
- Yo me llamo Rosa y tengo sesenta años
  My name is Rose and I'm sixty years old
- Soy directora de márquetin y trabajo en un hospital
  I'm a marketing director and I work in a hospital
- Llevo estudiando español tres meses y medio
  I've been learning Spanish for three and a half months
- A mí me gusta ver series de televisión y pasear por el campo
  I like watching TV series and walking through the countryside
- Yo estaré en Sevilla hasta pasado mañana
  I'll stay in Seville since the day after tomorrow

More practice!

- Hola. Soy Silvia. Soy de Berlín
  Hello. I'm Silvia. I'm from Berlin
- Llevo viviendo en Galicia dos años para mejorar mi español
  I've been living in Galicia two years to improve my Spanish
- Me gusta la comida típica de aquí. Es muy sabrosa
  I like the typical food from here. It's yummy
- Mañana voy a Berlín a visitar a mi familia durante una semana
  Tomorrow I'm going to Berlin to visit my family for a week

Have you noticed that in this last introduction we are not saying "me llamo" (my name is) but we are saying "Soy" (I am). Yes, you can use both when introducing your self. You can say "Me llamo" and then your name or start saying "Soy" and your name".

Now prepare and practice some sentences about you!

2.3 Apologise/thank someone

When we are socializing with people, we have to learn some vocabulary to develop our social skills as well in a foreigner language.
It's important to know how to apologise and to thank someone, so let's do it!

Disculparse (Apologise)

Lo siento	I'm sorry
Disculpa	Excuse me
Perdona	Pardon
Siento lo ocurrido	I regret what happened
Lo lamento	I'm sorry
No sabes cuánto lo siento	You don't know how sorry am
Mis disculpas	My apologies
Me disculpo por ...	I apologise for ...
Espero que me perdones	I hope you forgive me
Te debo una disculpa	I own you an apologise
Estoy muy apenado por ...	I'm very sorry for ...

Now let's practice these expressions in sentences:

Lo siento. No quería despertarte (I'm sorry. I didn't want to wake you up)
Disculpa, ¿me dejas pasar? (Excuse me, can you let me through?)
Perdona, no te he oído bien. ¿Puedes repetir, por favor? (Pardon, I didn't hear you well. Can you repeat, please?)
Siento lo ocurrido, no quería discutir contigo (I regret what happened. I didn't want to argue with you)
No sabes cuánto lo siento. No quería que llegaras tarde (You don't know how sorry I am. I didn't want you to be late)
Llego tarde. Mis disculpas. Había mucho tráfico (I'm late. My apologies. There was a lot of traffic)

Me disculpo por llegar tarde. Me equivoqué de estación de metro (I apologise for being late. I made a mistake with the underground station)

No quería ofenderte. Espero que me perdones (I didn't mean to offend you. I hope you forgive me)

Te debo una disculpa. Podría haberte avisado de que llegaba tarde (I own you an apologise. I could tell you I was going to be late)

Estoy muy apenado por la pérdida de tu perro (I'm very sorry for the loss of your dog)

Now that we know how to apologise in Spanish, let's learn how to say thanks. There's more than one way to say thanks and to answer that in Spanish. Take a look:

Gracias	Thanks	
Muchas gracias	Thank you very much	
Mil gracias	A thousand of thanks	Very popular expression in Spain. There's no equivalent form in English.
Gracias por todo	Thanks for everything	
Te lo agradezco	I thank you	
Muchísimas gracias	Thanks a lot / Thanks so much / Thanks a lot	
Te doy las gracias	I give you thanks	
De nada	You are welcome / No worries	
No hay de qué	Don't mention it	
No hay problema	No problem	

Let's practice now the different ways to say thanks in Spanish with these sentences:

¿Necesitas ayuda con el cochecito? (Do you need help with the pushchair?)
Gracias, eres muy amable (Thanks, you are very kind)

Te he traído tu tarta favorita (I have brought your favourite pie)
¡Muchas gracias! ¡Me encanta! (Thank you very much! I love it!)

No te preocupes, he llamado para avisar de que llegas tarde (Don't worry, I have called to say you are running late)
¡Mil gracias! No sé qué haría sin ti (A thousand of thanks! I don't know what I would do without you)

Aquí tenéis la cuenta. Espero que os haya gustado la cena (Here you have the bill. I hope you liked the dinner)
Sí. Gracias por todo. Estaba delicioso (Yes. Thanks for everything. It was delicious)

He comprado leche de camino a casa (I have bought milk on my way home)
Te lo agradezco porque yo no me he acordado (I thank you because haven't remembered to buy it)

¡Feliz cumpleaños! Este regalo es para ti. Espero que te guste (Happy birthday! This present is for you. I hope you like it)
¡Muchísimas gracias! (Thanks a lot!)

Te doy las gracias por haber cuidado de mi gato (I give you thanks to take care of my cat)

We are going to practice again the thanks sentences but adding now the response:

¿Necesitas ayuda con el cochecito? (Do you need help with the pushchair?)
Gracias, eres muy amable (Thanks, you are very kind)
No hay de qué (Don't mention it)

Te he traído tu tarta favorita (I have brought your favourite pie)
¡Muchas gracias! ¡Me encanta! (Thank you very much! I love it!)
De nada (You're welcome)

No te preocupes, he llamado para avisar de que llegas tarde (Don't worry, I have called to say you are running late)
¡Mil gracias! No sé qué haría sin ti (A thousand of thanks! I don't know what I would do without you)
No hay de qué (Don't mention it)

Aquí tenéis la cuenta. Espero que os haya gustado la cena (Here you have the bill. I hope you liked the dinner)
Sí. Gracias por todo. Estaba delicioso (Yes. Thanks for everything. It was delicious)
De nada (You're welcome)

He comprado leche de camino a casa (I have bought milk on my way home)
Te lo agradezco porque yo no me he acordado (I thank you because haven't remembered to buy it)
No hay problema (No problema)

¡Feliz cumpleaños! Este regalo es para ti. Espero que te guste (Happy birthday! This present is for you. I hope you like it)
¡Muchísimas gracias! (Thanks a lot!)
De nada (You're welcome)

Te doy las gracias por haber cuidado de mi gato (I give you thanks to take care of my cat)
No hay de qué (Don't mention it)

There's no rule to use one way or another to say "thanks" and to answer that. Try to learn the different ways and use it the same way you would do in your own language.

2.4 Complimenting

Compliments can do amazements in people when these are given at the appropriate time and use the correct language. Let's learn some compliments considering the culture that surrounds Spanish speaking countries.

"Hacer un cumplido" means "make a compliment"

Cumplidos personales	Personal compliments
Eres muy guapo	You are very handsome
Eres muy guapa	You are very pretty
Eres muy amable	You are very kind
Eres muy simpático	You are very nice
Eres muy simpática	You are very nice
Estas muy guapo	You look very nice
Estas muy guapo	You look very nice
Este traje te queda muy bien	This suit looks great on you
Este vestido te queda estupendo	This dress looks great on you

Cumplidos profesionales	Professional compliments
Tu trabajo es increíble	Your work is amazing
Bien hecho, sigue así	Well done, keep going
La presentación ha sido genial	The presentation was great
Tu equipo es muy eficiente	Your team is very efficient
Has superado las expectativas	You went over the expectations

Cumplidos para ocasiones especiales	Special occasions compliments
La comida que has hecho estaba deliciosa	The meal you made was delicious
La paella que has hecho estaba increíble	The paella you cooked was amazing
La fiesta ha sido muy divertida	The party has been very fun
El concierto ha sido asombroso	The gig has been amazing
La obra de teatro ha sido muy entretenida	The play has been very entertaining

Let's practice some sentences about complimenting:

- Espero que no te moleste que te lo diga, pero eres muy guapo
  I hope you don't mind I tell you this, but you are very handsome
- Eres muy guapa. Pareces una actriz de cine
  You are very pretty. You look like an actress
- Gracias por ayudarme. Eres muy amable
  Thanks for helping me. You are very kind
- Me gusta hablar contigo. Eres muy simpático
  I like talking with you. You are very nice
- Estoy encantada de haberte conocido. Eres muy simpática
  I'm glad to meet you. You are very nice
- No seas tonto, estás muy guapo
  Don't be silly, you look very nice
- No te cambies de ropa, estás muy guapa
  Don't change your clothes, you look very nice
- ¡Oh! Este traje te queda muy bien
  Wow! This suit looks great on you
- No tengo palabras. Este vestido te queda estupendo
  I have no words. This dress looks amazing on you
- El jefe está muy contento. Tu trabajo es fantástico
  The boss is very happy. Your work is fantastic.
- Bien hecho, sigue así. No has cometido ningún error
  Well done, keep going. You haven't done any mistake
- El cliente está encantado. La presentación fue genial
  The client is delighted. The presentation was great
- ¡Felicidades! Tu equipo es muy eficiente
  Congratulations! Your team is very efficient
- Estamos sorprendidos. Has superado las expectativas
  We are surprised. You went over the expectations
- Estoy llena. La comida que has hecho estaba deliciosa
  I'm full. The food you made was delicious
- He comido de maravilla. La paella que has hecho estaba increíble
  I have eaten wonderfully. The paella you cooked was amazing

- La fiesta ha sido muy divertida. Eres muy buen anfitrión
  The party has been very fun. You are a very good host
- Tu banda de música toca genial. El concierto ha sido asombroso
  Your music band plays great. The concert has been amazing
- La obra de teatro ha sido muy entretenida. Los actores son buenísimos.
  The play has been very entertaining. The actors were great.

Well! Now you know some compliments that can be handy to know to use in some situations.

2.5 Greetings, farewells and courtesy

There are a lot of different forms to greet and farewell in Spanish. We can say that every Spanish speaking country could have their own form for that, but we are going to learn the most typical expressions. There is not always an equivalent form in English, so to know what we are saying, the translation in English can sound strange.

Let's take a look!

Saludos	Greetings
Hola	Hello
Buenas	There's no form in English for this expression. It's used in informal conversations and it's like saying "good"
¿Qué tal?	What's up?
¿Qué pasa?	What happen?
¿Todo bien?	Everything alright?
Buenos días	Good morning
Buenas tardes	Good afternoon and evening. In Spanish we say "buenas tardes" from after lunch to when is dark.
Buenas noches	Good night. In Spanish we use "buenas noches" when is dark, to greet and farewell.
¿Qué te cuentas?	Do you have something to tell me?
¿Como te va?	How is it going?

Despedidas	Farewells
Adiós	Bye
Hasta luego	See you later
Hasta mañana	See you tomorrow
Hasta la vista	This expression, that you already know if you have seen Terminator 1, it is used to farewell someone who you don't expect to see again, at least in short time.
Nos vemos	See you
Hasta la próxima	See you next time
Hasta otra	See you in other occasion
Que tengas un buen día	Have a good day
Cuídate	Take care

Let's practice the followings conversations:

- Hola Carlos, ¿cómo te va? (Hello Carlos, how is it going?)
- Muy bien. Y tú, ¿qué te cuentas? (Very well. And you, something new to tell?)
- Pues nada nuevo (Nothing new)
- ¿Quedamos mañana para tomar un café? (Would you like to meet for a coffee tomorrow?)
- Vale. Nos vemos a las diez. Hasta mañana (Ok. See you at ten. See you tomorrow)
- Hasta mañana (See you tomorrow)

- Buenos días, Ana. ¿Como estas? (Good morning Ana, how are you?)
- Buenos días, María. Estoy bien, ¿y tú? (Good morning Maria. I'm fine. And you?)
- También, gracias (Me too, thanks)
- ¿Vendrás a la fiesta esta tarde? (Are you coming to the party this evening?)
- Sí. pero llegaré un poco tarde (Yes, but I'll be a little bit late)
- Vale, nos vemos luego (Ok, I see you later)
- Hasta luego (See you later)

Now imagine the following situation. There is a small bar. Juan goes always to have a coffee before starting to work. Juan knows the bar man from a long time ago.

- ¡Buenas! ¿Me pones un café, Paco? (Hi! Can I have a coffee, Paco?)
- Claro Juan. ¿Todo bien? (Sure Juan. Everything alright?)
- Sí, pero hoy me espera un día duro (Yes, but I will have a hard day)
- Pues a tomárselo con calma (Take it easy, then)
- Gracias Paco. ¡Que tengas un buen día! (Thanks Paco. Have a good day!)
- Tú también Juan, cuídate. (You too Juan, take care)

Now it's time to talk about courtesy. It's true that in Spain, people usually speak directly and through an informal way, but it will be useful to know the following courtesy forms in case we need them for a formal conversation.

Por favor	Please
Gracias	Thanks

Usted	"Usted" Is the second person singular that we use in Spanish instead of "tú" when we are talking to someone we haven't met before or older than us and the conversation is formal
Podrías	Is the condicional form "could" that in Spanish is used in formal conversations

Cartas y correos electrónicos formales	**Formal letters and emails**
Querido / Estimado Señor/Señora	Dear Sir/Madam
Reciba un cordial saludo	Kind/Best regards
Atentamente	Attentively

La pregunta del millón de dólares (the million dollar question):
When we use "tú" and when we use "usted"?
Well, there is no rule, only common sense. If you are in a conversation and feel the person in front of you needs a formal way and respectful way of telling things (e.g. the boss, an old wise man...) then use "usted" except if the other person ask you to treat him with "tú", that you can do it without fear.

Let's practice the "usted" form.
Do you remember when we learn how to ask questions to know people?
Now we are going to learn how to ask them using "usted". You will notice that the form of the verb and some pronouns change to third person singular.

¿Cómo se llama (usted)? (What's your name?)
¿Cuántos años tiene (usted)? (How old are you?)
¿De dónde es (usted)? (Where are you from?)
¿Dónde vive (usted)? (Where do you live?)

Note: It's not necessary to use the pronoun "usted" in all the questions since can be understood because of the verbal tense used

THIRD CHAPTER: Jobs and common situations (Trabajo y situaciones comunes)

3.1 Make an appointment (Pedir una cita)

Making an appointment can be quite easy if we are prepared and we know the vocabulary to use.
Let's see different situations where we need to make an appointment.

Pedir hora con el doctor (Make an appointment with the doctor)

- Buenos días, quería pedir hora con el doctor (Good morning, I would like to make an appointment with the doctor)
- Muy bien. Voy a mirar la agenda del doctor (Very well. Let me check doctor's timetable)
  ¿Cuándo prefiere venir, por las mañanas o por las tardes? (When do you prefer to come, mornings or afternoons?)
- Por las tardes, por favor (Afternoons, please)
- ¿El próximo martes a las tres y media? (Next Tuesday at half past three?)
- Perfecto, gracias (Perfect, thanks)
- ¿Me dice su nombre y su número de teléfono, por favor? (Can you tell me your name and your telephone number, please?)
- Jorge Fernández. Y mi teléfono es 546789201 (Jorge Fernandez. And my telephone is five, four, six, seven, eight, nine, two, zero, one)
- Muchas gracias. Hasta el martes a las tres y media entonces (Many thanks. See you on Tuesday at half past three, then)
- Gracias, hasta el martes (Thanks, see you on Tuesday)

Pedir hora para la revisión del coche (Make an appointment for a car service)

- Buenas tardes. Necesito pedir hora para la revisión del coche (Good afternoon. I need an appointment for a car service)
- Buenas tardes. ¿Me da el número de matrícula de su coche? (Good afternoon. Can you give me your car number registration?)
- La matrícula es JKL23AVV (The car registration number is JKL23AVV)
- ¿Es un Renault Clio? (Is it a Renault Clio?)
- Sí (Yes)
- Perfecto. Tenemos disponibilidad el miércoles a las 9 y cuarto de la mañana (Perfect. We have availability on Wednesday at a quarter past nine in the morning)
- Me va bien. Allí estaré (It Works for me. I'll be there)
- Vale. Hasta entonces (Ok, see you then)

Pedir hora para realizar un trámite en el ayuntamiento (Make an appointment council service)

- Hola. Buenos días. Necesito pedir hora para realizar un trámite en el ayuntamiento
(Hello. Good morning. I need to make an appointment to do a request in the council)
- Buenos días. Tienes que pedir hora online, en la web del ayuntamiento
(Good morning. You have to make the appointment online, on the council's website)
- Ah, vale. ¿Me puedes dar la dirección web, por favor?
(Ah, ok. Can you give the website, please?)
- www.ayuntamiento.com
Note: in Spanish the dot is "punto", the @ is "arroba", the slash (-) is "guión"
- Perfecto, gracias. Que tengas un buen día (Perfect, thanks. Have a good day)
- Igualmente (Likewise)

Pedir hora en la peluquería (make an appointment at the hair saloon)

- Hola. Me gustaría cortarme el pelo. ¿Tenéis horas disponibles?
  (Hello. I would like to cut my hair. Do you have available appointments?)
- Hola. Si quieres puedes esperar diez minutos ahora y te atendemos
  (Hello. If you want, you can wait now for ten minutes and we will serve you)
- Ahora no puedo. ¿Qué tal mañana?
  (I can't now. What about tomorrow?)
- ¿Mañana a las doce y cuarenta y cinco?
  (Tomorrow at twelve forty-five?)
- Sí, genial
  (Yes, great)
- ¿Me dices tu nombre y tu móvil?
  (Can you give your name and your mobile?)
- Soy Carmen. Mi móvil es el 999765112
  (I'm Carmen and my mobile is 999765112)
- Genial. Nos vemos mañana
  (Great. See you tomorrow)
- Hasta mañana
  (See you tomorrow)

In all this kind of situations would be helpful to be prepared. It can be a good idea to write down all
we want to say. Anyway, don't hesitate to ask anyone to repeat again what they are saying using
"¿Puedes repetir, por favor?" (Can you repeat, please?) or "¿Puedes repetir más despacio, por favor?" (Can you repeat slowly, please?)

3.2 Make an Interview (Hacer una entrevsita)

You have made the decision to start working in a Spanish speaking country and you have a job interview. Let's learn basic vocabulary to do it great!

Salario	Salary
Compañía	Company
Horario	Working hours / Schedule
Currículum	Resumé / CV
Entrevista	Interview
Contrato	Contract / Agreement
Referencias	References
Título	Degree
Jefa / Jefe	Boss / Manager
Anuncio de trabajo	Job advertisement
Descripción de trabajo	Job description
Permiso de trabajo	Work permit

Tengo experiencia…	I have experience…	Como actriz / actor (Acting)
		En la fotografía (In photography)
		En trabajo de oficina (In office work)
		Como vendedora / vendedor (In sales)
		Como secretaria / secretario (In secretarial work)
		En la enseñanza (Teaching)
		En el diseño (In design)
		En trabajos de limpieza (Cleaning)
		En la construcción (In construction work)
		Como camarera / camarero (As a waitress/waiter)

Estoy cualificada para…	I am qualified for…
Estoy buscando trabajo…	I'm looking for work …
A tiempo parcial	Part-time
A tiempo completo	Full-time
Esporádico	Casual Work
¿Cuál es el salario?	What's the salary?
¿Cómo me van a pagar?	How is the salary paid?
¿Cada cuánto me van a pagar?	How often would I get paid?
¿Cuál es el horario?	What are the working hours?
Seguro médico	Health insurance
Pago de horas extras	Overtime pay
Vacaciones pagadas	Paid vacation
Impuestos	Income tax

Let's see some typical questions that you can hear in a job interview:

- ¿Por qué deberíamos contratarte a ti? (Why should we hire you?)

- ¿Qué te hace diferente a los demás candidatos? (What makes you different from the other candidates)

- ¿Por qué deseas trabajar en esta empresa? (Why do you wish to work in this company?

- ¿Cuáles son tus 3 fortalezas y tus 3 debilidades? (What are your 3 strengths and 3 weakness?)

- ¿Qué sabes de la empresa y del puesto? (What do you know about the company and the position)

- ¿Cómo resolverías la siguiente situación? (How would you resolve this situation?)

To have exit in a job interview you have to be prepared whatever the language is. Now you know basic vocabulary and typical questions to work with.
Here's a sample dialogue. Notice that both speakers are using the "Usted" form because it is a formal situation.

Una Entrevista de Trabajo:

Entrevistador: Bueno, en su currículo dice que ha trabajado en diseño por más de 10 años.
Entrevistado: Así es. Empecé a trabajar en diseño cuando acabé la universidad.
Entrevistador: ¿Qué es lo que más le gusta del diseño?
Entrevistado: Lo que más me gusta es la creatividad. Desde pequeño que me ha gustado dibujar y crear.
Entrevistador: ¿Y por qué le gustaría trabajar con nosotros?
Entrevistado: Estoy convencido que, con mi experiencia en el área, puedo contribuir con nuevas y frescas ideas para ofrecer a sus clientes.
Entrevistador: ¿Conoce con qué tipo de clientes solemos trabajar?
Entrevistado: Si, he visto en su porfolio que trabajan sobre todo con compañías relacionadas con el deporte.
Entrevistador: ¿Y qué le parece?
Entrevistado: Bastante emocionante. El mundo del deporte es una de mis aficiones.

What have you understood from this interview? Let's check!

What is the interviewee job?
How many years of experience does he have?
With which kind of clients does the company use to work?
Is the interviewee happy with that? Why?

Now listen the translation in English and check your answers.

A job interview:

Interviewer: Well, in your resume it says you have worked in design for more than 10 years.
Interviewee: That's right. I started working on design when I finished college.
Interviewer: What do you like most about design?
Interviewee: What I like most is creativity. Since I was little I liked to draw and create.
Interviewer: And why would you like to work with us?
Interviewee: I am convinced that with my experience in the area, I can contribute with new and fresh ideas to offer to your clients.
Interviewer: Do you know what kind of clients we usually work with?
Interviewee: Yes, I have seen in your portfolio that you work mainly with companies related to sports.
Interviewer: And how do you feel about that?
Interviewee: Pretty excited. Sport is one of my hobbies.

How it went with the questions about the Spanish text?
Do not worry if it was difficult. Learning a language is challenging and the only secret to be good at that is practice, practice and practice.

You can try now to prepare your answers for a job interview following the dialog and using the vocabulary we have seen.

3.3 Different Occupations (Distintos trabajos y oficios)

Now we are going to learn about different occupations and some specific vocabulary for each one. Keep in mind that in Spanish occupations have gender, so it will be differently said if it's a female or a male. For example a teacher in English, in Spanish will be "una profesora" if it's a female teacher or "un profesor" if it's a male teacher.

Profesión en femenino	Profesión en masculino	Translation
profesora	profesor	teacher
abogada	abogado	lawyer
la agente de policía	el agente de policía	police officer
doctora	doctor	doctor
la piloto	el piloto	pilot
mecánica	mecánico	mechanic
peluquera	peluquero	hairdresser
veterinaria	veterinario	vet
directora	director	director
administrativa	administrativo	administrative
ingeniera	ingeniero	engineer
la astronauta	el astronauta	astronaut
pintora	pintor	painter
actriz	actor	actress, actor
bailarina	bailarín	dancer
cuidadora	cuidador	carer
enfermera	enfermero	nurse
cocinera	cocinero	cooker
programadora	programador	programmer

Let's read the following sentences regarding different occupations:

La profesora y el profesor enseñan en escuelas, institutos y universidades
The teachers teach in schools, institutes and universities

La abogada y el abogado defienden casos de accidentes laborales
The lawyer defends working accidents cases

Los agentes de policía patrullan las calles
Police officers patrols the street

La doctora y el doctor tratan enfermedades
Doctors treat illness

La piloto y el piloto se preparan para la carrera de coches
Pilots are getting ready for the cars racing

La mecánica y el mecánico arreglan el coche de carreras
The mechanics are fixing the racing car

La peluquera y el peluquero cortan el pelo gratis a las personas sin casa
The hairdressers are doing hair cuts for free for homeless

La veterinaria y el veterinario cuidan los animales del zoo
The vets take care of the animals of the zoo

La directora y el director dirigen el departamento de administración
The director leads the administration department

La administrativa y el administrativo trabajan en el departamento de administración
Administrative works in the administration department

La ingeniera y el ingeniero diseñan puentes
Engineers design bridges

La astronauta y el astronauta se entrenan para ir a Marte
Astronauts are training to go to Mars

La pintura y el pintor pintan cuadros de paisajes
Painters paint landscapes pictures

La actriz y el actor actúan en películas, series de televisión y obras de teatro
Actress and actors performance in movies, TV shows and theatre

La bailarina y el bailarín bailan en la ópera
Dancers dance in the opera

La cuidadora y el cuidador cuidan a los ancianos
Carers take care of elderly people

La enfermera y el enfermero trabajan en el hospital
Nurses work in the hospital

La cocinera y el cocinero cocinan en un restaurante muy famoso

Cookers cook in a very famous restaurant

La programadora y el programador trabajan en Madrid
Programmer work in Madrid

Now that we know some more occupations, let's see how to say something about our experience if we were...

Profesora o profesor (Teacher)
Tengo experiencia en diseñar currículos de lenguas extranjeras
I have experience in design modern foreigner language curriculums

Abogada o abogado (lawyer)
Tengo cinco años de experiencia en defender casos medioambientales
I have five years of experience in defending environmental cases

Agente de policia (police officer)
No tengo mucha experiencia, pero aprendo rápido
I do not have a lot of experience, but I learn quick

Doctora o doctor (doctor)
Mi especialidad es la dermatología
My speciality is dermatology

Piloto (pilot)
Soy piloto de aviones desde hace diez años
I'm a plane pilot for ten years now

Mecánica o mecánico (mechanic)
He trabajado para Ferrari durante cinco años
I have worked for Ferrari for five years

Peluquera o peluquero (hairdresser)
Desde pequeño he querido ser peluquero. Siempre peinaba a toda la familia.
I wanted to be a hairdresser since I was a kid. I always was doing all family hair.

Veterinaria o veterinario (Vet)
Siempre me han encantado los animales. Por eso me hice veterinario
I always have loved animals. This is way I became a vet

Directora o director (director)

Llevo dirigiendo equipos desde el año dos mil
I have been leading teams since the year two thousand

Administrativa o administrativo (administrative)
Tengo experiencia con bases de datos y traducción de documentos
I have experience in data bases and documents translations

Ingeniera o ingeniero (engineer)
Trabajé de ingeniera diez años, pero ahora doy clases en la universidad
I worked as engineer for ten years, but now I'm teaching at university

Astronauta (astronaut)
Me he entrenado duro para ir a Marte el próximo año
I have been training hard to go to Mars next year

Pintora o pintor (painter)
Tengo experiencia en pintar usando la técnica modernista
I have experience in painting using the modernist technique

Bailarina o bailarín (dancer)
He sido el bailarín principal del Ballet Nacional de Moscú durante tres años
I've been the first dancer at the National Moscow Ballet for three years

Cuidadora o cuidador (carer)
He trabajado en residencias de ancianos toda mi vida
I have worked at old people residences for all my life

Enfermera o enfermero (nurse)
He sido enfermero en el departamento de ginecología durante dos años
I have been a nurse in the gynaecology department for two years

Cocinera o cocinero (cooker)
He cocinado junto a los mejores chefs de España
I have cooked side by side with the best chefs in Spain

Programadora o programador (programmer)
Empecé a programar cuando acabé la universidad
I started programming when I finished the university

3.4 At the Restaurant (En el restaurante)

We already know food and meals vocabulary from the first book. **Now, we are going to practice some new vocabulary to be able to communicate successfully in some specific cases.**

- We are in a restaurant and the waiter has just bring us a bill that is not ours -

- Disculpe, debe de haber un error. Esta cuenta no es nuestra
  (Excuse me, there must be a mistake. This bill is not ours)
- Déjame ver. Tenéis razón. Mis disculpas. Ahora os traigo la vuestra
  (Let me see. You are right. My apologies. I'll bring yours now)

- We have been waiting to much for a plate -

- Disculpe camarero, ¿hay algún problema con nuestra comida? Llevamos esperando más de media hora
  (Excuse me waiter. Is there any problem with our food? We've been waiting for more than half an hour)
- Les pido disculpas. Estamos un poco saturados hoy porque vamos corto de personal
  (I'm so sorry. We are over saturated today because we are short of staff)

- We want the waiter to advise us what to eat -

- ¿Qué nos recomiendas para comer hoy?
  (What do you recommend us to eat today?
- Si os gusta la carne, el solomillo, y si preferís pesado, el bacalao.
  (If you are meat lovers, the steak, if you prefer fish, the cod)

- The food is cold -

- Disculpe. Esta comida esta fría. ¿Podrían traerme la comida caliente, por favor?
  (Excuse me, the food is cold. Could you bring me the food warm, please?)
- Enseguida

(Right away)

- We want a dessert -

- Perdone. ¿Nos puedes traer la carta de postres?
  (Excuse me. Can we have the dessert menu?)
- Claro, aquí tenéis. Avisadme cuando sepáis lo que queréis
  (Sure, there you are. Let me know when you know what you want)

- One more person is coming to have dinner with us -

- Buenas noches, tenemos una reserva para cuatro, pero al final seremos cinco
  (Good evening, we have a reservation for four, but we are going to be five)
- No hay problema. Si se esperan cinco minutos, les preparamos la mesa para cinco
  (No problem. If you wait five minutes, we will set the table for five)

- We have a food allergy -

- ¿Perdone, llevan gluten estas patatas fritas? Soy alérgica al gluten
  (Excuse me, is any trace of gluten on these chips? I have gluten allergy)
- No llevan gluten
  (These are gluten free)
- Perfecto, gracias
  (Perfect, thanks)

3.5 At the Hotel (En el hotel)

Now let's practice some situations in a hotel:

- Changing reservation/booking dates -

- Hola, buenos días. Tengo una reserva. Necesito cambiar las fechas
  (Hello, good morning. I have a reservation. I need to change the dates)
- Buenos días, no hay problema. ¿Me dice su nombre, por favor?
  (Good morning, no problem. Can you tell me your name, please?)
- Sí, claro. Marta Ferrer

- (Yes, of course. Marta Ferrer)
- Aquí está. ¿Qué fechas necesita cambiar?
  (Here it is. What dates do you need to change?)
- Llegaremos el martes catorce como originalmente, pero estaremos dos noches más. Nos iremos el domingo diecinueve.
  (We will arrive on Tuesday 14th as originally but we will stay for two more nights. We will depart on Sunday 19th)
- No hay problema, ya lo he anotado. ¿Algo más?
  (No problem, I have registered the change. Anything else?)
- No, eso es todo. Gracias
  (No, that's all. Thanks)
- Hasta la semana que viene
  (See you next week)

- There is a light not working in our room -

- Recepción. ¿En qué puedo ayudarle?
  (Reception. How can I help you?)
- Hay una luz fundida en nuestra habitación. Es una luz del baño
  (There is a cast light. It's a light from the bathroom)
- ¿Me da su número de habitación?
  (Can you give me your room number?)
- El 340 (tres cientos cuarenta)
  (It's 340 (three hundred forty))
- Perfecto. Lo arreglaremos hoy mismo
  (Perfect. We'll fix it today)

- Gracias
  (Thanks)
- De nada
  (You're welcome)

- We want to book a table for dinning at the hotel restaurant -

- Hola. Nos gustaría reservar una mesa en el restaurante del hotel para cenar mañana por la noche
  (Hello. We would like to book a table at the hotel restaurant for dining tomorrow night)
- Tienen que hacerlo directamente en el restaurante.

- (You have to do it directly on the restaurant)
  - ¿Podemos llamar por teléfono o tenemos que pasarnos?
    (Can we give them a call or we have to stop by?)
  - Podéis llamar por teléfono. ¿Tenéis el numero?
    (You can give them a call. Have you got the number?)
  - ¿No, nos lo puedes dar?
    (No, can you give it to us?)
  - Claro. Es el 789667823
    (Sure. It's 789667823)
  - Mil gracias
    (Thank you very much)

- We want to ask some advice to visit the city -

- Buenas tardes. ¿Qué nos recomienda que veamos mañana? Solo estaremos en Barcelona tres días.
  (Good evening. What do you advised us to visit tomorrow? We will stay in Barcelona for only three days)
- ¿Qué es lo que más les interesa? ¿Arquitectura, gastronomía, ocio, deportes…?
  (What are you interested in? Architecture, gastronomy, leisure, sports?)
- De todo un poco
  (A little bit of everything)
- Muy bien. Empezad por la Sagrada Familia y luego visitad el barrio del Born. Allí podréis comer bien
  (Very well. Start visiting the Sagrada Familia and after that you can visit "El Born" neighbourhood. You will eat well there)
- Al día siguiente podéis visitar Montjuic y subir al palacio. Por la tarde pasear por la playa.
  (The following day you can visit Montjuic and go up to the palace. You can go for a walk by the beach in the afternoon)
- Y el último día podéis visitar el Camp Nou si sois seguidores del Barcelona.
  (The last day you can visit the "Camp Nou" if you are Barcelona football team fans)
- ¡Genial! Muchas gracias
  (Great! Many thanks)

- We have lost the purse and we want to ask if anyone has returned to reception -

- Hola. Siento molestar. He perdido el monedero. ¿Os han traído alguno que alguien se haya encontrado?
  (Hi. Sorry to interrupt you. I have lost my purse. Does anyone has found one and give it to you?)
- Déjame comprobarlo
  (Let me check)
- ¿De qué color es?
  (What colour is it?)
- Es rojo con topos blancos
  (It's red with white spots)
- Aquí está.
  (Here you have)
- ¡Qué bien! Muchísimas gracias.
  (Oh, great! Thanks a lot!)

3.6 At the shop floor (En la tienda)

Let's practice now some situations inside a shop.

- Pidiendo ayuda para encontrar algo (Asking for help to find something) -

- ¿Disculpa, me puedes ayudar?
  (Excuse me, can you help me?)
- Estoy buscando la mantequilla, pero no la encuentro.
  (I'm looking for butter, but I can't find it)
- ¿Me puedes decir en qué pasillo está?
  (Can you tell me in which aisle it is?)
- Sí, claro. En el pasillo cuatro, al lado de los quesos
  (Yes, sure. Aisle four, next to the cheese)
- Genial. Gracias
  (Great. Thanks)

- En la pescadería (At the fishmonger) -

- Hola, buenos dias.
  (Hello, good morning)
- ¿Qué pescado fresco tienes del día?
  (What is the fresh fish of the day?)

- o Hoy tenemos bacalao
  (We have cod today)
- o Perfecto, ponme un bacalao, pues
  (Perfect, I want a cod, then)
- o ¿Me lo puedes cortar a filetes, por favor?
  (Can you cut steaks, please?)
- o Claro, ¿algo más?
  (Sure, anything else?)
- o No, eso es todo
  (No, that's all)

- En el mercado tradicional de comida (In a traditional food market) -

- o Pedro, vayamos primero a la tienda de fruta y después iremos a la carnicería.
  (Pedro, let's go first to the fruit shop and after that to the butcher shop)
- o Hola, me pones un quilo de naranjas, ¿por favor?
  (Hi, can I have a kilo of oranges, please?)
- o Claro, ¿algo más?
  (Sure, anything else?)
- o Si, una sandía, por favor
  (Yes, a watermelon, please)
- o ¿Es todo?
  (Is that all?)
- o Sí, ¿cuánto es?
  Yes, how much is it?
- o Son 7,38€|
  (It's 7,38 €)
- o Aquí tienes. Gracias
  (Here you have it. Thanks)

- o Hola. ¿Tienes hamburguesas para hacer a la barbacoa?
  (Hi. Have you got burgers for barbecue?)
- o Sí, tengo con cebolla y sin cebolla
  (Yes, I've got with and without onion)
- o Ponme dos con cebolla y dos sin
  (I'll take two with onion and two without onion)
- o Aquí tienes. Son 10 €
  (Here you have. It's 10 €)
- o Gracias (thanks)

FOURTH CHAPTER: Free time & Fun (Tiempo libre y diversión)

4.1. Food and drink (Comida y bebida)

We learnt food and drink vocabulary and some basic sentences in the first book. **Let's now practice different situations about food and drink to learn more!**

- We are in a party -

- Hola Graciela. Gracias por invitarme a tu fiesta.
  (Hello Graciela. Thanks for inviting me to your party)
- La fiesta es maravillosa
  (The party is wonderful)
- Gracias, Sara. ¿Te traigo algo para comer o beber?
  (Thanks Sara. Can I bring you something to eat or drink?)
- Sí, gracias, pero mejor voy contigo y miro lo que hay
  (Yes, thank you, but I better come with you to see what there is)
- ¡Vale, vamos!
  (Ok, let's go!)

- Planning to cook paella and buying the ingredients -

- Pedro me ha dado la receta de paella de su madre
  (Pedro has given to me his mother's paella recipe)
- ¡Qué bien! ¿Y que tenemos que comprar?
  (That's great! And what we have to buy?)
- Déjame leer de nuevo la receta
  (Let me read again the recipe)
- Vamos a ver... necesitamos arroz, tomates, cebolla, pimiento rojo, pollo, calabacín, berenjena y alcachofas

    (Let's see... we need rice, tomatoes, onions, red pepper, chicken, courgette, aubergine and artichoke)
- ¡Oh! ¿No es una paella de marisco?
    (Oh. It's not a seafood paella, is it?)
- No, es una paella mixta de pollo y vegetales. Pero está muy buena. Te lo prometo
    (No, but it's a 'mixta' paella with chicken and vegetables. But it's delicious. I promise)
- Te creo. ¡Pero quiero probarla!
    (I believe you. But I want to try it!)
- Claro
    (Sure)

- We are in a cocktail bar and the barman is asking us what we want for drink -

- Hola. ¿Qué queréis tomar?
    (Hi! What you want for drink?)
- No lo sabemos. ¿Qué nos recomiendas?
    (We don't know. What do you recommend us?)
- ¿Qué licor os gusta?
    (What spirit do you like?)
- A mí me gusta la ginebra y él prefiere el ron
    (I like gin and he prefers rum)
- Muy bien. Os prepararé dos cócteles especiales, uno con ginebra y otro con ron
    (Very well. I'll make two special cocktails for you, one with gin and the other one with rum
- Sentaos en la mesa. Yo os los llevo
    (Seat down to table. I'll bring them to you)

- We are having a barbecue with friends -

- ¿A qué hora vendrán Juan y Paula?
    (What time are Juan and Paula coming?)
- Dijeron que vendrían a las seis y media
    (They said they were coming at six thirty)
- Genial. Aun tenemos tiempo para acabar de preparar todo
    (Great. We still have time to finish preparation)
- Ya tenemos las salchichas, las hamburguesas, las patatas y el maíz preparados

(We have sausages, hamburgers, potatoes and corn ready)
- Y hay refrescos, cerveza y vino en la nevera
  (And there are soft drinks, beer and wine in the fridge)
- Perfecto. ¿Y el pan?
  (Perfect. And bread?)
- Esta aquí, junto a la ensalada
  (It's here, next to the salad)
- ¿Y las salsas?
  (And sauces?)
- Preparadas también
  Ready as well

4.2 Holidays, celebrations and Partying (Vacaciones, celebraciones y fiestas)

Well, it's now time to go for a holiday, celebrate special occasions and attend parties in Spanish!
Are you ready? **Let's practice the following situations:**

In a travel agency (En una agencia de viajes): We are planning a trip to Costa Rica (Planeando un viaje a Costa Rica)

- Hola, buenas tardes, nos gustaría hacer un viaje a Costa Rica
  (Hello, good afternoon. We would like to travel to Costa Rica)
- Buenas tardes. Perfecto. Tomen asiento y vamos a organizar un viaje maravilloso
  (Good afternoon. That's perfect. Take a sit and let's organise a wonderful trip)
- ¿Cuántas personas van a viajar?
  (How many people are going to travel?)
- Nosotros dos
  (We both)
- ¿Y cuánto tiempo queréis viajar?
  (And for how long would you like to travel?)
- ¿Qué mes quereis viajar?
  (What month do you want to travel?)
- No nos importa
  (We don't mind)
- Quince días estaría bien
  (Fifteen days should be fine)
- Perfecto, voy a ver qué paquetes y ofertas tengo

- (Perfect, I'm checking what packages and offers I have)
    - Bien. Tengo una oferta para el mes de mayo. ¿Os iría bien?
    (Well. I have an offer for May. Will this work for you?)
    - Sí, perfecto
    (Yes, perfect)
    - El viaje incluye los vuelos de ida y vuelta a San José, los traslados del aeropuerto al hotel y las excursiones al volcán "el Arenal", al parque Nacional "Tortuguero" y a la reserva natural Monteverde
    (The travel package includes flights to and from San Jose, airport transfer, and visits to El Arenal volcano, Tortuguero National Park and Monteverde natural reserve)
    - Fantástico. ¿Y cuánto cuesta por persona?
    (That's fantastic. And how much does it cost per person?)
    - Son 1.450 € por persona
    (It's 1.450 € per person)
    - Y os puedo ofrecer un 15% (quince por ciento) de descuento
    (And I can offer you a 15% discount)
    - Genial. Nos gustaría hacer la reserva del viaje
    (Great. We would like to reserve the trip)
    - Muy bien. Vamos a ello, pues
    (Very well, let's do it, then)

Now that you are in San Jose **you have to check in at the hotel**. Let's refresh vocabulary!

- Bienvenidos al hotel Monteverde. ¿En qué les puedo ayudar?
(Welcome to Monteverde Hotel. How can I help you?)
- ¡Hola! Tenemos una reserve a nombre de Smith
(Hello. We have a booking with name Smith)
- Déjenme ver. Aquí está. Una habitación doble para dos semanas
(Let me check. Here it is. A double bedroom for two weeks)
- Eso es
(That's it)
- Tienen el desayuno incluido. El desayuno se sirve en la cafetería de la planta baja, de 7:30 a 10 de la mañana
(You have the breakfast included. The breakfast is served in the ground floor cafeteria from 7:30 am to 10:00 am)
- Perfecto, muchas gracias
(Perfect, thanks a lot)

- Disfruten de su estancia
  (Enjoy your staying)

Now we are in Mexico and there is a big celebration "El día de Muertos" (The day of the death).
How you heard about that before? **Let's learn a little bit more about "el día de Muertos"**.

- ¿Qué es el día de Muertos?
  (What is the day of the death?)
- Es una celebración popular mexicana para honrar a los muertos
  I(t's a popular Mexican celebration to honour the deaths)
- ¿En qué consiste?
  (What is this about?)
- Se celebra el 1 y 2 de noviembre
  (It's celebrated the 1st and 2nd of November)
- Crean altares para honrar y recordar a los familiares que han muerto con fotografías
  (They create altars with pictures to honour and remember family who passed away)
- También cocinan platos tradicionales y van a comerlos al cementerio
  (They also cook traditional meals and they go to eat them to the cemetery)
- También llevan aquellas cosas favoritas de las personas fallecidas a sus tumbas
  (They also bring the deceased's favourite things to their graves)
- Es una celebración muy colorida por la decoración
  (It's a very colourful celebration)
- Pasan la noche entera en el cementerio, pero es más una fiesta alegre que triste
  (They spend the whole night in the cemetery, but it's more a happy celebration rather than sad)

Well. The world is plenty of different kind of celebrations. Let's talk another one. The famous carnival in Venice, Italy.
We've been invited to the Carnival in Venice. (Nos han invitado al Carnaval de Venecia)

- Gracias por invitarme al carnaval Carlo
  (Thanks for inviting me to the Carnival Carlo)
- Pero tienes que explicarme en qué consiste, porque no he ido nunca
  (But you have to explain what this is about because I haven't never been there)

- Es un festival anual y dura diez días. Nos disfrazamos y salimos a pasear
  (It's an annual festival and it goes for ten days. We dress up and we go out)
- Los disfraces son trajes de época y llevamos máscaras
  (The costumes are other period clothes and we wear masks)
- Estoy seguro de que habrás visto alguna foto o vídeo
  (I'm pretty sure you have seen some pictures or videos)
- Una tarde asistiremos a una fiesta y verás como todos van disfrazados con sus trajes y sus máscaras
  (One evening we will be attending a party and you will see everyone is dressing up with costumes and masks)
- ¡Estoy súper excitada por disfrazarme!
  (I'm very excited to dress up!)
- Será divertido, ya verás
  (It will be fun, you will see)

4.3 Shopping (De compras)

Now let's go for shopping and **let's practice some situations such as asking to advise, exchanges and refunds and asking for a shop**.

- We are looking for something special -

- Buenos días. ¿Puedo ayudarte en algo?
  (Good morning. Can I help you with anything?)
- Estoy buscando algo especial para hacer un regalo
  (I'm looking for something special to make a present)
- Muy bien. ¿Cuál es la ocasión?
  (Very well. What's the occasion?)
- Es para un cumpleaños. Va a cumplir cuarenta años y está un poco bajo de ánimos
  (It's for a birthday. He's going to turn forty years old and is feeling a little bit down)
- Veamos si encontramos algo. ¿Qué aficiones tiene?
  (Let's see if we can find something. What are his hobbies?)
- Le gusta el deporte, la tecnología, viajar... hacer puzzles le relaja
  (He likes sports, technology, traveling... and he makes puzzles to relax)
- ¿Por qué no le haces un puzzle con una foto que le guste?
  (Why don't you get him a puzzle from a picture he likes?)
- ¡Es una buena idea!
  (That's a good idea!)
- ¿La foto necesita especificaciones concretas?
  (Does the picture have any specific requirements?)
- No, pero tiene que tener calidad suficiente para hacer el puzzle del tamaño que quieras
  (No, but it needs a good quality to make the puzzle any size you want)
- Genial. ¿Y cuánto tardáis en hacer el puzzle?
  (Great. How long it takes to make the puzzle?)
- Un par de horas
  (A couple of hours)
- Perfecto. Voy a elegir la foto y vuelvo
  (Perfect. I'm going to choose the picture and I'll come back)
- Muy bien. Hasta luego
  (Very well. See you later)
- Hasta luego. Gracias
  (See you later. Thanks)

- We need to exchange something -

- Hola. Me gustaría cambiar estos pantalones
  (Hello. I would like to exchange these trousers)
- No hay problema. ¿Qué cambio quieres hacer? ¿Talla, modelo?
  (No problem. What kind of exchange do you want to make? Size, model?)
- Necesitaría una talla menos. Estos me quedan un poco grandes
  (I would need one size less. These are a bit large for me)
- De acuerdo. Ahora te los traigo
  (I see. I'll bring it now)
- Espero aquí
  (I wait here)
- Aquí tienes los pantalones en una talla menos
  (Here you have the trousers one size less)
- ¿Quieres probártelos?
  (Do you want to try it on?)
- No, no es necesario
  (No, it's not necessary)
- Muy bien. Pues aquí tienes
  (Very well. Here you have it)
- Gracias
  (Thanks)

- We want to make a refund -

- Hola, buenas tardes, Quiero devolver esto
  (Hello, good afternoon. I want to return this)
- Muy bien. ¿Tiene el tiquet y la tarjeta con la que pagó?
  (Very well. Do you have the ticket and the card with which you payed?)
- Si. Aquí están
  (Yes. Here they are)
- Déjemelos para tramitar la devolución
  (Leave them to me to process the refund)
- Ya está. Firme aquí, por favor
  (All done. Sign here, please)
- Muchas gracias
  (Thanks a lot)
- De nada. Que pase un buen día

(You're welcome. Have a good day)

- We are asking someone for a shop we can't find in a shopping centre -

- Hola. Quizás puedea ayudarme
  (Hello. Maybe you can help me)
- Estoy buscando la tienda de bolsos "Cat Noir" pero no la encuentro. ¿Sabes dónde está?
  (I'm looking for the "Cat Noir" handbags shop but I can't find it. Do you know where it is?)
- Si. Está en el segundo piso. Si coges estos ascensores, está justo enfrente
  (Yes, it is in the second floor. If you take these lifts, it's just in front of them)
- Genial. Muchas gracias
  (Great. Thanks a lot)
- No hay de qué
  (Don't mention it)

4.4 Clothing

There will be some occasions that you will need to talk about clothes. Maybe in a shop, maybe to borrow something to attend a celebration or maybe because you have left something in a bar, so **let's practice all these situations to know the specific vocabulary**.

- En la tienda de ropa (At the clothing store) -

- o Gracias por venir conmigo Aurora
  (Thanks for coming with me Aurora)
- o Necesito comprarme un vestido para una boda y tú me puedes ayudar
  (I need to buy a dress for a wedding and you can help me)
- o Confío en ti
  (I trust you)
- o ¿Qué te parece este?
  (What do you think about this?)
- o Me gusta, pero no parece tu estilo
  (I like it but it doesn't seem to be your style)
- o Piensa que tendrás que llevarlo durante mucho rato, así que busca un vestido que sea cómodo de llevar
  (Be aware you'll have to wear it for a long period of time, so look for a comfortable dress to wear)
- o ¿Y este?
  (And this?)
- o Este creo que te puede quedar muy bien. ¿Por qué no te lo pruebas?
  (I think this can look great on you. Why don't you try it on?)
- o ¿Qué tal estoy?
  (How do I look?)
- o ¡Perfecta! ¡Estás muy elegante y guapa!
  (Perfect! You look elegant and pretty!)
- o Pues me llevo este
  (Then I buy this)

- Pidiendo prestado algo a un amigo (Borrowing something from a friend) -

- Dani, tengo una cena formal este viernes. ¿Tienes alguna corbata para prestarme?
  (Dani, I have a formal dinner on Friday. Do you have any tie I can borrow?)
- Seguro que sí. ¿De qué color es el traje y la camisa que vas a llevar?
  (Sure. What colour is the suit and shirt you are going to wear?)
- El traje es gris oscuro y la camisa es rosa claro
  (The suit is dark grey, and the shirt is light pink)
- Creo que tengo tres que te pueden ir bien
  (I think I have three can suit you)
- Tengo esta morada, esta gris oscura o esta de rayas
  (I have this purple one, this grey one or this one with stripes)
- Creo que me gusta más la gris
  (I think I like more the grey one)
- Vale. Pues llévatela y ya me la devolverás
  (Ok then, take it and you will bring it back to me)
- Mil gracias
  (Many thanks)

- Olvidando cosas (Forgetting things) -

- Ostras Alberto, me he olvidado la chaqueta en el restaurante
  (Oops Alberto, I have forgotten the jacket at the restaurant)
- ¿Te importa si volvemos a buscarla?
  (Do you mind if we come back to look for it?)
- No hay problema
  (No problem)
- Disculpe, hemos cenado aquí hace un rato y me he olvidado una chaqueta roja. ¿La han visto?
  (Excuse me, we had dinner here early and I forgot a red jacket. Have you found it?)
- ¿En qué mesa se han sentado?
  (In what table were you sitting?)
- En la de la esquina izquierda
  (The one in the left corner)
- Déjenme preguntar al camarero de esa zona
  (Let me ask to the waiter there)
- Dice que sí la tiene, ahora la trae
  (He says he does have it. He's taking it now)

- Aquí la tiene
  (Here you have)
- Muchas gracias. Ha sido muy amable
  (Thank you very much. You were very kind)

- Encontrando cosas que alguien ha olvidado (Founding things someone has forgotten) -

Disculpe, acabo de encontrarme este abrigo en el suelo.
(Excuse me, I just have found this coat on the floor)

¿Perdona, es tuyo este pañuelo?
(Excuse me, is this foulard yours?)

Esa señora acaba de perder el jersey.
(That woman has just lost her jumper)

¿Perdona, has visto un bolso marrón?
(Excuse me, have you seen a brown handbag?)

Avisa a ese señor porque se le acaba de caer la bufanda.
Warn that man because his scarf has just fallen.

FIFTH CHAPTER: Expressions, proverbs and sayings

In Spanish, as in any other language there is a lot of typical expressions, popular sayings and proverbs impossible to translate literally into English because they will sound strange and will seem not making sense. But Spanish speakers use them a lot, so let's learn the expressions and what they mean.

We will translate as literally as possible to know what they are saying but this won't be the actual meaning of the sentence, keep that in mind. We are going to explain the meaning of the expression and we will use it in an example.

1. **A buenas horas mangas verdes** (Good hours, green sleeves): this expression is used to say that is too late for something. For example: A buenas horas mangas verdes, Juan. Ya he enviado yo la carta por correo (what we are saying is that I already have sent the letter by post because Juan is always late for everything)
2. **A palabras necias, oídos sordos** (To foolish words, deaf ears): used to say that you don't have to care about some people say. Example: No te preocupes por lo que diga Carola, porque está celosa. A palabras necias, oídos sordos (here we are saying that you have not to care about what Carola is saying because is jealous)
3. **A Dios rogando y con el mazo dando** (To God begging, and with the hammer hitting): this expression is used to say that you can ask God for help, but you have to do everything is in your hand. Example: Pablo es muy trabajador, pero tiene mala suerte con sus parejas. Por eso siempre está a Dios rogando y con el mazo dando. (Pablo is very hard worker, but he's very unlucky with his partners. This is why he's asking God to help him although he'll continue doing his best)
4. **A fin de cuentas** (At the end of the day): This expression is used to clarify that what we are going to say a conclusion. For example. Rosa ha dejado el trabajo, a fin de cuentas, vivía muy lejos y cada día tardaba dos horas en llegar (Rosa has left the job because, at the end of the day, she spent a loto f time on her way to the office)
5. **A caballo regalado no le mires el dentado** (To a horse given, don't look at its teeth): this expressions is used to say that if something is given to you for free, someone give you something for free, you can't complain. Example: La moto que te ha dado Rafa tiene algún arañazo pero a caballo regalado no le mires el dentado (the motorbike has scratches but is a gift so focus on the positive)

6. **A otra cosa, mariposa** (To other thing, butterfly): we use this expression when we want to change the subject in a conversation, or to jump into a different task or status. Example: Si esta relación no funciona, a otra cosa, mariposa (we'll leave the relationship if it does not work)
7. **Al mal tiempo, buena cara** (If bad weather, good face): we are telling someone that has to be strong despite a bad experience. Example: Has suspendido el examen, pero al mal tiempo buena cara (Someone has failed an exam and we are saying to him or her to be strong and positive)
8. **A palo seco** (Dry stick): This is easy to understand. It's used when we have an alcoholic drink without mixing. Example: Me gusta el whisky a palo seco (I like whiskey with nothing else)
9. **A vivir que son dos días** (To live that it's only two days): we use this expression to say don't worry too much and enjoy living because life is short. Example: ¡Olvidate de la discusión que has tenido y a vivir que son dos días! (Forget about the argument you have just had and enjoy the life!)
10. **Al pan, pan y al vino, vino** (Bread to bread, wine to wine): we mean that everything must be called by its own name. Example: Lo que ha dicho Javier ha sido para hacer daño. Al pan, pan y al vino, vino (Javier has spoken with the only aim to hurt)
11. **¡Anda ya!** (Come on!): When it's hard to believe what we are hearing we say "anda ya". It's like saying "It can't be true". Example: ¿ Has aprobado el examen de conducir a la primera? ¡Anda ya! (You have passed the driving test at the first try. It can't be true!)
12. **A quien madruga, Dios le ayuda** (Who wakes up early, God will help him) If you want God's help, don't be lazy. Example: Como sabes, a quien madruga, Dios ayuda, así que levántate de la cama y empieza a estudiar (If you need help or luck at your studies, you also have to do your part)
13. **Bajar la guardia** (Put down the guard): It's to relax, not to pay enough attention to something. Example: Confiaban mucho en su superioridad así que bajaron la guardia y perdieron (you can put down the guard when you trust excessively on yourself and, therefore, losing unexpectedly a game)
14. **Cada maestrillo tiene su librillo** (Every little master has his own little book) It means that no one makes things exactly same way. Example: Aunque el trabajo era idéntico, la forma de llevarlo a cabo era muy distinta (There are different paths that heads you to the same place)
15. **Caer en saco roto** (To fall down in a broken bag): Despite your efforts, you're not going to achieve your goal. Example: Hizo una muy buena entrevista, pero todos sus esfuerzos cayeron en saco roto y no consiguió el trabajo (We are saying that he made a really good interview but didn't get the job)

16. **Cantar las cuarenta** (To sing the forty): We use it when someone has done something bad and we are going to scold him because of that. Example: Le he dejado el coche a José y me lo ha devuelto con un arañazo, le voy a cantar las cuarenta. (We are saying we have lent our car to Jose, and he has returned the it with a big scratch. So, we are mad at him)
17. **Como agua de mayo** (Like water in May): It's said when something is very opportune or convenient. Example: El aumento de sueldo me va como agua de mayo (The salary rise is very opportune to me)
18. **Como Pedro por su casa** (Like Peter at his house): we use this expression when someone feels quickly pretty comfortable in a new space. Example: Marta lleva solo un día trabajando aquí y se mueve como Pedro por su casa. (We are saying Marta has just started working here and she already feels very comfortable)
19. **Con la miel en los labios** (With honey on the lips): when we are going to do something we love and it's cancelled at the very last moment. Example: Me dijo que iríamos al concierto de Bruce Springsteen, pero al final no consiguió entradas y me quede con la miel en los labios (I was very excited because he told me we were going to Bruce Springsteen concert but he couldn't get tickets)
20. **Costar un ojo de la cara** (Cost an eye of the face): Used when something is very expensive. Example. El abrigo es precioso pero me ha costado un ojo de la cara (Nice coat but super expensive)
21. **Costar un huevo** (Cost an egg): something is going to take a lot of effort. Example: Hacer el pastel me costó un huevo (I spent a lot of time and effort on making that cake)
22. **Quedar dos telediarios** (Remaining two newscasts): when there is barely time left. Example: A Marisol le quedan dos telediarios, el lunes ya empieza las vacaciones (We are saying that Marisol is going on holidays next Monday so there are just a few days left)
23. **Es otro cantar** (It's another sing): we use this expression to say something is different and difficult .Example: Hemos conseguido que la empresa nos reduzca el horario y ahora trabajemos de 9 a 5, pero conseguir que los viernes nos dejen salir a las tres durante todo el año va a ser otro cantar. (We are saying that we have agreed with the company a new workday from 9 to 5, but it's not going to be easy to get Fridays we can go at 3 all year round)
24. **Dar en el clavo** (Hit the spot): This expression means we are right about something or we have guessed right. Example: Has dado en el clavo, tengo 45 años. (You are right, I'm 45 years old)
25. **De cara a la galería** (Facing the gallery): we use this expression when someone acts differently when is exposed and look for recognition. Example: Carla siempre

está feliz de cara a la galería, pero después siempre se está quejando de todo. (Carla seems pretty happy in front of others, but then she's always complaining about everything)

26. **De tal palo tal astilla** (Like wood like stick): used to refer that someone is very alike to a family member, usually older. Example: Mi hermana es mandona como mi madre, de tal palo tal astilla. (My sister is bossy as my mother)

27. **Déjame en paz** (leave me alone): the same as "leave me alone" in English. Example: ¡Déjame en paz! No quiero hablar ahora. (Leave me alone. I don't want to talk right now)

28. **Diálogo de besugos** (Bream dialog): when having a conversation that makes no sense because no one is listening. Example: Llevamos diez minutos hablando y cada uno hablamos de temas distintos. Esto parece un diálogo de besugos. (We both are talking about different matters and not listening each other. This conversation makes no sense)

29. **Dios los cría y ellos se juntan** (God made them, and they get along): This expression means when people who are very alike but not related, get along. Example: ¡Dios los cría y ellos se juntan, se acaban de conocer y parece que sean amigos de toda la vida! (We are saying that they have just known each other but they are getting along and seem they know for a long time)

30. **Dormir como un lirón** (to sleep like a dormouse): We say that when someone is sleeping no matter what: noise, warm, is late... Example: Rocio duerme como un liron, no se despierta ni con el ruido de la excavadora. (Rocio is sleeping like a dormouse; she's not waking up even with the noise of the excavator)

31. **Dormir la mona** (Sleeping the monkey): Well this means we have got a rough night (partying, drinking until late) and we need are sleeping. Example: No creo que venga a desayunar, está durmiendo la mona. (I don't think she's coming for breakfast and without specifying someone were going to sleep very late, if we say "dormir la mona" we understand that)

32. **Echar leña al fuego** (Put Wood in the fire): when someone is trying to upset someone talking about matters that can be hurtful. Example: Tu hermano ha suspendido el examen, no eches más leña al fuego, no se lo recuerdes más. (Your brother has failed the exam and you don't have to be reminding it to him)

33. **El horno no está para bollos** (The oven is not for buns): when it is not a good moment for something. Example: El Horno no está para bollos Silvia, el jefe esta de muy mal humor, no le pidas las vacaciones ahora (We are saying that is not a good moment to talk about holidays because the boss is very crossed)

34. **El mundo es un pañuelo** (The world is a tissue): We use this expression when we bump or meet someone very far away from the common space. Example: No

esperaba encontrarte aquí en Paris, el mundo es un pañuelo (I wasn't expecting to bum pinto you here in Paris)

35. **El que algo quiere, algo le cuesta** (If you want something, it's going to cost you): This expression means pretty much what the translation into English says. Example: El que algo quiere, algo le cuesta. Si quieres que te suban el sueldo, tienes que demostrar lo que has aprendido en este tiempo. (We are saying that if you want a salary raise you have to show what you have learnt during this time)

36. **El quinto pino** (the fifth pine): we use this expression to say something is far away. Example: La catedral está en el quinto pino. Es mejor que vayas en autobús. (The cathedral is far away. Better take the bus)

37. **En boca cerrada no entran moscas** (In shout mouth flies don't go in): Sometime it's better say nothing. Example: Si te pregunta, no digas nada de que la viste anoche. En boca cerrada no entran moscas. Y así no te metes en líos. (We are saying that if she asks you don't tell you saw her last night to avoid troubles)

38. **En todas partes cuecen habas** (Everywhere are cooking beans): this expression means that there are difficult situations everywhere. Example: No te creas que somos la única familia que discutimos, en todas partes cuecen habas. (Here we are saying that we are not the only family who argue with each other, it happens in a lot of families)

39. **Entre ceja y ceja** (Between eyebrow and eyebrow): We say that someone has something "entre ceja y ceja" between eyebrows when is obsessed with something. Example: No para de hablar de la nueva vecina. La tiene entre ceja y ceja. (He can't stop talking about the new neighbour, He's obsessed about her)

40. **Entre pitos y flautas** (Between whistles and flutes): This means for a reason or another, Let's see the example: Entre pitos y flautas todavía no he hecho los deberes. (For a reason or another I haven't done yet the homework)

41. **Estar en la gloria** (To stay in the glory): It means that we are feeling very comfy. Example: Estoy en la Gloria aquí tumbada en la playa sin hacer nada. Esto es relax. (I'm very comfy here on the beach, laying down and doing nothing)

42. **Éramos pocos y parió la abuela** (We were a few and then granny gave birth): when in a situation seems can't go worst and then, the worst happens. Example: Eramos pocos y pario la abuela. Tengo el coche en el taller y ahora también la moto. Me he quedado sin transporte para repartir los paquetes. (My car is in the mechanic and now the motorbike too. I have no transport to deliver the parcels)

43. **Es peor el remedio que la enfermedad** (I t's worst the remedy than the sickness): when the solution produces more troubles than the original issue. Example: Si no me presento al examen va a ser peor el remedio que la enfermedad porque no me dejaran presentarme el mes que viene. (We are

meaning that if we don't go the exam it will be worst because they are going to let me to go in another occasion)

44. **Estar como pez en el agua** (To be like a fish in water): with this expression we are saying that we are in the best place for us to stay, like a fish in water. Example: Me gusta vivir en Madrid, me siento como pez en el agua. (I like living in Madrid. I feel really comfortable there)

45. **Estar como una cuba** (To be like a tub): when someone has drunk too much. Example: Ramon esta como una cuba. No se aguanta de pie. (Ramos is drunk. He can't stay standing)

46. **Estar patas arriba** (To be upside down): when a room is "patas arriba" means that is a mess. Example: Mi piso esta patas arriba y tengo que recoger porque tengo visita esta tarde. (My house is a mess and I have to tidy up because I am having visits this afternoon)

47. **Faltar un tornillo** (Missing a screw): when someone is a little bit crazy or is doing silly things. Example: Va disfrazado a la playa. Yo diría que le falta un tornillo. (he's going all dressed up to the beach. He's crazy)

48. **Ha pasado un ángel** (An angel has passed): When suddenly nobody says anything and there is a silence we say "ha pasado un ángel". Example: Vaya, ha pasado un ángel, de repente nos hemos quedado todos callados. (Oh, an angel has passed, suddenly we all stopped talking)

49. **Hacer borrón y cuenta nueva** (To erase and start a new account) we say that, when we believe it is necessary to forgive someone and start over. Example: No seas rencoroso, haz borrón y cuenta nueva. No era su intención hacerte daño. (Don't be rancorous. Forgive him and start over. He didn't mean to harm you)

50. **Hacer la pelota** (Make the ball): when someone is always making compliments to someone, usually the boss, to profit himself, we say he's is being "un pelota". Example: Susana es una pelota. Siempre se rie de los chistes del jefe. ¡Y son muy malos! (Susana is being "una pelota" She's always laughing at boss' jokes. And they are too bad!)

51. **Hacerse la boca agua** (make mouth water): to understand this expression will be easier through an actual situation. Imagine you are going home from work and starving, and you pass a bakery with delicious pastries in the window. And you look at them and you can feel how your mouth is producing more saliva. Well this is it! Let's make an example now: Tengo tanta hambre que se me hace la boca agua con tan solo leer el menú. (We are saying that we really hungry and with only reading the menu we are feeling the sensation of producing more saliva)

52. **Ir con pies de plomo** (Go with lead feet): The "plomo" (lead) is a very heavy metal. This expression means to do things very carefully and slowly, step by step. Example: Ten cuidado al montar el mueble, ve con pies de plomo, no vayas a

tener un accidente. (Be carefully when assembling the furniture, not to have an accident)

53. **Ir pisando huevos** (Go treading eggs): To say someone is going very unusually slowly or/and erratic. Example: Este coche debe de tener algún problema porque va pisando huevos. (This car may have a problem because is going unusually slowly)

54. **Ir con la música a otra parte** (Go with the music to another side): this expression is used when someone is feeling what he is saying is not listened by the others and then decides to go away with it. It's like no one is listening to your music so you packed your instrument and change location. Example: Bueno, como nadie me escucha, me voy con la música a otra parte. (We are saying as no one is listening to me, I'm going)

55. **Irse por los cerros de Úbeda** (Go for the Ubeda hills): when someone is going "por los cerros de Ubeda" is because she has started talking about something and she has changed the topic without ending the first matter. Example: Clara te has ido por los cerros de Úbeda. Has empezado contándome lo que te paso el lunes y me estás hablando ahora de lo que vas a hacer para cenar. Acaba de contarme lo del lunes. (Here we are saying that Clara started to tell us about she was doing on Monday and now she was talking about she was going to have for dinner. She has to finish to tell us about her Monday)

56. **La avaricia rompe el saco** (The avarice breaks the bag): If you want more and more, you could end with nothing. Example: Ya has ganado una apuesta. La avaricia rompe el saco. Coge el dinero y vete a casa, no apuestes más o lo puedes perder todo. (This sentence means that you have won a bet, so take the money and go home. If you bet again you could lose everything)

57. **La gota que colmó el vaso** (The drop that filled the glass): this expression refers to something that has done our patience gone. Example: Cada día igual David, tu despertador suena durante mas de media hora y nos despierta a todos menos a ti. Esto es la gota que colma el vaso. O cambias de actitud o tendrás que buscar otros compañeros de piso. (We are saying that it's always the same. David's alarm clock sounds every morning for more than half an hour and wakes up everyone but him, and David's sharing flat partners are tired of that)

58. **La media naranja** (The half orange): when someone has a partner and feels that is "the one" we say is "la media naranja". Example: Mi mujer es mi media naranja, nos complementamos en todo. (My wife is my better half; we complement each other in everything)

59. **Lágrimas de cocodrilo** (Crocodile tears): when someone is faking to be sad and cry, we say she's crying "lágrimas de cocodrilo". Example: No me vengas con esas lágrimas de cocodrilo Marta. Ya te dije que si no recogías tu habitación no

saldrías por la noche. (Don't come to me with your fake tears. I told you, you wouldn't go out tonight without tidy up your room)

60. **Llevar la voz cantante** (Bring the singer voice): we use this expression to refer to the one who is the leader of a situation. Example: Silvia lleva la voz cantante. Desde el principio ha organizado la fiesta de graduación (Silvia is the leader because since the beginning she's been planning the graduation party)

61. **Llover sobre mojado** (Rain on wet): in a bad situation something happens that makes that situation even worse. Example: Llueve sobre mojado, ha caído enferma mientras cuidaba a su padre enfermo (she falls ill while taking care of her sick father)

62. **Mala hierba nunca muere** (Weeds never die): used to highlight how resistant seem to be the bad guys. Example: No le des importancia a lo que ha dicho Jose, ya sabes que mala hierba nunca muere. (We are saying that you don't be upset about Jose told. You know he's always like that)

63. **Mas vale tarde que nunca** (Better late than never): the English translation is clear. Example: Por fin ha llegado el paquete que estábamos esperando. ¡Mas vale tarde que nunca! (Finally, the parcel we were waiting for is here. Better late than never!)

64. **Matar dos pájaros de un tiro** (To kill two birds with one shot): it means that with one action you are sorting out more than one thing. Example: Con la mesilla nueva mato dos pájaros de un tiro: me deshago de una vieja y fea y gano más espacio para guardar cosas. (I have bought a new bedside table so I'll have more space plus I can take the ugly old one away)

65. **Me está tomando el pelo** (She's taking my hair): when some is lying about something to someone, maybe joking, we say she is "tomando el pelo". Example: Sé que me estás tomando el pelo porque he mirado yo antes en el congelador y quedan helados. (I know you are lying to me because I have looked before in the freezer and there were ice creams)

66. **Matar el gusanillo** (To kill the worm): Do you know the sensation when you are starting to feel hungry? We call this "el gusanillo". So "matar el gusanillo" is to eat just something to remove that sensation. Example: Ya sé que hemos quedado para comer en una hora pero es que tengo hambre. Voy a comer una fruta para matar el gusanillo (I know we're going to have lunch in an hour, but I'm hungry so I'm going to eat a fruit to wait until then)

67. **Me ha salido rana** (I got frog): we use this expression when didn't get the result we expected for something. Example: La paella me ha salido rana. Pensaba que estaría mas buena de lo que está. (We are saying we have cooked a paella but the paella doesn't taste as we expected, it's not as good as it seemed)

68. **Más claro que el agua** (Clearer than water): to say that something has been clearly understood. Example: ¿Has entendido lo que te he explicado? Si, gracias, me ha quedado más claro que el agua (Have you understood what I have just explained? Yes, thanks, clear as water)
69. **Meter cizaña** (Put darnel plant): saying something with the aim of creating a conflict. Example: Ya está Paola metiendo cizaña. Les dice a todos que soy yo la que no quiere ir este verano a Tailandia, cuando no es verdad. (What we are saying is that Paola is lying when telling everyone I don't want to go to Thailand this summer, so gets them upset with me)
70. **Mucho ruido y pocas nueces** (much ado about nothing): Expression very well known. Example: El nuevo rector de la Universidad prometió aulas nuevas y al final no han cambiado nada. Mucho ruido y pocas nueces. (The new rector of the university promised new classrooms and, in the end, nothing has changed. Much ado about nothing)
71. **Ni fu ni fa**: There is no translation for these words because actually they aren't words with meaning. This expression is used to say that something is anodyne, it lacks interest or importance. It's not bad, it's not good. Example: ¿Te ha gustado la última película de Tarantino? Pues ni fu ni fa. (Did you like the last Tarantino movie? And the answer is neither yes nor no)
72. **Ni harto de vino** (Not fed up with wine): if we say that we are not going to do something "ni harto de vino", means that there is no way we are going to do that. Example: ¿Quieres venir a hacer paracaidismo conmigo? ¡Ni harta de vino! (Do you want to come skydiving with me? No way!)
73. **Ni me va ni me viene** (neither goes nor comes to me): when something means nothing to us or lacks importance. Example: ¿Qué opinas del dinero que se gastan los equipos de fútbol para fichar nuevos jugadores? La verdad es que ni me va ni me viene. (What do you think about the money football clubs spend in getting news players? It's not important to me)
74. **No hay mal que por bien no venga** (There's no harm that for good do not come): when something bad happens, something good will come. Example: Desde que tengo el coche en el mecanico, camino más y me siento más ágil. No hay mal que por bien no venga. (Since my car is at the mechanic, I'm walking more and am feeling more agile. This is a good thing because of a bad thing, isn't it)?
75. **No pegar ni con cola** (They don't stick even with glue): when there is no way two people get along because of differences we say they "no pegan ni con cola". Example: Mi hermana y mi marido no pegan ni con cola. Piensan tan distinto que ni se hablan. (My sister and my husband they don't get along. They think so differently that they don't speak to each other)

76. **No ser trigo limpio** (Don't be clean wheat): we say someone "no es trigo limpio" when we suspect or know she's faking and she's untrustworthy. Example: Mi nuevo compañero de trabajo no es trigo limpio. Va de simpático y luego te critica con los demás. (My new work partner is untrustworthy. He seems nice but he criticizes everyone)
77. **No tener abuela** (Not to have granny): when someone flatters himself a lot we say that he has no granny, because grannies are always flattering their grandchildren. Example: La verdad es que soy bueno jugando a rugby. EL equipo estaría perdido sin mí. ¡Simón, parece que no tengas abuela! (I'm very good at playing Rugby. I don't know what the team would do without me. Simon, it seems you don't have grandmother!)
78. **Ojalá**: it can't be translated literally but the meaning is similar to hopefully, I hope so, I wish that. Example: He comprado un billete de lotería. ¡Ojalá me toque! (I have bought a lottery ticket. I hope I win)
79. **Ojos que no ven, corazón que no siente** (If eyes can't see, heart can't feel): you can guess the meaning of this expression. If someone doesn't see something, he won't suffer for that. Example: Si vieras un amigo engañando a su pareja, ¿se lo dirías a la pareja o piensas que ojos que no ven, corazón que no siente? (If you see a friend cheating on his partner, would you let the partner know, or you think if eyes can't see, heart can't feel?)
80. **Pasar página** (Pass the page): well, life can be tough and when something bad happens and we achieve to be over it, to keep going, we say the that we "pasamos página". Example: Perder el trabajo fue muy duro, pero he pasado página. Ahora ya estoy preparada para mi próximo reto profesional. (Losing the job was very hard but I'm over it. I'm ready for a new professional challenge)
81. **Pedir peras al olmo** (To ask for pears to the elm): this expression means that someone is asking for the impossible. Example: No me pidas que aprenda chino en un mes porque es como pedir peras al Olmo. (We are saying not to ask me to learn Chinese in one month because is as to ask pears to a tree that doesn't get pears, to the elm)
82. **Ponerse las pilas** (Put on batteries): when the deadline is around the corner and you are starting to run short of time. You have then to hurry up to finish the work on time. We say then, you have to "ponerse las pilas". Example: Ponte las pilas con el español o no aprobarás el examen. Solo te queda una semana para estudiar. (Hurry up with the Spanish or you won't pass the exam. You only have one week left to study)
83. **Ponerse morado** (become purple): We use this expression when we are full of food, drink and everything. For example, like in the Christmas's dinner. We likely eat and drink a lot so we feel we can't eat anything else or we will explode.

Example: ¿Quieres postre Carlota? No gracias, me he puesto morada. No puedo comer nada más (Do you want a dessert Carlota? No thanks, I'm full. I can't eat anything else)

84. **Por si las moscas** (By the flies): this expression means "just in case". Example: He cogido un jersey por si las moscas (I have taken a sweater, just in case)

85. **Que me quiten lo bailado** (To take away from me what I have danced): to understand this expression let's imagine that we have partied last night, and we had great fun. We are working today, feeling tired and sleepy, but we think that it was still worth last night because was great. No one can't steal us what we "danced" last night, can they? Example: Buf, estoy muy cansada hoy y se me va a hacer el día largo, pero que me quiten lo bailado. (Oh, I'm super tired today and it's going to be a long day but they can't steal from me what I danced)

86. **Quedarse a cuadros** (Stay as a sqaure): we say that when someone is astonished for some reason. Example: Le he dicho a mi madre que estoy embarazada y se ha quedado a cuadros. (I told my mother I'm pregnant and she's atonished)

87. **Quedarse frito** (Stay fried): When someone is really tired and can't avoid falling sleep, we say that "se ha quedado frito". Example: Ha salido del hospital de trabajar una jornada de veinticuatro horas. Al llegar a casa se ha quedado frito. (He has gone off the hospital, after working 24 hours turn. He felt asleep just arriving home)

88. **Quien siembre vientos, recoge tempestades** (Who sows winds, will pick up thunderstorms): This expression means that if someone is doing always bad things, one day he will get a very big bad thing. Example: Rosario siempre ha tenido celos de María y le ha hecho la vida imposible. Al final quien siembra vientos, recoge tempestades. Ahora María es su jefa y no se lo pone fácil. (Rosario has always been jealous of Maria and made her life impossible. Now Maria is her boss and that doesn't make it easy for her)

89. **Rascarse la barriga** (Scratch the belly): Said when someone is doing nothing and being lazy. Example: Ha sido un trimestre tan duro que tengo ganas de que acabe para rascarme la barriga. (It's been a really hard term. I just want to finish it and do nothing)

90. **Romper el hielo** (Break the ice): when we are in a tense situation, we just want to get over it as soon as possible. Like the first day of a course. We don't know each other and for some people is not easy to interact with new people. So, there's always and ice breaker activity. Example: Bienvenidos a todos a este curso de español. Para romper el hielo y conocernos todos un poco más, vamos a jugar al bingo. (Welcome all to this Spanish course. To break the ice and to know each other a little bit more, let's play bingo)

91. **Rizar el rizo** (Loop the loop): We use this expression when someone wants to make something more complicated, something already difficult will get it more difficult yet. Example: El tenista perdió un punto por querer rizar el rizo. (The tennis player lost a point because he wanted to it complicated)
92. **Saber a gloria** (Taste as glory): when something tastes delicious tastes as glory. Example: Esta tarta de manzana sabe a gloria. Es la mejor tarta que he comido nunca (This apple pie tastes as glory. Is the best pie I have ever eaten!)
93. **Sacar las castañas del fuego** (Take off the chestnut form the fire): when we solve other's problem or we face the consequences for another person, we say we are "sacando las castañas del fuego"). Example: Gracias por sacarme las castañas del fuego. No sabía cómo salir de esta. Sin tu ayuda no sé qué habría hecho. (We are thanking someone to solve my problem. I didn't know how to get off from this. I don't know what I would have done without your help)
94. **Salvarse por los pelos** (Save by the hair): we use this expression when someone has been near to a disaster and he escaped last minute. Example: Ese niño iba a cruzar la calle sin mirar y estaba viniendo un coche muy deprisa. Por suerte ha parado en el último momento y se ha salvado por los pelos. (That kid was going to cross the Street without looking at any side and a car was coming fast. Luckily, he stopped at the last moment)
95. **¡Salud!** (Health!): when someone sneezes, we say ¡salud!
96. **Ser como un libro abierto** (To be like an open book): when someone is easy to read, so we know exactly what he's thinking and feeling in every moment, we say that he "es como un libro abierto". Example: Luis es como un libro abierto. Su cara siempre refleja cómo se siente y hasta puedes adivinar lo que está pensando. (Pedro is like an open book. His face shows how is he feeling, and you can even guess what is he thinking)
97. **Se me ha ido el santo el cielo** (The saint has gone to the sky): we use this expression to say we have lost track of time. Example: Siento llegar tarde, estaba leyendo en la biblioteca y se me ha ido el santo al cielo. (Sorry to be late, I was reading at the library and I lost track of time)
98. **Ser la oveja negra** (To be the black sheep): this means to be the different within a group (family, friends...). Example: En mi familia todos son abogados, pero yo soy la oveja negra. Yo soy arquitecto. (In my family they all are lawyers, but I'm the black sheep. I'm an arquitect)
99. **Ser pan comido** (To be eaten bread): when something is very easy, we say is like to eat bread. Example: No te preocupes mamá, soy capaz de prepararme la cena. Es pan comido (Don't worry mum, I'm able to prepare my dinner. Is like to eat bread)

100. **Ser un aguafiestas** (To be a killjoy): We say someone is an "aguafiestas" when breaks down a party or a situation where we're having fun. Meaning that the party was going wonderfully, and he has done something to finish that. Example: Nos los estábamos pasando de maravilla en la fiesta, cuando Carlos empezó a reírse de todo el mundo porque iba borracho y la diversión se terminó. Fue un aguafiestas. (We were enjoying so much the party, when Carlos started laughing at everyone because he was drunk, and then the fun stopped. He was a killjoy)

CONCLUSIONS

Well, now you have finished the book!
You have covered a lot. The tricky thing will be to remember everything. The key is and will be to practice what you are learning. If not, it's easy to forget.

The good thing now, that you know the basic vocabulary and have read and learnt a lot of sentences, is that you are getting used to real Spanish, the Spanish language that is spoken by people in the street!
If you are listening this book as an audiobook this will also help you to get used to the speaking Spanish accent and pronunciation, and this will help to understand Spanish speakers talking.
If you are reading this book by yourself, you are learning as well how Spanish is written so it will be easy for you to read signs and stuff when you are in a Spanish speaking country.

With the first and the second books you have lots and lots of vocabulary and sentences, so if you are not able to practice in the short time, try to read and/or listen again the book. And repeat as much as you can!

Why not starting to practice writing some dialogs in Spanish? You know the words and you have sentences that can guide you to do that. Maybe you can try to translate some simple conversation you have had recently. Google translate will help you with the words you don't know, but watch out with the translator since it's useful as dictionary but not such good when translation text and sentences!

If you already have started to watch TV shows and movies in Spanish with English subtitles, this could be the perfect time to switch to Spanish subtitles. You have to listen and try to match the key words you are hearing with the subtitles.

It's time now as well to work with the sounds you are struggling. You can make lists with the trickiest words and practice them loud. You can practice as well to make sentences with these words.
Try to learn your routines in Spanish, the things you are using every day, etc.
The more Spanish used during your everyday, the better!
The way is long but the hardest step is the first one and you did it so keep going!
And keep going.
And practise in between.
And keep going!

Thank you for making it through to the end of "Learn Spanish in your car – Level 2", let's hope it was informative and able to provide you with all of the tools you need to achieve your goals whatever they may be.

We really hope you enjoyed this guide, customer satisfaction for us is very important.
If you found this book useful in any way, a review on Amazon is always appreciated! ☺

LEARN SPANISH IN YOUR CAR
for Intermediates

The Ultimate Easy Spanish Learning Guide: How to Learn Intermediate Spanish Language Vocabulary like crazy with over 500 Useful Phrases.

Lesson 11-20
level 3

INTRODUCTION

Hola! Either if this is your third book or if you are starting now because you already know some Spanish, you are more than welcome!
This third book is created for an intermediate level. What does it mean? Is it right for you?
It supposes you already know the basics and you are able to listen and understand basic questions and you feel confident answering. You also can read and write known words and basic sentences. If you can do that, you are in the right place!

What are we going to learn here?
First of all, we will refresh pronunciation and we will be practicing and focusing on the struggling sounds.
After that, it's time for some grammar. You can think grammar is tough, well, it's not the funniest topic to learn, but if you want to continue your Spanish learning journey and progress through that, you need to learn grammar. You know a lot of vocabulary and sentences and all that is really helpful, but now you are going to learn how to make the sentences by yourself.
When we say grammar, we mean to know how conjugate regular and irregular verbs in different verb tenses. Consider that when learning all the verb tenses, you will be able to speak not only in present but in past and even to express your ideas for the future!
We will take a look at the famous Spanish subjunctive, but don't freak out and run away, we will try to make it as simple and understandable as possible.
With all verb tenses, we will use examples, and we will also give you some verbs for you to practice on your own. As always, you will have to practice as much as you can!
Well, don't waste more time and let's move on, or better said let's continue, our Spanish learning journey!

FIRST CHAPTER: Back to Pronunciation

As you know through your Spanish learning journey, pronunciation is one of the aspects that needs more practice in Spanish. There are a lot of sounds different from English, and struggling with those can make someone not to feel enough confident to speak Spanish when there is the opportunity.
So, to try to minimise the "pronunciation panic attack", let's refresh the letter's sounds.

First, **let's remind the alphabet** and how to pronounce each letter:

Letra (letter)	Nombre (name)	Consejos de pronunciación (pronunciation tips)
a	a	This letter sounds like *a* in "*cat*".
b	be	This letter sounds like an English *b*.
c	ce	If before *a, o, u* sounds like the English *k in "kite"*. But before *e* or *i*, sounds similar to *th* in "*think*".
d	de	Like English, "*done*"
e	e	Sounds like the *e* in "*bed*".
f	efe	Like English, "*fancy*"
g	ge	Sounds like an English *g* when before *a, o or u*, and similarly to the English *h* when before *e* or *i*.
h	hache	This letter is mute in Spanish, except when follows a *c* that sounds like English *ch*.
i	i	Sounds like *i* in "*him*".
j	jota	Similar to English *h* in "*hello*".

k	ca	Like in English, *"kite"*
l	ele	Like in English, *"lemon"*
m	eme	Like in English, *"mouse"*
n	ene	Like in English, *"nose"*
ñ	eñe	*There is not any English correspondence, but the sound is similar to ny in "canyon", best example can be found in the word "España".*
o	o	This letter sounds like *o* in "song".
p	pe	Like in English, *"pencil"*
q	cu	Always followed by the letter *u* and sounds like English *k*.
r	erre	Like in English, *"rock"*
s	ese	Like in English, *"salmon"*
t	te	Like in English, *"tea"*
u	u	This letter sounds like *u* in "flu".
v	uve	Sounds like an English *b*.
w	uve doble	This letter has been imported from English to Spanish, hence sounds similar to English *w*.
x	equis	Like in English, *"xylophone"*
y	ye	Sounds like the *y* in English *"yes"*.

z	zeta	Sounds similar to *th* in *"think"*.

Now that we have refreshed the alphabet and the sounds, **let's practice**!

The following sentences have been written to practice the sounds that can be confusing. You'll see that the meaning of the sentence can be a bit odd, but focus on the pronunciation that is what these sentences are for. Read and repeat slowly, focusing on each sound. No shortcuts as we were singers. Every letter must have a sound!

- Cecilia es celosa (Cecilia is jealous)
- La piscina municipal está cerrada (The public swimming pool is closed)
- A Cecilia le gusta el zumo de cerezas (Cecilia likes cherry juice)
- La voz de Marcelo me fascina (I'm fascinated by Marcelo's voice)
- Susana, Sonia y Cecilia cenan pastel de zanahoria (Susana, Sonia and Cecilia are dinning carrot cake)
- A Pablo le gusta que le cuente un cuento antes de irse a dormir (Pablo likes me to tell him a story before going to sleep)
- En Cuenca y Cáceres hay casas de colores (There are colourful houses in Cuenca and Caceres)
- Explícame cómo has perdido el móvil en el taxi (Explain to me how you have lost the mobile phone in the taxi)
- El examen tenía un texto para leer sobre la xenofobia (The exam had a text about xenophobia to read)
- Charo come chocolate con leche (Charo eats chocolate with milk)
- He visto a Chema e iba vestido con chándal y chanclas (I've seen Chema and he was wearing suit track and slippers)
- Adela y Daniel se adoran desde siempre (Adela and Daniel adore each other since always)
- ¿Dónde decías para ir a desayunar? (Where were you saying to go for breakfast?)
- Lola saluda a Laura diciendo hola (Lola greets Laura saying hello)
- Falta luz en esta habitación, tendremos que comprar una lámpara (There isn't enough light in this bedroom, we will have to buy a lamp)
- Llevo las llaves en el llavero (I have my keys in the keyring)
- La calle está llena de gente (The street is full of people)
- Ya llega mayo (May it's almost here)
- Al llegar ha llamado a Yolanda (When she got here, she has called Yolanda)

- Si la ensalada está sosa siempre puedes echar más sal (If the salad is bland you can always add more salt)
- Sandra siempre esta sana (Sandra is always healthy)
- La araña que he visto esta mañana era grande (The spider I have seen this morning was big)
- En la cabaña hay muchas arañas (There are a lot of spiders in the cabin)
- El perro y el zorro corren juntos (The dog and the fox run together)
- Ramón ha traído rosas del rosal de Rosa (Ramon has brought roses from Rosa's rosebush)
- Es raro que Roberto ronque cuando duerme (It's strange that Roberto snores when he's sleeping)
- El bebé bebe leche con su biberón (The baby drinks milk with his bib)
- Valencia y Barcelona tienen playa (Valencia and Barcelona have beach)
- ¿Vas a venir o prefieres que vaya yo? (Are you coming, or you prefer me going?)
- Pedro pela patatas y pepinos (Pedro is peeling potatoes and cucumbers)
- Paris y Pamplona empiezan por P (Paris and Pamplona start with P)
- A Gabriel le gusta la guitarra (Gabriel likes the guitar)
- El gato de Gabi es muy goloso (Gabi's cat is very gourmand)
- Juan y Julia comen jamón juntos (Juan and Julia eat ham together)
- La jirafa come hojas del árbol (The giraffe eats leaves from the tree)
- La gente hace burbujas con el jabón (People are doing bubbles with soap)
- Fernando come falafel y frambuesas (Fernando eats falafel and raspberries)
- Fabian tiene un Ferrari (Fabian has a Ferrari)
- La fábrica fabrica fichas de ajedrez (The factory makes chest pieces)
- Manuel me mandó un mensaje (Manuel sent me a message)
- Mi marido me manda flores todas las mañanas (Mi husband sends me flowers every morning)
- No negocies ningún contrato con él (Don't negotiate any contract with him)

Now that we have been practicing the sentences focusing in sounds, **let's do more practice**.
Now we are going to read longer sentences.

- Cuando llegué a Santiago de Chile, me sorprendió que aun hablando también español como yo, que soy de España, tuviéramos tantas palabras y expresiones distintas (When I arrived at Santiago de Chile, it surprised me that even speaking

Spanish like me as I'm from Spain, we had a lot of different words and expressions)

- Me dijo que cogería el tren de las cinco, pero no llegó a tiempo y tuvo que coger el tren de las siete (He told me he was going to take the five o'clock train but he was late, and had to take the train at seven)

- No me digas que no has podido comprar la fruta, porque has pasado por delante del supermercado de camino a casa (Don't tell me you couldn't buy fruit, because you passed in front of the supermarket in your way home)

- Xavi toca el xilofón, Gabriel toca la guitarra, Anabel toca el acordeón y Patricia toca el piano (Xavi plays the xylophone, Gabriel plays the guitar, Anabel plays the accordion and Patricia plays the piano)

Well done! Don't hesitate to repeat and practice again and again. The only secret for a good pronunciation is doesn't be nervous and practice a lot!

SECOND CHAPTER: Regular verbs in present, past and future

Spanish verbs are a complex area of Spanish grammar, with many combinations of tenses, aspects and moods.

The mood of a verb indicates the way it is used in a sentence. There are four moods in Spanish: indicative (*indicativo*), subjunctive (*subjuntivo*), conditional (*condicional*) and imperative (*imperativo*).

The indicative mood is used for expressing reality. This mode is made up of the present, past and future tenses.

The subjunctive mood is used for expressing desires, doubts, the unknown, the abstract, and emotions.

The conditional mood is used to express conditional sentences relying on conditions being met.

The imperative mood is used to express an order, request or prohibition.

Now that we know how the Spanish verbs are classified, let's start with the **indicative** mode.

We will learn how conjugate Spanish regular verbs in present, past and future. Don't worry, we'll be going step by step, verb tense by verb tense. We will learn when we are using each tense, how to conjugate the verbs and we will practice with a lot of examples.

But before starting with the present tense, we have to know that in Spanish the verbs are divided in three groups or three conjugations, depending on their ending.

The first group or first conjugation are the verbs ending with "AR" like cantar (to sing), comprar (tu buy), hablar (to talk), pensar (to think).

The second group or second conjugation, are the verbs ending with ER, like beber (to drink), leer (to read), comer (to eat) or correr (to run).

The third group or third conjugation, are the verbs ending with IR, like vivir (to live), reir (to laugh), compartir (to share) or salir (to go out).

Let's see if you can say which conjugation are the following verbs:

Robar (to steal)
Esconder (to hide)
Bailar (to dance)

Sonreir (to smile)
Ver (to see)
Mirar (to watch)
Escribir (to write)
Enviar (to send)
Estudiar (to study)
Comer (to eat)

Remember: first conjugation all the verbs ending in AR, second conjugation all the verbs ending in ER and third conjugation all the verbs ending in IR.
But, does this means that all the Spanish verbs always end in AR, ER or IR? Yes, the infinitive form does.
Let's see now how conjugate the verbs now.

El presente simple (Simple present)

This tense is used to talk about actions are happening now, habitual actions and routines or nearly future actions when we specify when is going to happen. Let's see some examples:

Actions happening now:
La tienda está cerrada (The shop is closed)
Juana come manzanas (Juana eats apples)
Javier canta una canción (Javier sings a song)

Habitual actions and routines:
Cada día desayuno tostadas con mantequilla y un café (Every day I eat for breakfast toast and butter and a coffee)
Los martes voy al gimnasio (I go to the gym on Tuesdays)
Mi hermana hace yoga los lunes (My sister practices yoga on Mondays)

Nearly future actions:
El domingo juego a bádminton (I play badmilton on Sunday)
La semana que viene tengo el examen (I have the exam next week)
Tengo la cita con el medico el próximo jueves (I have the appointment with the doctor next Thursday)

Now that we have seen when we use the present tense in Spanish and some examples, let's learn how to form the present tense.
To form the present what we have to do is take off the ending of the verb (AR, ER o IR) and then use the appropriate ending depending on the subject.

So, for example, we have the verb CANTAR (to sing), ending in AR (i.e. first conjugation), we remove the ending AR, having now CANT, and then we form the present adding different endings like this:

Yo cant<u>o</u> (I sing)
Tú cant<u>as</u> (You sing)
Él/Ella cant<u>a</u> (He/She sings)
Nosotros/Nosotras cant<u>amos</u> (We sing)
Vosotros/Vosotras cant<u>áis</u> (You sing)
Ellos/Ellas cant<u>an</u> (They sing)

And all the regular verbs from the first conjugation will be the same. That means that removing the ending AR from the verb and using the appropriate ending for each subject, we will have the present tense.
Note: We are talking about regular verbs, don't forget that!

Examples:

	cantar	*bailar*	*hablar*	*saltar*
	to sing	*to dance*	*to speak*	*to jump*
yo	canto	bailo	hablo	salto
tú	cantas	bailas	hablas	saltas
él/ella/usted	canta	baila	habla	salta
nosotros/-as	cantamos	bailamos	hablamos	saltamos
vosotros/-as	cantáis	bailáis	habláis	saltáis
ellos/ellas/ustedes	cantan	bailan	hablan	saltan

Let's make sentences in present:

Yo canto en un coro los lunes por la noche (I sing in a choir on Mondays evening)
¿Cantas en el grupo del instituto? (Do you sing in the high school band?)
La verdad es que ella canta muy bien (The truth is that she sings very good)
El próximo fin de semana cantamos en la feria de verano del pueblo (Next weekend we sing in the village summer fair)

Vosotros cantáis ahora y nosotros cuando acabéis (You sing right now, and we'll sing when you finish)
Ellos cantan a capella desde que formaron el grupo (They sing a capella since the group was created)

Now, pay attention at the ending of the following verb forms to know what pronoun is correct.
We will work with the verb "olvidar" (to forget). Let's start!

Olvidamos... is "nosotros", we forget
Olvido... is "yo", I forget
Olvidáis... is "vosotros", you forget
Olvidan... is "ellos or ellas", they forget
Olvidas... is "tú", you forget
Olvida... is "el or ella", he or she forget

Now try again with "decorar" (to decorate):

Decoro... is "yo", I decorate
Decoran... is "ellos or ellas", they decorate
Decoras... is "tu", you decorate
Decora... is "el or ella", he or she decorate
Decoramos... is "nosotros", we decorate
Decoráis... is "vosotros", you decorate

Great! You know how to from the present tense with all regular verbs from the first conjugation, ending with AR.
And how do we form the second and third conjugation verbs? We have to separate the ending as well, ER for the second conjugation, and IR for the third conjugation, and then use the following endings depending on the pronoun.

	aprender	*vivir*
	to learn	*to live*
yo	aprend<u>o</u>	viv<u>o</u>
tú	aprend<u>es</u>	viv<u>es</u>
él/ella/usted	aprend<u>e</u>	viv<u>e</u>
nosotros/-as	aprend<u>emos</u>	viv<u>imos</u>

vosotros/-as	aprend**éis**	viv**ís**
ellos/ellas/ustedes	aprend**en**	viv**en**

As you can notice, the pronouns yo (I), tú (you), él and ella (he and she) and ellos y ellas (they), have the same ending in both conjugations, and Nosotros (we) and vosotros (you) have different endings. Verbs ending with ER will use "emos" and "éis", like in aprend<u>emos</u> and aprend<u>éis</u>, and verbs ending with IR will use "imos" ans "ís", like in viv<u>imos</u> and viv<u>ís</u>.

Let's conjugate a couple of more verbs!

	vender	*compartir*
	to sell	to share
yo	vendo	comparto
tú	vendes	compartes
él/ella/usted	vende	compartes
nosotros/-as	vendemos	compartimos
vosotros/-as	vendéis	compartir
ellos/ellas/ustedes	venden	comparten

Now it's time to make sentences to practice the present tense.

- Yo vendo zapatos en una zapatería (I sell shoes in a shoe shop)
- Tú vendes tu moto porque no la usas (You sell your motorbike because you don't use it)
- Ella vende flores de su jardín (She sells flowers from her garden)
- Nosotros compartimos piso con una estudiante alemana (We share the flat with a German student)
- Vosotros compartís el coche con los compañeros de Erasmus (You share the car with your Erasmus partners)
- Ellos comparten casa desde hace cinco años (They share the house for five years)

Now is your turn to try to form the present tense for the following verbs:

SALUDAR (to greet): yo saludo, tú saludas, él/ella saluda, nosotros saludamos, vosotros saludáis, ellos saludan

BEBER (to drink): yo bebo, tú bebes, él/ella bebe, nosotros bebemos, vosotros bebéis, ellos beben

ASISTIR (to assist): yo asisto, tú asistes, él/ella asiste, nosotros asistimos, vosotros asistís, ellos asisten

Now it's time for the past tense!!

We are going to learn three different past tenses: the "**pretérito indefinido**" that in English is like the simple past (I went → yo fui), the "**pretérito perfecto**" that in English is like the present perfect tense (I have eaten → yo he comido) and the "**pretérito imperfecto**" with no direct equivalence in English (I was working →yo trabajaba).

Step by step, let's start with the "**pretérito indefinido**".

This verb tense is used for completed past actions, facts or general truths in the past, or to express an action that interrupts a second action.

Example for a completed action from the past:
El año pasado **fui** a Varsovia y allí **conocí** a Paula (Last year I went to Versova and I met Paula there).

Example for an action that interrupts a second action:
Justo cuando empezaba a divertirme, **tuve** que irme (Just when I started getting fun, I had to leave).

As in the present tense, to form this past tense, we have to remove from the infinitive form the ending AR, ER or IR, and add the corresponding ending for each person:

person	hablar	aprender	vivir
	to speak	to learn	to live
yo	hablé	aprendí	viví
tú	hablaste	aprendiste	viviste
él/ella/usted	habló	aprendió	vivió

nosotros/-as	habl<u>amos</u>	aprend<u>imos</u>	viv<u>imos</u>
vosotros/-as	habl<u>asteis</u>	aprend<u>isteis</u>	viv<u>isteis</u>
ellos/ellas/ustedes	habl<u>aron</u>	aprend<u>ieron</u>	viv<u>ieron</u>

Let's conjugate more verbs!

- **Saludar** (to greet): yo saludé, tu saludaste, él/ella saludó, nosotros/nosotras saludamos, vosotros/vosotras saludasteis, ellos/ellas saludaron
- **Cantar** (to sign): yo canté, tu cantaste, él/ella cantó, nosotros/nosotras cantamos, vosotros/vosotras cantasteis, ellos/ellas cantaron
- **Beber** (to drink): yo bebí, tu bebiste, él/ella bebió, nosotros/nosotras bebimos, vosotros/vosotras bebisteis, ellos/ellas bebieron
- **Emprender** (to undertake): yo emprendí, tu emprendiste, él/ella emprendió, nosotros/nosotras emprendimos, vosotros/vosotras emprendisteis, ellos/ellas emprendieron
- **Permitir** (to allow): yo permití, tu permitiste, él/ella permitió, nosotros/nosotras permitimos, vosotros/vosotras permitisteis, ellos/ellas permitieron
- **Escribir** (to write): yo escribí, tu escribiste, él/ella escribió, nosotros/nosotras escribimos, vosotros/vosotras escribisteis, ellos/ellas escribieron

Now that we know how to form the "**pretérito indefinido**", **let's practice with some sentences**:

- Ayer **vi** y **saludé** a Carlos en el metro (I saw and greeted Carlos yesterday in the underground)
- (Tú) **cantaste** muy bien en el concierto del domingo (You sang very well on Sunday's concert)
- Ella no **escribió** el informe antes de irse y hoy tendrá problemas (She didn't write the report before leaving and today she'll be in trouble)
- Por suerte, nosotros no **enfermamos**, si no, hubiéramos tenido que anular las vacaciones (Luckily, we didn't get sick, or we would have to cancel the holidays)
- Vosotros **engañasteis** al profesor porque ya sabíais las preguntas del examen (You cheated the professor because you already knew the questions from the exam)

- Ellas **vivieron** en Nueva Zelanda antes de mudarse a Australia (They lived in New Zealand before moving to Australia)

Now is your turn to try to form the past tense, "pretérito indefinido", for the following regular verbs.
Remember, remove the ending and use instead the correspondent ending for each person.

Cancelar (to cancel)
Yo cancelé, tú cancelaste, él/ella canceló, nosotros/nosotras cancelamos, vosotros/vosotras cancelasteis, ellos/ellas cancelaron

Añadir (to add)
Yo añadí, tú añadiste, él/ella añadió, nosotros/nosotras añadimos, vosotros/vosotras añadisteis, ellos/ellas añadieron

Encoger (to shrink)
Yo encogí, tú encogiste, él/ella encogió, nosotros/nosotras encogimos, vosotros/vosotras encogisteis, ellos/ellas encogieron

Do you remember when we use the **"pretérito indefinido"** now?

For completed actions and events that took place in the past.
And for an action which interrupts another action already taking place.

Let's learn now the **"pretérito perfecto"** that, as we have said, is like the present perfect in English.
First of all, when we use this past tense?

- Actions completed within a period of time that is still considered as the present such as "esta mañana" (this morning), "esta semana o este mes" (this week or month), or "este año, este verano, este siglo" (this year, this summer, this century)

Ejemplos:

Esta mañana he ido a trabajar en autobús (This morning I have gone to work by bus)

Esta semana he ido al gimnasio tres días (This week I have been at the gym three days)

Este mes he aprobado el examen de conducir (This month I have passed my driving test)

- Completed actions whose results influence the present or future.

Ejemplos:

Pablo ha ordenado su habitación. Ha planeado mantener el orden en el futuro (Pablo has tidied up his room. He has planned to keep it neat for the future)

He empezado a ir al gimnasio para ponerme en forma (I have started to go to gym to be fit)

Ella ha empezado a aprender español porque se va a vivir a México (She has started to learn Spanish because she's going to live in Mexico)

We know when we use the tense, now we'll learn how to form the "**pretérito perfecto**".

To form this tense we need two verbs: an auxiliary verb and a main verb. The auxiliary we use in Spanish is HABER (to have, in English), and the main verb will be used in its past participle form.

Starting with the auxiliary verb, let's see how to conjugate it.

person	*haber*
	to have
yo	he
tú	has

él/ella/usted	ha
nosotros/-as	hemos
vosotros/-as	habeis
ellos/ellas/ustedes	han

And how we form the past participle from an infinitive form?

If the infinitive ends in AR, we change the ending for ADO:
Comprar – comprado (to buy – bought)
Hablar – hablado (to speak – spoken)

If the infinitive ends in ER or IR, we change the ending for IDO:
Beber – bebido (to drink – drank)
Aprender – aprendido (to learn – learnt)
Vivir – vivido (lo live – lived)
Compartir – compartido (to share – shared)

And then let's put the two verbs, auxiliary and main verb, together!

person	haber	past participle
yo	he	hablado / aprendido / vivido
tú	has	hablado / aprendido / vivido
él/ella/usted	ha	hablado / aprendido / vivido
nosotros/-as	hemos	hablado / aprendido / vivido
vosotros/-as	habéis	hablado / aprendido / vivido
ellos/ellas/ustedes	han	hablado / aprendido / vivido

Some examples:

Este año **he estado** en Argentina dos veces (This year I've been in Argentina two times)
¿Qué **has desayunado** esta mañana? (What have you got for breakfast this morning?)
¿**Has ido** al médico esta semana? (Have you been at the doctor this week?)
He venido andando, por eso estoy tan cansada (I have come walking, this is why I'm so tired)
Nosotros **hemos estado** en Colombia este verano (We have been in Colombia this summer)
Vosotras **habéis estudiado** mucho durante la semana (You have studied a lot during the week)
Ellos **han aprendido** español y chino en la escuela (They have learnt Spanish in the school)

Now is your turn to practice and form the past participle for the following verbs:

Aparcar (to park): aparcado
Compartir (to share): compartido
Aprender (to learn): aprendido
Enchufar (to plug): enchufado
Alquilar (to let): alquilado
Perder (to lose): perdido
Permitir (to allow): permitido
Aplaudir (to clap): aplaudido
Aplicar (to apply): aplicado
Practicar (to practice): practicado
Pretender (to pretend): pretendido
Escoger (to choose): escogido
Prohibir (to forbid): prohibido

Some verbs have an irregular and/or regular participle form. These can be found in the following list:

verb	perfect participle		translation
	Irregular form	Regular form	
abrir	abierto		opened
decir	dicho		said

escribir	escrito		written
hacer	hecho		done/made
freír	frito	freído	fried
imprimir	impreso	imprimido	printed
morir	muerto		died
poner	puesto		placed/put
proveer	provisto	proveído	provided
suscribir	suscrito		subscribed
ver	visto		seen
volver	vuelto		returned

Now **practice** putting auxiliary verb and main verb together to form the "**pretérito perfecto**"

Yo+haber+practicar = yo he practicado
Tú+haber+cantar = tú has cantado
Él+haber+aprender = él ha aprendido
Ella+haber+aparcar = ella ha aparcado
Nosotros+haber+comer = nosotros hemos comido
Nosotras+haber+dormir = nosotras hemos dormido
Vosotros+haber+escoger = vosotros habéis escogido
Vosotras+haber+hablar = vosotras habéis hablado
Ellos+haber+beber = ellos han bebido
Ellas+haber+aparcar = ellas han aparcado

It's time now to learn about the "**pretérito imperfecto**". As we have said before, this past tense is a Spanish past tense and it doesn't exist in English in the same way. The "**pretérito imperfecto**" is used to talk about past actions that were habitual such as past routines and to talk about repeated actions.

Let's see some examples:

Cuando era pequeña **jugaba** al futbol (When I was a kid, I played football)
We can say that the idea of this Spanish past tense is similar to when we use the English form "we used to do an action", i.e. it was a past routine or a past action that was habitual in our lives.

Los martes **estudiaba** alemán (On Tuesdays I used to learn German)
It was a routine for us to go to learn German every Tuesday.

Before start learning how to form the "**pretérito imperfecto**", you must be wondering about the difference between the "**pretérito indefinido**" and the "**pretérito imperfecto**" as this is one of the topics that cause more confusion among the Spanish learners.
Let's compare both past tenses with an example to see the different meanings:

Explicar la situación a sus hijos **fue** complicado (To explain the situation to her kids was complicated)
Fue is the "**pretérito indefinido**" form for the verb SER.

Explicar la situación a sus hijos **era** complicado (To explain the situation to her kids was complicated)
Era is the "**pretérito imperfecto**" form for the verb SER.
.
Both sentences are correct, but the meaning is different.
In the first sentence we are specifying that the action was done and finished.
In the second one we mean that it's (or used to be) difficult to talk about the situation, but we are not saying if it happened or not and if it's finished.

Hopefully this explanation has made clearer the difference between the both past tenses.

Let's learn now how to form the "**pretérito imperfecto**" for regular verbs.

persona	Hablar	Aprender	Vivir
	To speak	*To learn*	*To live*
yo	hablaba	aprendía	vivía
tú	hablabas	aprendías	vivías
el/ella/usted	hablaba	aprendía	vivía

nosotros/-as	habl**ábamos**	aprend**íamos**	viv**íamos**
vosotros/-as	habl**abais**	aprend**íais**	viv**íais**
ellos/ellas/ustedes	habl**aban**	aprend**ían**	viv**ían**

As with the other tenses, what we must do is remove the ending AR, ER or IR from the infinitive and use the correspondent ending for each person.

The first conjugation, infinitives ending in AR, will be like this:

APARCAR (to park): yo aparcaba, tú aparcabas, él/ella aparcaba, nosotros/nosotras aparcábamos, vosotros/vosotras aparcabais, ellos/ellas aparcaban.

BAILAR (to dance): yo bailaba, tú bailabas, él/ella bailaba, nosotros/nosotras bailábamos, vosotros/vosotras bailabais, ellos/ellas bailaban.

The second conjugation, infinitives ending in ER, and the third conjugation, infinitives ending in IR, will be both the same way:

BEBER (to drink): yo bebía, tú bebías, él/ella bebía, nosotros/nosotras bebíamos, vosotros/vosotras bebíais, ellos/ellas bebían.

APRENDER (to learn): yo aprendía, tú aprendías, él/ella aprendía, nosotros/nosotras aprendíamos, vosotros/vosotras aprendíais, ellos/ellas aprendían.

COMPARTIR (to share): yo compartía, tú compartías, él/ella compartía, nosotros/nosotras compartíamos, vosotros/vosotras compartían, ellos/ellas compartían.

PERMITIR (to allow): yo permitía, tú permitías, él/ella permitía, nosotros/nosotras permitíamos, vosotros/vosotras permitíais, ellos/ellas permitían.

Now **let's practice** the "**pretérito imperfecto**" with sentences:

Yo **jugaba** en el parque de al lado de casa mis padres (I used to play at the park near my parent's house)

Tú **cantabas** en el coro del instituto (You used to sing in the high school's choir)
Él siempre **ordenaba** la habitación cuando acababa de jugar (He used to tidy up the room when he finished playing)
Ella **hablaba** francés cuando era pequeña (She spoke French when she was a kid)
Nosotros **veraneábamos** en la playa (We used to spend the summer on the beach)
Nosotras **viajábamos** en tren cada verano (We used to travel by train every summer)
Vosotros **aparcabais** en la segunda planta (You used to park in the second floor)
Vosotras **celebrabais** el fin de año en Madrid (You used to celebrate New Year's Eve in Madrid)
Ellos **fumaban** un paquete de cigarrillos diario (They smoked a packet of cigarettes daily)
Ellas **bailaban** en el ballet de la ópera (They used to dance in the opera's ballet)

Yo **bebía** café cada mañana, pero ahora bebo té (I used to drink coffee every morning, but I drink tea now)
Tu **aprendías** más rápido que yo (You used to learn quicker than me)
Él se **creía** que era Superman (He thought he was superman)
Ella **rompía** los zapatos muy fácilmente (She used to break her shoes easily)
Nosotros **tosíamos** siempre al entrar en el restaurante (We used to cough always when we get into the restaurant)
Nosotras **comíamos** helado de postre los domingos (We used to eat ice cream for dessert on Sundays)
Vosotros **leíais** el periódico cuando desayunabais (You used to read the newspaper when you get breakfast)
Vosotras siempre **respondíais** lo mismo a todas las preguntas (You used to answer the same to all questions)
Ellos **corrían** todos los fines de semana (They used to run all weekends)
Ellas **vendían** pasteles durante el festival de verano de su pueblo (They used to sell cakes during the summer fair in their village)

Yo **vivía** y **estudiaba** en Paris (I lived and studied in Paris)
Tu **abrías** la cafetería los martes y los jueves (You used to open the cafeteria on Tuesdays and Thursdays)
Él **escribía** una columna en el periódico (He used to write a column on the newspaper)
Ella **asistía** a todas las clases del profesor Gutiérrez (She used to attend to all the professor Gutierrez's classes)
Nosotros **discutíamos** por todo (We used to argue for everything)
Nosotras **subíamos** el volumen de la televisión (We used to raise the television's volume)

Vosotros **decidíais** todo juntos (You used to decide everything together)
Vosotras no **admitíais** nunca que no teníais razón (You didn't use to admit you were wrong)
Ellos **recibían** regalos de su tía por sus cumpleaños (They used to receive presents from their auntie when it was their birthday)
Ellas siempre **descubrían** donde estaba escondido el chocolate (They always used to discover where the chocolate was hidden)

Well, you have seen three different Spanish past tense. There is a lot to remember and a lot to keep practicing, to make clear when use one or another, but let's try to make a mini summary to recap what we have learnt.

We have seen three different past tenses: el "**pretérito indefinido**", el "**pretérito perfecto**" y el "**pretérito imperfecto**".

Look at these three sentences.

- **Desayuné tostadas con mantequilla.** (I ate for breakfast toast with butter)
- **Esta mañana he desayunado tostadas con mantequilla** (This morning I have eaten for breakfast toast with butter)
- **Cuando era pequeña desayunaba tostadas con mantequilla** (I used to eat for breakfast toast with butter when I was a kid)

As you can see all three sentences are written in past tense, but all are different and the meaning of each one is different too.

Can you figure it out which past tense is using each sentence and why?

Desayuné tostadas con mantequilla (I ate for breakfast toast with butter) is "**pretérito indenido**", like the simple past in English. We are talking about and action from the past that is finished and completed.

Esta mañana he desayunado tostadas con mantequilla (This morning I have eaten for breakfast toast with butter), is "**pretérito perfecto**", like the present perfect in English. It's an action from the past but it's considered part of the present. In this case, it happened on the morning, so it's still today.

Cuando era pequeña desayunaba tostadas con mantequilla (I used to eat for breakfast toast with butter when I was a kid), "**pretérito imperfect**". We are talking about an action that was habitual in the past, and we are not specifying if it's finished or not.

Well, it's time now to start with the future tense. Let's start for the simple future.

The "**futuro simple**" expresses a forthcoming action, an intention or a probability. We can use the future tense to express:

- ✓ an intention regarding the future:
  Mañana **ordenaré** mi habitación (Tomorrow I will tidy up my bedroom)

- ✓ a supposition about the future:
  No lo **acabarás** en un día (You won't finish in one day)

- ✓ a supposition about the present:
  Me imagino que tu habitación todavía **estará** desordenada (I suppose your bedroom is still messy)

Once me know when we use the simple future, let's see how to form this tense for the regular verbs.

person	Hablar	Aprender	Vivir
	To speak	*To learn*	*To live*
yo	hablar**é**	aprender**é**	vivir**é**
tú	hablar**ás**	aprender**ás**	vivir**ás**
el/ella/usted	hablar**á**	aprender**á**	vivir**á**
nosotros/-as	hablar**emos**	aprender**emos**	vivir**emos**
vosotros/-as	hablar**éis**	aprender**éis**	vivir**éis**
ellos/ellas/ustedes	hablar**án**	aprender**án**	vivir**án**

For this tense, instead of separating the ending from the infinitive, we have to add to the full infinitive the correspondent ending for each person. But the good news is that all three conjugations have the same endings for each subject.

Let's see some other verbs:

COMPARAR (to compare): yo compararé, tú compararás, él/ella comparará, nosotros/nosotras compararemos, vosotros/vosotras comparareis, ellos/ellas compararán.

BARRER (to sweep): yo barreré, tú barrerás, él/ella barrerá, nosotros/nosotras barreremos, vosotros/vosotras barreréis, ellos/ellas barrerán.

COMPARTIR (to share): yo compartiré, tú compartirás, él/ella compartirá, nosotros/nosotras compartiremos, vosotros/vosotras compartiréis, ellos/ellas compartirán.

Now that we know how to form the future simple with regular verbs, let's see some sentences to **practice** the different uses of the tense:

- ✓ an intention regarding the future:

    El mes que viene **empezaré** a estudiar español (Next month I will start to learn Spanish)

Mañana **llevarás** el coche al mecánico (tomorrow you will bring the car to the garage)

El año que viene ella **comprará** un piso (Next year she will buy a flat)

Él **vendrá** pronto mañana (He will come early tomorrow)

Nosotros **actuaremos** en el concierto (We will act in the concert)

Nosotras **traeremos** bebida y aperitivos para la fiesta (We will bring drinks and snacks for the party)

Vosotros **compartiréis** habitación durante el viaje (You will share a room during the travel)

Vosotras **viajaréis** mañana en el tren de las dos (You will travel tomorrow by train at 2)

Ellos **comerán** con nosotros la semana que viene (They will have lunch with us next week)

Ellas **vivirán** en Roma el próximo curso (They will live in Rome next course)

- ✓ a supposition about the future:

  No lo **acabarás** en un día (You won't finish in one day)

  Creo que **llegarás** tarde, como siempre (I think you will be late, as always)

  No **vendrá** a cenar porque **saldrá** tarde (He won't come to dinner because he'll finish late)

  Supongo que ellas **traerán** los regalos que compramos (I suppose they will bring the presents we bought)

  Imagino que **aprobaré** el examen (I imagine I will pass the exam)

- ✓ a supposition about the present:

Me imagino que tu habitación todavía **estará** desordenada (I suppose your bedroom is still messy)

Supongo que todavía **estará** de camino (I suppose he's still on his way)

Creo que la reunión **acabará** en breve (I think the meeting is nearly finished)

Imagino que **vendrás** a comer a casa hoy, ¿no? (I imagine you are coming to have lunch at home today, don't you?)

Supongo que **estarás** arreglada ya (I suppose you are ready)

Now you know how to form the simple future. **Practice** to conjugate the following verbs:

EXISTIR (to exist): yo existiré, tú existirás, él/ella existirá, nosotros/nosotras existiremos, vosotros/vosotras existiréis, ellos/ellas existirán

BUCEAR (to dive): yo bucearé, tú bucearás, él/ella buceará, nosotros/nosotras bucearemos, vosotros/vosotras bucearéis, ellos/ellas bucearán

LEER (to read): yo leeré, té leerás, él/ella leerá, nosotros/nosotras leeremos, vosotros/vosotras leeréis, ellos/ellas leerán

Great! We know the simple future so let's learn now the future perfect, the **"futuro perfecto"**.

The **"futuro perfecto"** is used in Spanish to express a forthcoming action that will have concluded before another future action. It may also express the assumption that an action would have occurred in the past.

Let's put the explanation in context:

¿Por qué está cambiando una rueda Belén? (Why is Belen changing the tire?)
Se **habrá pinchado** la rueda (The tire must have been punctured)

¡Oh, no! En una hora queríamos ir al cine y necesitamos el coche (Oh, no! We would like to go to the cinema in an hour and we need the car)
¡No te preocupes! Para entonces ya la **habrá cambiado** (Don't worry! It will be changed by then)
To conjugate the perfect future we have to use the auxiliary verb "HABER" (to have) in future tense plus the past participle. Do you remember how we form the past participle?

If the infinitive ends in AR, we change the ending for ADO
Comprar – comprado (to buy – bought)
Hablar – hablado (to speak – spoken)

If the infinitive ends in ER or IR, we change the ending for IDO.

Beber – bebido (to drink – drank)
Aprender – aprendido (to learn – learnt)
Vivir – vivido (lo live – lived)
Compartir – compartido (to share – shared)

And also remember the verbs that has irregular forms for the past participle:

verb	perfect participle		translation
	irregular	regular	
abrir	abierto		open
decir	dicho		say
escribir	escrito		write
hacer	hecho		do/make
freír	frito	freído	fry
imprimir	impreso	imprimido	print
morir	muerto		die
poner	puesto		place/set
proveer	provisto	proveído	provide
suscribir	suscrito/suscripto		sign/subscribe
ver	visto		see
volver	vuelto		return

Once this has been refreshed, let's conjugate the perfect future:

person	haber	past participle
yo	habré	Hablado / aprendido / vivido
tú	habrás	Hablado / aprendido / vivido
él/ella/usted	habrá	Hablado / aprendido / vivido
nosotros/-as	habremos	Hablado / aprendido / vivido
vosotros/-as	habréis	Hablado / aprendido / vivido
ellos/ellas/ustedes	habrán	Hablado / aprendido / vivido

Let's do some examples:

Cuando vengas a buscarme, ya **habré acabado** (When you pick me up, I will have finished)
Estoy segura de que la película **habrá terminado** ya (I'm sure the film is already finished)
Después de esta lección, nosotros **habremos entendido** el futuro perfecto (After this lesson, we will have understood the perfect future)
Con esta reunión, ellos **habrán conseguido** llegar a un acuerdo (With this meeting, they will have got an agreement)

As you can imagine, the only secret to know how to use the verb tenses is practising. You can conjugate regular verbs and try to make sentences with them.

Here you can find a list of the one hundred more useful regular verbs in Spanish:

to answer	**contestar**	to pass	**pasar**

to arrive	**llegar**	to pay	**pagar**
to ask	**preguntar**	to permit	**permitir**
to attend	**asisitir**	to practice	**practicar**
to believe	**creer**	to present	**presentar**
to annoy	**molestar**	to prohibit	**prohibir**
to break	**romper**	to promise	**prometer**
to burn	**quemar**	to read	**leer**
to buy	**comprar**	to receive	**recibir**
to call	**llamar**	to respond	**responder**
to change	**cambiar**	to rest	**descansar**
to clean	**limpiar**	to return	**regresar**
to go up	**subir**	to check	**revisar**
to comprehend	**comprender**	to ride	**montar**
to congratulate	**felicitar**	to run	**correr**
to consist	**consistir**	to see	**ver**
to cook	**cocinar**	to sell	**vender**
to cry	**llorar**	to send	**mandar**
to dance	**bailar**	to share	**compartir**
to deliver	**entregar**	to sing	**cantar**
to wish	**desear**	to skate	**patinar**
to draw	**dibujar**	to ski	**esquiar**
to drink	**beber**	to smoke	**fumar**
to drive	**manejar**	to speak	**hablar**
to eat	**comer**	to talk	**hablar**
to end	**terminar**	to spend	**gastar**
to enter	**entrar**	to steal	**robar**
to explain	**explicar**	to rob	**robar**
to take out	**sacar**	to put away	**guardar**
to fill	**llenar**	to study	**estudiar**
to fix	**arreglar**	to sweat	**sudar**
to get off	**bajar**	to sweep	**barrer**
to get down	**bajar**	to swim	**nadar**
to give a gift	**regalar**	to take care	**cuidar**
to greet	**saludar**	to take	**tomar**
to guess	**adivinar**	to eat or drink	**tomar**
to have dinner	**cenar**	to take	**llevar**
to help	**ayudar**	to wear	**llevar**

183

to hide	**esconder**	to carry	**llevar**
to hug	**abrazar**	to teach	**enseñar**
to insist	**insistir**	to touch	**tocar**
to kiss	**besar**	to play	**tocar**
to know facts	**saber**	to travel	**viajar**
to last	**durar**	to treat	**tratar**
to leave	**dejar**	to turn off	**apagar**
to lend	**prestar**	to use	**usar**
to listen	**escuchar**	to vary	**variar**
to live	**vivir**	to verify	**verificar**
to look at	**mirar**	to visit	**visitar**
to watch	**mirar**	to wait	**esperar**
to look for	**buscar**	to walk	**andar**
to need	**necesitar**	to wash	**lavar**
to occur	**ocurrir**	to win	**ganar**
to open	**abrir**	to earn	**ganar**
to owe	**deber**	to work	**trabajar**
to paint	**pintar**	to write	**escribir**

THIRD CHAPTER: Vocabulary review

During your Spanish learning journey, you have heard and read a lot of new vocabulary. It's very hard to remember everything, and, in fact, it's not necessary nowadays because we can always count on translation apps to give us a hand when needed.
But to keep carry on with our learning, it's good to try to memorise some new words each day/week/month. One of the best methods to learn vocabulary is through lists and flashcards.

We want you to refresh some vocabulary and to learn new words to keep expanding your Spanish wordbook.
Here you'll find a list with useful words in Spanish and examples in context. At same time you are reading and/or listening all these words and examples, use your Spanish knowledge to try to identify what kind of word is.
Is it a noun? Or maybe a verb? An adjective?

a	at, to	Voy a trabajar (I'm going to work)
abajo	downstairs, below, down	La tienda que buscas está abajo (The shop you're looking for is downstairs)
abandonar	to leave a place, to abandon	No me gusta la gente que abandona a los animales (I don't like people who abandon animals)
abierto	unlocked, open	EL súper todavía está abierto (The supermarket is still open)
abrir	to open	Abren a las 10 (They open at 10 am)
absolutamente	completely, absolutely	Lo que te dije ayer era absolutamente cierto (What I told you yesterday was absolutely true)
absoluto	absolute	Él es un absoluto cretino (He's an absolute idiot)
acceso	entry, access	El acceso norte está cerrado (North access is closed)

accidente	accident	Hay un accidente en la autopista (There is an accident in the highway)
acción	action	Me gustan las películas de acción (I like action movies)
aceptar	to accept	Aceptaré su oferta de trabajo (I will accept his job offer)
acercar	to get closer	Esta tarde me acercaré a tu casa (I'll pass by your house this afternoon)
acompañar	to accompany	Te acompañaré al médico para que no vayas sola (I'm coming with you to the doctor not to leave you alone)
acontecimiento	event	La victoria del equipo ha sido un acontecimiento en el pueblo (The victory of the team has been a big event at the town)
acordar	to agree	Acordamos salir pronto hoy (We agreed to leave soon today)
actitud	attitude	No me gusta su actitud (I do not like her attitude)
actividad	activity	La profesora preparó una actividad para sus alumnos (The teacher set up an activity for her learners)
acto	act	Vamos a llegar tarde al segundo acto (We are going to be late to the second act)
actual	current	¿Cuál es el valor actual del dólar? What is the current dollar value?
actuar	to act	Desde que era pequeña que le gusta actuar (Since she was a kid that she likes acting)

acudir	to attend	Tengo que acudir a la reunión de las cuatro (I have to attend the four o'clock meeting)
adelante	further, forward	Sigue adelante y gira a la derecha (Go further and turn right)
además	besides, as well, also	Compra café además de leche (Buy coffee as well as milk)
adquirir	to acquire / buy / purchase	La empresa va a adquirir un nuevo servidor (The company is going to purchase a new server)
agosto	August	Hago vacaciones en Agosto (I'm on holidays on August)
agua	water	Tengo sed, voy a beber agua (I'm thirsty, I'm going to drink some water)
agudo	sharp	Su respuesta ha sido muy aguda (Her answer has been very sharp)
ahí	there	Déjalo ahí para que no moleste a nadie (Leave it there it not to bother anyone)
ahora	now	Ramon ha dicho que venía ahora (Ramon has said he's coming now)
aire	air	Necesito tomar el aire (I need fresh air)
alcanzar	to each	Para alcanzar su nivel tienes que estudiar más (To reach her level you need to study more)
alegría	happiness, joy	Que alegría me da que hayas aprobado el examen (I'm glad you passed the exam)

algo	somewhat, something	Mira a ver si queda algo para comer en la nevera (Take a look if there is something to eat in the fridge)
allá	over there, there	He visto que has dejado tus llaves allá. Así las perderás (I have seen you have left your keys over there. You're going to lose them)
alma	soul / spirit	Elisa es el alma de la fiesta (Elisa is the spirit of the party)
alto	high, tall	Mi hermano es diez centímetros más alto que yo (My brother is ten centimetres taller than me)
ambiente	environment	Cuidar el medio ambiente es una prioridad hoy en día (Take care of the environment is a priority nowadays)
americano	American	Supongo que era americano por su acento (I suppose he was American for his accent)
amor	love	Dicen que el amor es capaz de mover montañas (They say love can move mountains)
analizar	to analyse	Laura lo analiza todo antes de tomar una decisión (Laura always analyses everything before making a decision)
animal	animal	Mi animal favorito es el delfín (My favourite animal is the dolphin)
año	year	Este año nos vamos a Vietnam (We are going to Vietnam this year)

anterior	previous	El invierno anterior hizo mucho frio (The previous winter was very cold)
antiguo	ancient, old	Esta casa tiene cien años, es muy antigua (This house is 100 hundred years old, it's very old)
aparecer	to appear	Apareció cuando menos se lo esperaba (He appeared when he wasn't expected)
aplicar	to apply	He aplicado para el puesto de profesor de español (I have applied for the Spanish teacher job position)
apoyo	backing, support	SI decides presentarte a las elecciones, tienes todo mi apoyo. (If you are running for elections, you have all my support)
aprobar	to pass a test	Acabo de aprobar el examen de conducir (I just have passed the driving test)
aquel	that	Aquel coche es el mío. Este no se de quién es (That car is mine. I don't know whom it is that one)
árbol	tree	Podemos hacer el picnic debajo de ese árbol (We can have the picnic under that tree)
argumento	argument	Su argumento fue el mejor (Her argument was the best)
artículo	item, article	En esta tienda hay muchos artículos de regalo (There are a lot of gifts items in this shop)

asegurar	insure, secure, to assure	Tengo que asegurar el coche antes de llevármelo de la tienda (I have to insure the car, before taking it from the store)
aspecto	appearance, aspect	Conocí a su marido y tiene muy buen aspecto (I met her husband and he has good appearance)
atención	attention	Prestad atencion, por favor (Pay attention, please)
atrás	behind, back	Si mueves el coche hacia atrás, podre pasar (If you move your car backwards, I'll be able to pass)
autor	author, writer	El autor del artículo del periódico es muy famoso (The newspaper article author is very famous)
avanzar	progress, to advance	Es imposible avanzar si no nos ponemos de acuerdo en nada (It's impossible to progress if we don't agree anything)
ayuda	aid, help	Si necesitas ayuda, no dudes en pedírmela (If you need help, don't hesitate to ask for it to me)
azul	blue	El ladrón llevaba una camisa azul (The thief was wearing a blue shirt)
barco	ship, boat	Hemos visto un barco enorme atracado en el puerto (We have seen a huge ship docked at the port)
bastante	quite a bit, fairly, rather, enough	Hay bastante bebida para la fiesta, no hace falta que compres más (There are drinks enough for the

		party, it's not necessary to buy more)
bien	well	Me encuentro bien, gracias, pero me siento un poco cansada (I'm feeling well, thanks, but a bit tired)
blanco	white	El coche blanco es el que ha golpeado el árbol (The white car is the one who bumped into the tree)
brillante	sparkling, shiny, brilliant	Has tenido una idea brillante (You have had a brilliant idea)
bueno	well…	Ya te dije que llegaría tarde hoy, no sé por qué te enfadas (I told you I was going to be late today; I don't know why you are mad at me)
cabeza	head	Me duele la cabeza, me voy a tumbar un rato (I have a headache, I'm going to lay down for a bit)
cadena	chain	Tengo que comprar una cadena para la bicicleta (I have to buy a chain for my bike)
caja	box	¿Tienes una caja para prestarme para guardar los adornos de navidad? (Do you have a box to lend me to keep the Christmas decorations?)
calle	street	En la calle donde vivo hay muchos árboles (There are a lot of trees in the street I live)
cambiar	to change	Tengo que cambiarme de ropa antes de ir a cenar

		(I have to change my clothes before going for dinner)
camino	path, route, road	Si sigues este camino, llegarás al lago (If you follow the path, you will arrive to the lake)
capacidad	capacity	El maletero de tu coche tiene más capacidad que el mío (Your car's trunk has more capacity than mine)
cara	face	Su cara estaba bronceada por el sol (His face was tanned by the sun)
carrera	race	La carrera de coches empezará a las seis y media (The car race will start at half past six)
casa	house	Si quieres comprar una casa, primero tienes que ahorrar (If you want to buy a house, you have to save money first)
casi	nearly, almost	El pavo está casi hecho, así que ya podemos sentarnos a la mesa (The turkey is almost done, so we can seat for dinner)
causa	cause	Su enfermedad es la causa du sus ausencias laborales (Her sickness is the cause of her work absences)
cerca	near, close	La biblioteca está cerca, podemos ir andando (The library is close, we can go walking)
cerrado	closed	EL restaurante de la esquina está cerrado por vacaciones The corner's restaurant is closed for holidays)

cielo	sky	Me gustan los días con el cielo azul brillante (I like days with shiny blue sky)
cien	hundred	Pilar tiene ochenta años y sigue bailando salsa (Pilar is a eighty years old and she's still dancing salsa)
cinco	five	¡Choca esos cinco! (High five!)
cine	cinema	¿Quieres venir al cine conmigo? (Would you like to come to the cinema with me?)
ciudad	city	Me gusta vivir en la gran ciudad (I like living in the big city)
clase	class	Mi hijo está en la misma clase que el hijo de Raquel (My son is in the same class as Raquel's son)
clave	key	La clave para resolver el misterio estaba en la mesa del comedor (The key to solve the mystery was on the dining table)
coche	car	Hemos alquilado un coche para toda la semana (We have hired a car for all week)
colegio	school	Cuando era pequeño no me gustaba ir al colegio (I didn't like going to school when I was a kid)
comentario	comment	Me ha sentado mal su comentario sobre mi trabajo (His comment about my job has upset me)
comer	to eat	Voy a ir a comer con Sonia y Pedro. ¿Quieres venir con nosotros?

		(I'm going to have lunch with Sonia and Pedro. Do you want to come with us?)
comenzar	to start, to begin	¿Ha comenzado el partido? Todavía no (Has the match started? Not yet)
cómo	how?	¿Como te encuentras? (How are you feeling?)
compañía	company	La compañía cerrará por Navidad una semana (The company will close for a week during Christmas)
comprar	to buy	No puedo comprarme un coche nuevo porque no tengo dinero (I can't buy a new car, because I have no money)
comprobar	to check	¿Puedes comprobar que el paquete ya ha sido enviado? (Can you check if the parcel has already been sent?)
con	with	Voy a ir a la ópera con mi tía y mi prima (I'm going to the opera with my auntie and my cousin)
conocer	to know someone or a place	No conozco ningún restaurante hindú, pero le preguntaremos a Javi (I don't know any Hindu restaurant, but we'll ask Javi)
conocimiento	knowledge	Tengo algún conocimiento de alemán, pero no lo hablo bien (I have some knowledge of German, but I can't speak well)
conseguir	to get, to achieve	Si quieres conseguir tus objetivos, debes ser constante (If you want to achieve your goals, you must be constant)

conservar	to preserve, to conserve	Tenemos que conservar el planeta en el que vivimos (We have to preserve the planet where we are living)
construir	to build	Están construyendo un rascacielos de más de cien pisos (They are building a skyscraper with more than a hundred floors)
contar	To count, to tell	Le gusta que le cuentes un cuento antes de irse a dormir (He likes you to tell him a story before going to sleep)
contestar	To reply, to answer	Le envié el mail ayer, pero todavía no me ha contestado (I sent the email yesterday, but there is still no answer)
control	control	Hay bastante cola en control de seguridad del aeropuerto (There's queue at the airport security control)
corazón	heart	Mi padre sufrió hace dos años un ataque al corazón (My father suffered two years ago a heart attack)
cortar	to cut	¿Puedes cortar las patatas mientras yo bato los huevos? (Can you cut the potatoes meanwhile I'm scumbling the eggs?)
cosa	thing	¡Tu maleta pesa mucho! ¿Cuántas cosas llevas? (Your suitcase is so heavy! How many things did you packed?)
creer	to think, to believe	Nunca he creído en hadas y duendes (I have never believed in fairies and elves)

cruzar	to cross	Mira a ambos lados antes de cruzar la calle (Look at both sides before crossing the street)
cuando	when	Cuando llegues a casa, preparamos juntos la cena (When you get home, we'll prepare the dinner together)
cuanto	regarding	En cuanto a mi carta de renuncia, te la traeré hoy (Regarding my resignation letter, I'll give it to you today)
cuarto	fourth	Carlos vive en el cuarto piso (Carlos lives in the fourth floor)
cuatro	four	Tengo cuatro hermanos, dos hermanas y dos hermanos (I have four siblings, two sisters and two brothers)
cuenta	account, bill	Nos puede traer la cuenta, ¿por favor? (Can you bring us the bill, please?)
cuidado	care	Ten cuidado cuando cortes jamón. El cuchillo está muy afilado (Be careful when cutting ham. The knife is very sharp)
cultura	culture	La cultura latina es muy diversa (The Latin culture is very diverse)
curiosidad	curiosity	Tengo curiosidad por saber cuál es la noticia que nos tiene que dar (I feel curiosity about what's the new he's going to tell us)
dar	to give	Me he encontrado con Amanda y me ha dado saludos para ti (I have bumped into Amanda

		and she has given greetings for you)
debajo	below, underneath	Pon la mochila debajo del asiento, por favor (Place your backpack below the seat, please)
decidir	to decide	Todavía tengo que decidir a donde voy a ir de vacaciones este verano (I still have to decide where I'm going on holidays)
dedo	toe, finger	Me he roto un dedo jugando a hockey (I have broken a finger playing hockey)
dejar	to leave, to let	Te he dejado el móvil en tu mesita de noche (I have left your mobile phone in your bedside table)
delicado	delicate	Yo no lavaría ese jersey en la lavadora. Es demasiado delicado (I wouldn't wash this jumper in the washing machine. It's too delicate)
dentro	inside	Quedamos a las siete en el bar de siempre, pero hace frio, estaré dentro (We'll meet at seven at the usual bar. But it's cold, I'll be inside)
depender	to depend on	No sé si iremos a Cambridge el viernes, depende del tiempo. (I don't know if we are going to Cambridge on Friday, depends on the weather)
desaparecer	to vanish, to disappear	¿Has visto mis llaves? Han desaparecido. No las encuentro (Have you seen my keys? They have vanished. I can't find them)

desarrollo	development	
descubrir	to discover	Han descubierto un planeta potencialmente habitable (They have discovered a potentially habitable planet)
desear	wish for, to desire	Deseo que estas Navidades puedas venir a cenar con nosotros (I wish you can come for dinner this Christmas)
despedir	to fire	Han despedido a Laura por haber robado información confidencial (Laura has been fired because of stealing confidential information)
después	after	Podemos ir a comer juntas después de la clase de yoga (We can go and have lunch together after yoga class)
detrás	behind	Puedes colgar el abrigo detrás de la puerta (You can hang the coat behind the door)
diario	daily	Tienes que comer fruta fresca a diario (You must eat fresh fruit daily)
diez	ten	Han dicho que la conferencia empezará a las diez en punto (We've been said the conference will start at ten o'clock)
dinero	money	Rubén apostó todo su dinero y lo perdió (Ruben bet all his money, and he lost everything)
dirección	address	Si me das tu dirección, te recojo para ir al cine

		(If you give me your address, I'll pick you up to go to the cinema)
distancia	distance	Mira la distancia que hay hasta el aeropuerto, para calcular cuánto tardamos. (Look the distance to the airport, to check how long is going to take to get there)
dividir	to divide	Han dividido la casa en dos apartamentos para alquilar (They have split the house into two apartments to let)
doctor	doctor	Tengo que irme un poco antes para ir al doctor (I have to leave a bit earlier to go to the doctor)
dolor	ache, pain	Tengo dolor en la espalda desde hace una semana (I'm feeling pain in my back for one week now)
dónde	where?	¿Dónde está el vestido que te preste? (Where is the dress I lent you?)
duda	doubt	Si tienes dudas, pregúntale antes de que sea demasiado tarde (If you have any doubts, ask him before it's too late)
durante	during	Ha dicho que enviaría el paquete durante esta semana (She said she would sent the parcel during the week)
duro	hard	Es muy duro trabajar con Juan, es muy exigente (It's very hard to work with Juan. He's very demanding)
economía	economics, economy	La economía del país está mejorando gracias a las nuevas

		políticas de empleo. (The country economy is improving thanks to the new work policies)
edad	age	¿A qué edad te puedes jubilar en tu país? (What age can you retire in your country?)
ejemplo	example	Este libro es un buen ejemplo de cómo está cambiando la sociedad (This book is a good example of how the society is changing)
elegir	to elect, to choose	Tenemos que elegir al representante del curso (We have to choose the class representative)
empezar	to start, to begin	Empezó en el nuevo trabajo la semana pasada (She started in the new job last week)
empleo	job, work, occupation	Está buscando empleo, pero todavía no ha encontrado nada (She's looking for a job, but she hasn't found anything yet)
encontrar	to find	¿Has encontrado los papeles que buscabas? (Have you found the papers you were looking for?)
energía	power, energy	Creo que necesito descansar un rato, estoy bajo de energía (I think I need to rest for a little bit. I'm low of energy)
enfermo	sick, ill	Ha llamado porque está enferma (She called because she is sick)
enorme	huge, enormous	Este camión es enorme, no creo que pueda aparcar allí

		(This truck is huge, I don't believe it could be parked there)
entender	to understand	No te entiendo. ¿Puedes hablar más despacio, por favor? (I don't understand you. Can you speak slowly, please?)
entrada	admission ticket, entrance	Ya guardo yo las entradas que tú siempre las pierdes (I'll keep the tickets, because you always lose them)
entre	among, between	Mi casa está entre la farmacia y la tienda de deportes (My house is between the pharmacy and the sports shop)
entregar	to deliver	Han confirmado que entregarán la carta mañana antes de la una (It's been confirmed the letter will be delivered by tomorrow at 1pm)
escribir	to write	Todavía tengo que escribir el informe de la reunión (I still have to write the meeting inform)
escuela	school	Esta semana han empezado todas las escuelas (This week all schools have started.)
esfuerzo	effort	Gracias a tu esfuerzo hemos conseguido acabar a tiempo. (Thanks to your effort we have managed to finish on time)
especial	special	Es una ocasión especial, así que no llegues tarde (It's a special occasion, so don't be late)
esperanza	hope	Dicen que la esperanza es lo último que se pierde

		(It's said hope is the last thing to lose)
espíritu	ghost, spirit	Todos los vecinos creen que hay un espíritu en la casa de la colina (All the neighbours believe there is a spirit in the hill's house)
establecer	to establish	Tenemos que establecer las normas de nuestra clase (We have to stablish our class rules)
este	this	Este libro me lo recomendó mi primo y la verdad es que me está gustando (My cousin recommended this book, and the truth is I like it)
estudiar	to study	¿Vas a seguir estudiando español este año? (Are you keep studying Spanish this year?)
examen	exam, examination	Esta vez el examen ha sido muy difícil, No sé si habré aprobado (This time the exam was very difficult. I don't know if I'll pass it)
existir	to exist	Si no existiera la siesta, yo mismo la inventaría (If nap time didn't exist, I would invent it myself)
experiencia	experience	Tirarme en paracaídas ha sido una experiencia súper emocionante (To do skydiving has been a very exciting experience)
explicar	to explain	Tienes que explicarme lo que te ha dicho Carmen (You have to explain me what carmen has told you)

exposición	display, exhibition	Hay una exposición de fotografía de los años 20, ¿quieres venir? (There is a photography exhibition from the twenties, do you want to come?)
extraño	strange	No sé cómo describirlo, era un ruido extraño (I don't know how to describe it. It was a strange noise)
facilidad	facility, ease	Tienes mucha facilidad para practicar cualquier deporte (You have a lot of ease to play any sport)
familia	family	¿Te apetece venir conmigo y mi familia a esquiar este fin de semana? (Would you like to come with me and my family to sky this weekend?)
favor	benefit, favour	¿Te puedo pedir un favor? ¿Puedes recoger a Clara en el colegio? (Can I ask you a favour? Can you pick up Clara from School?)
fecha	date	¿En qué fecha estamos? (What day is today?)
formación	education, formation	Hoy en día es importante tener formación y experiencia (Nowaday is important to have education and experience)
frío	cold	Si tienes frio, pon la calefacción (If you are cold, turn on the heating)
fuera	away, outside, out	Haz lo que tengas que hacer, yo te espero fuera

		(Do what you have to do, I'll wait for you outside)
futuro	future	¿Qué futuro crees que nos espera con lo del cambio climático? (What future do you think we would have considering the climate change?)
generación	generation	Tengo cuarenta años, Soy de una generación distinta a la tuya (I'm forty years old. I'm from another generation)
generalmente	usually, generally	Generalmente voy a trabajar en bicicleta, pero hoy nevaba (Generally I go to work by bike, but it was snowing today)
gesto	gesture	Cederle el asiento ha sido un gesto muy amable. (Give her your seat has been a very kind gesture)
golpe	punch, strike, hit	Me he golpeado la rodilla con la mesa (I hit my knee with the table)
grave	serious	Es una operación grave, tendrá que estar más de una semana en el hospital (It's a serious operation. She'll have to stay for more than a week at the hospital)
grupo	group	¿Quieres unirte a nuestro grupo de lectura? (Would you like to join our reading group?)
gusto	preference, taste, pleasure	Mucho gusto en conocerte (It's a pleasure to meet you)
habitación	bedroom, room	Necesitamos una habitación doble para la semana que viene

		(We need a double bedroom for next week)
hacer	to make, to do	¿Qué haces aquí? ¿No trabajabas hoy? (What are you doing here? Didn't you work today?)
hecho	happening, fact	De hecho, ha sido ella la que me ha dicho la verdad (In fact, it was her who told me the true)
hija	daughter	Su hija va conmigo a la universidad (Her daughter attends university with me)
historia	story, history	No me creo la historia que me ha contado (I don't believe the story he told)
hombre	man	Ese hombre se parece a un actor famoso (That man looks like a famous actor)
hora	hour	¿A qué hora nos vemos esta tarde? (At what time are we meeting this evening?)
hoy	today	Hoy no podremos quedar para tomar algo, pero mañana sí (We can't grab a drink today, but we can tomorrow)
idea	idea	Me gusta la idea de ir de camping este verano (I like the idea to go for a camping this summer)
idioma	language	¿Cuántos idiomas hablas? (How many languages do you speak?)
imaginar	to imagine	No me imaginaba que Javier aceptaría irse a vivir a Argentina

		(I wasn't imagining that Javier was going to live in Argentina)
imponer	enforce, to impose	Siempre tratas de imponer tus reglas, y esta clase es una democracia (You are always trying to impose your rules, and this classroom is a democracy)
importante	important	Es importante que escuches para saber lo que tienes que hacer (It's important you to listen to know what you have to do)
imposible	impossible	Es imposible que quepa todo el equipaje en el maletero (It's impossible that all luggage fits in the trunk)
indicar	to indicate	Me indicó que siguiera recto tres calles y entonces girara a la derecha (She indicated me to keep going straight for three streets and then turn right)
inmediatamente	immediately	¿Perdona, me puedes traer un café, por favor? Claro, inmediatamente (Excuse me, can I have a coffee, please? Sure, immediately)
inteligente	intelligent	Parece un chico muy inteligente, lo entiendo todo fácilmente (He seems very smart, he understands everything easily)
internacional	international	Trabajo en una compañía internacional. Las oficinas centrales están en París (I work in an international

		company. Headquarters are in Paris)
intervenir	to intervene	No quise intervenir en la discusión porque no era asunto mío (I didn't want to intervene in the argument because it wasn't my business)
invitar	to invite	Hemos invitado a todos los amigos de Julia a su fiesta sorpresa (We have invited all Julia's friend to her surprise party)
jamás	never	Jamás haré submarinismo. Me da terror el mar (I'm never going to dive. I'm scared of the sea)
jefe	manager, boss	El jefe esta refunfuñón hoy, así que mejor no le digas nada (The boss is grumpy today, so better don't say anything)
joven	young	Todavía eres joven para seguir jugando a fútbol. (You're still young to keep playing football)
jugar	to play	Desde pequeño que juego a baloncesto los fines de semana (I play basketball during the weekend since I was a kid)
lado	side	Sigue recto y veras la librería al lado del banco (Go straight and you'll see the book shop next to the bank)
largo	long	Tengo el pelo demasiado largo, tengo que ir a la peluquería (My hair is too long, I have to go to the hairdresser)

leche	milk	¿Quieres leche de vaca o leche de soja con el café? (Do you want cow milk or soya milk with your coffee?)
lengua	tongue	Me he mordido la lengua y la tengo hinchada (I have bitten my tongue and it's swollen)
libro	book	Quiero empezar a leer un libro nuevo. ¿Me recomiendas alguno? (I would like to start reading a new book. Do you advise me any?)
lista	list, ready	Mira en la lista de invitados en qué mesa estamos sentados (Look in the guests list in what table we are seating in)
llamada	call	Tengo una llamada de Judith. Cuando salga de trabajar, la llamo (I have a call from Judith. I'll call her back when I finish my work)
llegar	to arrive	Llegaré sobre las nueve, si quieres desayunamos juntos. (I will arrive around nine. If you want, we can have breakfast together)
llevar	to bring, to carry	¿Llevaras tú el pastel para la fiesta de Julia? (Will you bring Julia's birthday party cake?)
lograr	to achieve	Hemos logrado todos los objetivos del curso (We have achieved all course goals)

luego	afterwards, later	Nos vemos luego, ahora voy a una reunión (I'll see you later, I have a meeting now)
maestro	teacher	Esta mañana he visto al maestro que tuvimos en la escuela de secundaria (This morning I have seen the teacher we had at secondary school)
malo/mala	bad	Es una mala idea, a Andrea no le va a gustar (It's a bad idea, Andrea it's not going to like it)
mandar	to send	Este año han mandado las tarjetas de Navidad un poco tarde (This year they have sent the Christmas cards a little bit late)
manera	manner, way	De ninguna manera voy a hacerte los deberes. (No way I'm doing your homework)
mano	hand	Me echas una mano para recoger la habitación, ¿por favor? Can you give me a hand to tidy up the room, please?)
máquina	machine	La máquina de café no funciona. La arreglarán mañana (The coffee machine is broken. It will be fixed tomorrow)
marido	husband	Mi marido va a ver todos los partidos de hockey (Mi husband goes to watch all hockey matches)
materia	subject, matter	Las matemáticas eran la materia que menos me gustaba

		(Maths were the subject I liked less)
mayor	older	Mi hermana mayor está viviendo en Panamá desde hace tres años (My old sister is living in Panama since three years ago)
me	to me	Me puedes pasar una manzana, ¿por favor? (Can you get me an apple, please?)
medio	middle, half	No tengo demasiada hambre, con media pizza ya tengo bastante (I'm not very hungry. Half a pizza is enough for me)
memoria	memory	Tengo muy mala memoria, por eso me lo apunto todo en el calendario (I have a really bad memory, this is why I write down everything in the calendar)
mensaje	message	Te dejé un mensaje en el contestador. ¿Lo escuchaste? (I left a message in your voice mail. Did you hear it?)
mercado	market	Vamos a ir al mercado a comprar fruta y verdura fresca (We are going to the market to buy fresh fruit and vegs)
mesa	table	Vamos a poner la mesa que los invitados están a punto de llegar (Let's set the table as the guests are almost here)
mientras	meanwhile, while	Mientras tú estudias para el examen, yo hare la cena (Meanwhile you study for the exam, I'll make dinner)

mismo	same	Clara y Anabel llevan los mismos zapatos (Clara and Anabel are wearing the same shoes)
moderno	modern	Hemos ido al museo de arte moderno (We have been at the modern art museum)
momento	time, moment	De momento no sé qué voy a hacer, prefiero esperar unos días para decidir (At the moment I don't know what I'm going to do. I prefer to wait a few days before deciding)
mostrar	to show	Me mostró el camino a recepción el primer día, pero me he perdido (He showed me the way to reception on the first day, but I've got lost)
mover	to move	Este armario pesa mucho. Ayúdame a moverlo, por favor (This wardrobe is too heavy. Help me to move it, please)
mucho	many, much, a lot	No hay mucho que hacer en este pueblo (There is not much to do in this village)
muerto	dead	Cuando llegó la ambulancia, ya estaba muerto, no pudieron hacer nada. (When the ambulance arrived he was already dead. They couldn't do anything)
mundial	worldwide	El cambio climático nos afecta a nivel mundial

		(The climate change is affecting worldwide)
música	music	Me gustaría dedicarme a la música, pero no tengo tiempo para practicar (I would like to be a musician, but I don't have time to practice)
nacer	to be born	Nací en Argentina, pero ahora vivo en Uruguay (I was born in Argentina, but I'm living now in Uruguay)
nadie	anybody, nobody	Nadie que conozca toca el piano como tú (No one I know can play the piano like you)
naturaleza	nature	Me gusta pasar los fines de semana rodeado de naturaleza (I like to spend the weekend surrounded by nature)
necesario	necessary	Es necesario que rellenes los formularios antes de empezar a trabajar aquí. (It's necessary you fill in these forms before starting working here)
negar	refuse, to deny	Me niego a fregar los platos, siempre lo hago yo (I refuse to wash the dishes again, I'm always doing it)
nivel	level	Tendrás que hacer una prueba de nivel, para saber qué curso de español es el más adecuado (You'll have to do a level test to know what Spanish course is best for you)
noche	evening, night	Anoche me acosté tarde, pero esta noche me acostaré temprano

		(I went to sleep late last night, but I'll go early tonight)
nota	grade, note	¿Ya sabes qué nota has sacado en el examen? (Have you know what grade you had in your exam?)
nuestro / nuestra	our	Nuestro proyecto está entre los tres finalistas del concurso (Our project is one of the three contest finalist)
nuevo	new	¿Es nuevo este vestido que llevas? Nunca te lo había visto (Is it new the dress you are wearing? I haven't seen it before)
objetivo	objective	El objetivo de este curso es entender la gramática española (The objective for this course is to understand the Spanish grammar)
ocasión	occasion, opportunity	Voy a aprovechar la ocasión para felicitarle por su reciente ascenso (I'll take the occasion to congratulate him for his recent promotion)
ofrecer	to offer	Me han ofrecido un trabajo en el colegio de mi hijo (They have offered me a job in my son's school)
operación	operation	El doctor dijo que la operación había ido bien (Doctor said the operation went well)
opinar	be of the opinion, to think	Yo opino que es mejor votar y decidir entre todos

		(I think we have to vote and decide all of us)
oportunidad	chance, opportunity	Cuando tengas la oportunidad, llama a Esteban. Está esperando tu llamada. (When you have a chance, call Esteban. He is waiting for your call)
oscuro	obscure, dark	Está muy oscuro y no veo nada. Corre la cortina, por favor. (It's so dark I can see anything. Open the curtain, please)
padre	father	Ya conoces a mi padre, es un fanático del cricket (You already know my father, he's a cricket fanatic)
página	page	En la página 16 del libro está la fotografía de la universidad (On page 16 there is the university picture)
palabra	word	Desde la discusión, no nos hemos dirigido la palabra (Since we argued, we haven't talked to each other)
parecer	look like, to seem	Te pareces muchísimo a tu hermana y a tu madre (You look like your sister and your mother)
pared	wall	Tiene la pared llena de pósters de películas (He has the wall full of poster from movies)
participar	to participate / get involved	Voy a participar en el debate, por eso tengo que prepararme bien (I'm going to participate on the debate, so I'll need to be prepared)

pedir	request, to ask for	Me pidió que le guardara el móvil mientras hacía el examen (He asked to me for keeping his mobile phone while he was doing the test)
pensamiento	thinking, thought	Mi pensamiento está con las familias de las víctimas (My thoughts are with victim's families)
pequeño	small, little	Los números y las letras son tan pequeños que los veo borrosos (Numbers and letter are so small that I see them blurry)
perfectamente	perfectly	Te he entendido perfectamente, no hace falta que me lo vuelvas a explicar (I have understood you perfectly. It's not necessary that you explain to me again)
permitir	permit, to allow	No está permitido fumar en este edificio (Smoking is not allowed in the building)
persona	person	Solo necesito a una persona para este trabajo (I only need one person for the job)
personal	personal	Es un tema personal, prefiero hablar en privado (It's a personal matter. I prefer to talk privately)
plantear	present, to propose	He decidido plantearle al jefe mi nueva idea de negocio (I have decided to propose the boss my new business plan)
pobre	poor	Pobre niño, se ha caído del tobogán y se ha roto un pie

		(Poor boy, he felt down from the slide and broke his foot)
poder	to can, to be able to	No puedo hablar ahora, estoy en medio de una reunión (I can't talk right now, I'm in the middle of a meeting)
policía	police officer, police	El policía estaba buscando a un joven con una sudadera amarilla (The police was looking for a young guy with a yellow hoodie)
popular	popular	Es una canción muy popular. La oirás en todas las fiestas (It's a very popular song. You will hear it at all the parties)
porque	because	Al final no compré las botas porque no estaban en mi número (At the end I didn't buy the boots because they weren't in my size)
posible	possible	Coge el paraguas porque han dicho en la tele que es posible que llueva (Take the umbrella because they have said on the TV it's possible to rain)
positivo	positive	Sé positivo, seguro que encuentras trabajo pronto (Be positive, I'm sure you will find a job soon)
pregunta	question	No sabía que contestar a la pregunta que me hizo Rafa (I didn't know what to answer to Rafa's question)
premio	reward, prize	Valentina ha ganado el premio al mejor proyecto de ciencias (Valentina has won the prize for the best science project)

preparar	to prepare	Tengo que preparar un montón de cosas antes de salir a cenar (I have to prepare a lot of things before go out for dinner)
presentar	to introduce	¿Vendrás a la cena esta noche? Me gustaría presentarte a mi hermano (Are you coming for tonight's dinner? I would like to introduce you my brother)
prestar	to lend	¿Puedes prestarme 50 euros? (Can you lend me 50 euros?)
problema	problem	¿Se te ocurre alguna idea para solucionar el problema? (Do you have any ideas to solve the problem?)
profesor	teacher, professor	Mi profesor de español es de Caracas (My Spanish teacher is from Caracas)
programa	program, software	El programa de contabilidad que usamos ahora me gusta más que el anterior (I like the accountancy software we are using currently more than the old one)
próximo	next	La próxima vez que nos veamos, te invito yo a comer (Next time we meet up, I'll buy you lunch)
prueba	test, trial, proof	El periodo de prueba para este trabajo es de nueve meses (The probation period for this job is nine months)
pueblo	village	Cadaqués es un pueblo muy bonito de la Costa Brava (Cadaqués is a beautiful village from la Costa Brava)

quejar	to complain	Voy a quejarme porque me han roto la maleta (I'm going to make a complain because they have broken my suitcase)
quizás	maybe, perhaps	Quizás pueda venir un poco más pronto, pero todavía no lo sé seguro (Maybe I can come in a little bit earlier, but still not sure)
raro	scarce, rare, strange	Es muy raro que no te haya llamado. Seguro que le ha surgido algo (It's really strange she hasn't called you. Something must have happened)
realizar	to carry out	Él ha sido el responsable de realizar la presentación del nuevo producto. (He has been the responsible to carry out the presentation for the new product)
revista	journal, magazine	Me gusta leer revistas cuando voy a la peluquería (I like reading magazines at the hair salon)
saber	knowledge	Sabe mucho de historia. Se nota que es una de sus pasiones. (He knows a lot about history. You can tell it's one of his passions)
sala	hall, room	Espera en la sala que Sergio enseguida está contigo (Wait at the hall. Sergio will be with you shortly)
salir	go out, to leave	Voy a salir a dar un paseo. ¿Te apuntas?

		(I'm going out for a walk. Are you coming?)
salvar	rescue, to save	El vecino le salvó la vida. Fue él el que llamo a la ambulancia (The neighbour saved his life. He was who called the ambulance)
seguir	keep on, to follow	Ya que has llegado hasta aquí, sigue aprendiendo español (Now you are here, keep on learning Spanish)
semana	week	Nos veremos la semana que viene en casa de Ana (We'll see each other next week at Ana's house)
señalar	signal, to point	¿Me puedes señalar en el mapa dónde está la catedral? (Can you point on the map where the cathedral is?
sentar	seat, to sit down	Siéntate si estas cansada y descansa (Sit down if you are tired and get some rest)
tamaño	dimension, size	¿Sabes de qué tamaño necesitamos la caja para enviarle el cuadro? (Do you know the size we need for the box to send the picture?)
tampoco	either, nor, neither	Yo no quiero postre. Yo tampoco (I don't want a dessert. Neither do I)
tanto	so many, so much	¡Te quiero tanto! (I love you so much!)
tarea	job, task	Cuando acabes la tarea, podrás salir a jugar (When you finish your task, you can go out to play)

temperatura	temperature	Con esta temperatura es imposible dormir (It's impossible to sleep with this temperature)
título	heading, title	¿Recuerdas el título de la película? (Do you remember the title from the movie?)
todavía	yet, still	Todavía estoy esperando que se disculpe (I'm still waiting for him to apologise)
a través	through, over	No puedo ver nada a través de esta ventana (I can't see anything through the window)
último	final, last	El que llegue el último, paga las bebidas (The last one pay the drinks)
utilizar	utilize, to use	Estoy acostumbrada a utilizar la calculadora (I'm used to use the calculator)
vehículo	car, vehicle	Ese vehículo tiene una multa por estar mal aparcado (That vehicle has a fine to stay wrong parked)
vender	to sell	Quiere vender su piso para comprarse una casa más grande (She wants to sell her flat to buy a bigger house)
verdad	truth	La verdad es que la película me gusto mucho (The truth is I liked the movie very much)
viajar	to travel	Me gusta viajar en coche porque puedo parar donde quiera (I like travelling by car because I can stop wherever I want)

| vino | wine | ¿Quieres una copa de vino? ¿Tinto, rosado o blanco? (Do you want a glass of wine? Red, rose or white?) |
| visitar | to visit | Este fin de semana vamos a visitar a los primos de Jorge (This weekend we are going to visit Jorge's cousins) |

FOURTH CHAPTER: Irregular Verbs and how to conjugate

Well, in Spanish as in English there are irregular verbs. The **Spanish Irregular Verbs** are those **verbs** whose "raíces" or stems, change when they are conjugated in different tenses and with different personal pronouns. But, to be an irregular verb doesn't mean that the verb is irregular for all persons and tenses. The irregularity will be only in one tense or in one person.

We will learn here the most important irregular verbs in Spanish and how to conjugate them in the indicative mood, in present, past and future, as these are the most common tenses we are going to use when we speak.

Let's start to know what the 50 most common irregular verbs in Spanish are.

No.	Spanish	English
1	ser	to be (essential/permanent quality)
2	haber	to have (to do something, auxiliary verb)
3	estar	to be (health, location, state)
4	tener	to have
5	hacer	to do, make
6	poder	to be able, can
7	decir	to say, tell
8	ir	to go
9	ver	to see
10	dar	to give
11	saber	to know (information)
12	querer	to want, love
13	llegar	to arrive, come, reach
14	poner	to put, place, set
15	parecer	to seem, look, appear
16	creer	to believe
17	seguir	to follow, continue
18	encontrar	to find, encounter
19	venir	to come
20	pensar	to think

21	salir	to leave, go out
22	volver	to return, go back
23	conocer	to know (people, places)
24	sentir	to feel, regret
25	contar	to count, relate, tell
26	empezar	to begin, start
27	buscar	to search for, look for
28	escribir	to write
29	perder	to lose
30	producir	to produce
31	entender	to understand
32	pedir	to request, ask for
33	recordar	to remember, remind
34	aparecer	to appear, show up
35	conseguir	to get, obtain
36	comenzar	to begin, start, commence
37	servir	to serve
38	sacar	to take out, stick out
39	mantener	to maintain, get
40	leer	to read
41	caer	to fall
42	abrir	to open
43	oír	to hear
44	convertir	to convert, change
45	traer	to bring, to get, fetch, to carry
46	morir	to die
47	realizar	to achieve, attain, accomplish
48	suponer	to suppose
49	explicar	to explain
50	tocar	to touch, to play (an instrument)

SER and **ESTAR** (to be) are the two most common verbs in Spanish, and both have irregularities when conjugating them:

Ser	Presente	Pretérito indefinido	Pretérito imperfecto	Futuro simple
yo	soy	fui	era	seré
tú	eres	fuiste	eras	serás
él/ella/usted	es	fue	era	será
nosotros	somos	fuimos	éramos	seremos
vosotros	sois	fuisteis	erais	seréis
ellos/ellas/ustedes	son	fueron	eran	serán

Estar	Presente	Pretérito indefinido	Pretérito imperfecto	Futuro simple
yo	estoy	estuve	estaba	estaré
tú	estás	estuviste	estabas	estarás
él/ella/Usted	está	estuvo	estaba	estará
nosotros	estamos	estuvimos	estábamos	estaremos
vosotros	estáis	estuvisteis	estabais	estaréis
ellos/ellas/Ustedes	están	estuvieron	estaban	estarán

HABER *(to have as auxiliary verb)* is another irregular verb. Keep in mind that in the preterit, an "u" is used instead of an "a".

Haber	Presente	Pretérito indefinido	Pretérito imperfecto	Futuro simple
yo	he	hube	había	habré
tú	has	hubiste	habías	habrás
él/ella/usted	ha, hay	hubo	había	habrá
nosotros	hemos	hubimos	habíamos	habremos
vosotros	habéis	hubisteis	habíais	habréis
ellos/ellas/ustedes	han	hubieron	habían	habrán

DECIR (to say) and **HACER** (to do/to make) have one main thing in common, the soft "c." This means that they have similar irregularities.

1. The first person conjugation (yo) in the present tense requires a g for both decir and hacer.

2. In the preterit tense, they both change the vowel in their stems to "i".

Hacer	Presente	Pretérito indefinido	Pretérito imperfecto	Futuro simple
yo	hago	hice	hacía	haré
tú	haces	hiciste	hacías	harás
él/ella/usted	hace	hizo	hacía	hará
nosotros	hacemos	hicimos	hacíamos	haremos
vosotros	hacéis	hicisteis	hacíais	haréis
ellos/ellas/ustedes	hacen	hicieron	hacían	harán

Decir	Presente	Pretérito indefinido	Pretérito imperfecto	Futuro simple
yo	digo	dije	decía	diré
tú	dices	dijiste	decías	dirás
él/ella/usted	dice	dijo	decía	dirá

nosotros	decimos	dijimos	decíamos	diremos
vosotros	decís	dijisteis	decíais	diréis
ellos/ellas/ustedes	dicen	dijeron	decían	dirán

TENER (to have) and **PONER** (to put)

1. In the first person conjugation (yo) of the present tense there's a "g".

2. The preterit tense changes the stem vowel to "u" on both "poner" and "tener".

Tener	Presente	Pretérito indefinido	Pretérito imperfecto	Futuro simple
yo	tengo	tuve	tenía	tendré
tú	tienes	tuviste	tenías	tendrás
él/ella/usted	tiene	tuvo	tenía	tendrá
nosotros	tenemos	tuvimos	teníamos	tendremos
vosotros	tenéis	tuvisteis	teníais	tendréis
ellos/ellas/ustedes	tienen	tuvieron	tenían	tendrán

Poner	Presente	Pretérito indefinido	Pretérito imperfecto	Futuro simple
yo	pongo	puse	ponía	pondré
tú	pones	pusiste	ponías	pondrás
él/ella/usted	pone	puso	ponía	pondrá
nosotros	ponemos	pusimos	poníamos	pondremos
vosotros	ponéis	pusisteis	poníais	pondréis
ellos/ellas/ustedes	ponen	pusieron	ponían	pondrán

SENTIR (to feel) and **SEGUIR** (to follow) have the same irregularity in preterit: the "e" changes to "i" in both the singular and the plural third person conjugations. However, they have different irregularities in the present tense.

Sentir has "ie" instead of e in singular first and second person conjugations. This change doesn't occur in the plural first and second person conjugations.

Seguir has just an "i" instead of the "e" for four conjugations: first person plural and first, second and third person singular.

These irregularities are very common, and you will find them repeated often.
Other verbs which have the same irregularity as sentir ("e" to "ie"): empezar, comenzar, pensar, querer.
Other verbs like seguir ("e" to "i") are: pedir, elegir, medir.

Sentir	**Presente**	**Pretérito indefinido**	**Pretérito imperfecto**	**Futuro simple**
yo	siento	sentí	sentía	sentiré
tú	sientes	sentiste	sentías	sentirás
él/ella/usted	siente	sintió	sentía	sentirá
nosotros	sentimos	sentimos	sentíamos	sentiremos
vosotros	sentís	sentisteis	sentíais	sentiréis
ellos/ellas/ustedes	sienten	sintieron	sentían	sentirán

Seguir	**Presente**	**Pretérito indefinido**	**Pretérito imperfecto**	**Futuro simple**
yo	sigo	seguí	seguía	seguiré
tú	sigues	seguiste	seguías	seguirás
él/ella/usted	sigue	siguió	seguía	seguirá
nosotros	seguimos	seguimos	seguíamos	seguiremos
vosotros	seguís	seguisteis	seguíais	seguiréis
ellos/ellas/ustedes	siguen	siguieron	seguían	seguirán

Let's see how all the other irregular verbs are conjugated. To feel that you know how to use this verb you'll have to memorise the because there are no rules.

PODER - to can / to be able to

Presente	Pretérito Indefinido	Pretérito Imperfecto	Futuro
yo puedo	yo pude	yo podía	yo podré
tú puedes	tú pudiste	tú podías	tú podrás
él puede	él pudo	él podía	él podrá
nosotros podemos	nosotros pudimos	nosotros podíamos	nosotros podremos
vosotros podéis	vosotros pudisteis	vosotros podíais	vosotros podréis
ellos pueden	ellos pudieron	ellos podían	ellos podrán

DECIR - to tell

Presente	Pretérito Indefinido	Pretérito Imperfecto	Futuro
yo digo	yo dije	yo decía	yo diré
tú dices	tú dijiste	tú decías	tú dirás
él dice	él dijo	él decía	él dirá
nosotros decimos	nosotros dijimos	nosotros decíamos	nosotros diremos
vosotros decís	vosotros dijisteis	vosotros decíais	vosotros diréis
ellos dicen	ellos dijeron	ellos decían	ellos dirán

IR - to go

Presente	Pretérito Indefinido	Pretérito Imperfecto	Futuro
yo voy	yo fui	yo iba	yo iré
tú vas	tú fuiste	tú ibas	tú irás
él va	él fue	él iba	él irá
nosotros vamos	nosotros fuimos	nosotros íbamos	nosotros iremos

| vosotros vais | vosotros fuisteis | vosotros ibais | vosotros iréis |
| ellos van | ellos fueron | ellos iban | ellos irán |

VER - to see

Presente	Pretérito Indefinido	Pretérito Imperfecto	Futuro
yo veo	yo vi	yo veía	yo veré
tú ves	tú viste	tú veías	tú verás
él ve	él vio	él veía	él verá
nosotros vemos	nosotros vimos	nosotros veíamos	nosotros veremos
vosotros veis	vosotros visteis	vosotros veíais	vosotros veréis
ellos ven	ellos vieron	ellos veían	ellos verán

DAR - to give

Presente	Pretérito Indefinido	Pretérito Imperfecto	Futuro
yo doy	yo di	yo daba	yo daré
tú das	tú diste	tú dabas	tú darás
él da	él dio	él daba	él dará
nosotros damos	nosotros dimos	nosotros dábamos	nosotros daremos
vosotros dais	vosotros disteis	vosotros dabais	vosotros daréis
ellos dan	ellos dieron	ellos daban	ellos darán

SABER - to know

Presente	Pretérito Indefinido	Pretérito Imperfecto	Futuro
yo sé	yo supe	yo sabía	yo sabré
tú sabes	tú supiste	tú sabías	tú sabrás
él sabe	él supo	él sabía	él sabrá
nosotros sabemos	nosotros supimos	nosotros sabíamos	nosotros sabremos
vosotros sabéis	vosotros supisteis	vosotros sabíais	vosotros sabréis
ellos saben	ellos supieron	ellos sabían	ellos sabrán

QUERER - to want/to love

Presente	Pretérito Indefinido	Pretérito Imperfecto	Futuro

yo quiero	yo quise	yo quería	yo querré
tú quieres	tú quisiste	tú querías	tú querrás
él quiere	él quiso	él quería	él querrá
nosotros queremos	nosotros quisimos	nosotros queríamos	nosotros querremos
vosotros queréis	vosotros quisisteis	vosotros queríais	vosotros querréis
ellos quieren	ellos quisieron	ellos querían	ellos querrán

LLEGAR - to arrive

Presente	Pretérito Indefinido	Pretérito Imperfecto	Futuro
yo llego	yo llegué	yo llegaba	yo llegaré
tú llegas	tú llegaste	tú llegabas	tú llegarás
él llega	él llegó	él llegaba	él llegará
nosotros llegamos	nosotros llegamos	nosotros llegábamos	nosotros llegaremos
vosotros llegáis	vosotros llegasteis	vosotros llegabais	vosotros llegaréis
ellos llegan	ellos llegaron	ellos llegaban	ellos llegarán

PONER - to put

Presente	Pretérito Indefinido	Pretérito Imperfecto	Futuro
yo pongo	yo puse	yo ponía	yo pondré
tú pones	tú pusiste	tú ponías	tú pondrás
él pone	él puso	él ponía	él pondrá
nosotros ponemos	nosotros pusimos	nosotros poníamos	nosotros pondremos
vosotros ponéis	vosotros pusisteis	vosotros poníais	vosotros pondréis
ellos ponen	ellos pusieron	ellos ponían	ellos pondrán

PARECER - to seem

Presente	Pretérito Indefinido	Pretérito Imperfecto	Futuro
yo parezco	yo parecí	yo parecía	yo pareceré
tú pareces	tú pareciste	tú parecías	tú parecerás

él parece	él pareció	él parecía	él parecerá
nosotros parecemos	nosotros parecimos	nosotros parecíamos	nosotros pareceremos
vosotros parecéis	vosotros parecisteis	vosotros parecíais	vosotros pareceréis
ellos parecen	ellos parecieron	ellos parecían	ellos parecerán

CREER - to believe

Presente	Pretérito Indefinido	Pretérito Imperfecto	Futuro
yo creo	yo creí	yo creía	yo creeré
tú crees	tú creíste	tú creías	tú creerás
él cree	él creyó	él creía	él creerá
nosotros creemos	nosotros creímos	nosotros creíamos	nosotros creeremos
vosotros creéis	vosotros creísteis	vosotros creíais	vosotros creeréis
ellos creen	ellos creyeron	ellos creían	ellos creerán

SEGUIR - to follow

Presente	Pretérito Indefinido	Pretérito Imperfecto	Futuro
yo sigo	yo seguí	yo seguía	yo seguiré
tú sigues	tú seguiste	tú seguías	tú seguirás
él sigue	él siguió	él seguía	él seguirá
nosotros seguimos	nosotros seguimos	nosotros seguíamos	nosotros seguiremos
vosotros seguís	vosotros seguisteis	vosotros seguíais	vosotros seguiréis
ellos siguen	ellos siguieron	ellos seguían	ellos seguirán

ENCONTRAR - to find

Presente	Pretérito Indefinido	Pretérito Imperfecto	Futuro
yo encuentro	yo encontré	yo encontraba	yo encontraré
tú encuentras	tú encontraste	tú encontrabas	tú encontrarás
él encuentra	él encontró	él encontraba	él encontrará
nosotros encontramos	nosotros encontramos	nosotros encontrábamos	nosotros encontraremos
vosotros encontráis	vosotros encontrasteis	vosotros encontrabais	vosotros encontraréis
ellos encuentran	ellos encontraron	ellos encontraban	ellos encontrarán

VENIR - to come

Presente	Pretérito Indefinido	Pretérito Imperfecto	Futuro
yo vengo	yo vine	yo venía	yo vendré
tú vienes	tú viniste	tú venías	tú vendrás
él viene	él vino	él venía	él vendrá
nosotros venimos	nosotros vinimos	nosotros veníamos	nosotros vendremos
vosotros venís	vosotros vinisteis	vosotros veníais	vosotros vendréis
ellos vienen	ellos vinieron	ellos venían	ellos vendrán

PENSAR - to think

Presente	Pretérito Indefinido	Pretérito Imperfecto	Futuro
yo pienso	yo pensé	yo pensaba	yo pensaré
tú piensas	tú pensaste	tú pensabas	tú pensarás
él piensa	él pensó	él pensaba	él pensará
nosotros pensamos	nosotros pensamos	nosotros pensábamos	nosotros pensaremos
vosotros pensáis	vosotros pensasteis	vosotros pensabais	vosotros pensaréis
ellos piensan	ellos pensaron	ellos pensaban	ellos pensarán

SALIR - to go out

Presente	Pretérito Indefinido	Pretérito Imperfecto	Futuro
yo salgo	yo salí	yo salía	yo saldré
tú sales	tú saliste	tú salías	tú saldrás
él sale	él salió	él salía	él saldrá
nosotros salimos	nosotros salimos	nosotros salíamos	nosotros saldremos
vosotros salís	vosotros salisteis	vosotros salíais	vosotros saldréis
ellos salen	ellos salieron	ellos salían	ellos saldrán

VOLVER - to return / to go back

Presente	Pretérito Indefinido	Pretérito Imperfecto	Futuro
yo vuelvo	yo volví	yo volvía	yo volveré
tú vuelves	tú volviste	tú volvías	tú volverás
él vuelve	él volvió	él volvía	él volverá
nosotros volvemos	nosotros volvimos	nosotros volvíamos	nosotros volveremos
vosotros volvéis	vosotros volvisteis	vosotros volvíais	vosotros volveréis
ellos vuelven	ellos volvieron	ellos volvían	ellos volverán

CONOCER - to know people, places

Presente	Pretérito Indefinido	Pretérito Imperfecto	Futuro
yo conozco	yo conocí	yo conocía	yo conoceré
tú conoces	tú conociste	tú conocías	tú conocerás
él conoce	él conoció	él conocía	él conocerá
nosotros conocemos	nosotros conocimos	nosotros conocíamos	nosotros conoceremos
vosotros conocéis	vosotros conocisteis	vosotros conocíais	vosotros conoceréis
ellos conocen	ellos conocieron	ellos conocían	ellos conocerán

SENTIR - to feel

Presente	Pretérito Indefinido	Pretérito Imperfecto	Futuro
yo siento	yo sentí	yo sentía	yo sentiré
tú sientes	tú sentiste	tú sentías	tú sentirás
él siente	él sintió	él sentía	él sentirá
nosotros sentimos	nosotros sentimos	nosotros sentíamos	nosotros sentiremos
vosotros sentís	vosotros sentisteis	vosotros sentíais	vosotros sentiréis
ellos sienten	ellos sintieron	ellos sentían	ellos sentirán

CONTAR - to tell / to count

Presente	Pretérito Indefinido	Pretérito Imperfecto	Futuro
yo cuento	yo conté	yo contaba	yo contaré
tú cuentas	tú contaste	tú contabas	tú contarás
él cuenta	él contó	él contaba	él contará
nosotros contamos	nosotros contamos	nosotros contábamos	nosotros contaremos
vosotros contáis	vosotros contasteis	vosotros contabais	vosotros contaréis
ellos cuentan	ellos contaron	ellos contaban	ellos contarán

EMPEZAR - to start

Presente	Pretérito Indefinido	Pretérito Imperfecto	Futuro
yo empiezo	yo empecé	yo empezaba	yo empezaré
tú empiezas	tú empezaste	tú empezabas	tú empezarás
él empieza	él empezó	él empezaba	él empezará
nosotros empezamos	nosotros empezamos	nosotros empezábamos	nosotros empezaremos
vosotros empezáis	vosotros empezasteis	vosotros empezabais	vosotros empezaréis
ellos empiezan	ellos empezaron	ellos empezaban	ellos empezarán

BUSCAR - to search for

Presente	Pretérito Indefinido	Pretérito Imperfecto	Futuro
yo busco	yo busqué	yo buscaba	yo buscaré
tú buscas	tú buscaste	tú buscabas	tú buscarás
él busca	él buscó	él buscaba	él buscará
nosotros buscamos	nosotros buscamos	nosotros buscábamos	nosotros buscaremos
vosotros buscáis	vosotros buscasteis	vosotros buscabais	vosotros buscaréis
ellos buscan	ellos buscaron	ellos buscaban	ellos buscarán

ESCRIBIR - to write

Presente	Pretérito Indefinido	Pretérito Imperfecto	Futuro
yo escribo	yo escribí	yo escribía	yo escribiré
tú escribes	tú escribiste	tú escribías	tú escribirás
él escribe	él escribió	él escribía	él escribirá
nosotros escribimos	nosotros escribimos	nosotros escribíamos	nosotros escribiremos
vosotros escribís	vosotros escribisteis	vosotros escribíais	vosotros escribiréis
ellos escriben	ellos escribieron	ellos escribían	ellos escribirán

PERDER - to lose

Presente	Pretérito Indefinido	Pretérito Imperfecto	Futuro
yo pierdo	yo perdí	yo perdía	yo perderé
tú pierdes	tú perdiste	tú perdías	tú perderás
él pierde	él perdió	él perdía	él perderá
nosotros perdemos	nosotros perdimos	nosotros perdíamos	nosotros perderemos
vosotros perdéis	vosotros perdisteis	vosotros perdíais	vosotros perderéis
ellos pierden	ellos perdieron	ellos perdían	ellos perderán

PRODUCIR - to produce

Presente	Pretérito Indefinido	Pretérito Imperfecto	Futuro
yo produzco	yo produje	yo producía	yo produciré
tú produces	tú produjiste	tú producías	tú producirás
él produce	él produjo	él producía	él producirá
nosotros producimos	nosotros produjimos	nosotros producíamos	nosotros produciremos
vosotros producís	vosotros produjisteis	vosotros producíais	vosotros produciréis
ellos producen	ellos produjeron	ellos producían	ellos producirán

ENTENDER - to understand

Presente	Pretérito Indefinido	Pretérito Imperfecto	Futuro
yo entiendo	yo entendí	yo entendía	yo entenderé
tú entiendes	tú entendiste	tú entendías	tú entenderás
él entiende	él entendió	él entendía	él entenderá
nosotros entendemos	nosotros entendimos	nosotros entendíamos	nosotros entenderemos
vosotros entendéis	vosotros entendisteis	vosotros entendíais	vosotros entenderéis
ellos entienden	ellos entendieron	ellos entendían	ellos entenderán

PEDIR - to request / to ask for

Presente	Pretérito Indefinido	Pretérito Imperfecto	Futuro
yo pido	yo pedí	yo pedía	yo pediré
tú pides	tú pediste	tú pedías	tú pedirás
él pide	él pidió	él pedía	él pedirá
nosotros pedimos	nosotros pedimos	nosotros pedíamos	nosotros pediremos
vosotros pedís	vosotros pedisteis	vosotros pedíais	vosotros pediréis

| ellos piden | ellos pidieron | ellos pedían | ellos pedirán |

RECORDAR - to remind / to remember

Presente	Pretérito Indefinido	Pretérito Imperfecto	Futuro
yo recuerdo	yo recordé	yo recordaba	yo recordaré
tú recuerdas	tú recordaste	tú recordabas	tú recordarás
él recuerda	él recordó	él recordaba	él recordará
nosotros recordamos	nosotros recordamos	nosotros recordábamos	nosotros recordaremos
vosotros recordáis	vosotros recordasteis	vosotros recordabais	vosotros recordaréis
ellos recuerdan	ellos recordaron	ellos recordaban	ellos recordarán

APARECER - to appear / to show up

Presente	Pretérito Indefinido	Pretérito Imperfecto	Futuro
yo aparezco	yo aparecí	yo aparecía	yo apareceré
tú apareces	tú apareciste	tú aparecías	tú aparecerás
él aparece	él apareció	él aparecía	él aparecerá
nosotros aparecemos	nosotros aparecimos	nosotros aparecíamos	nosotros apareceremos
vosotros aparecéis	vosotros aparecisteis	vosotros aparecíais	vosotros apareceréis
ellos aparecen	ellos aparecieron	ellos aparecían	ellos aparecerán

CONSEGUIR - to get / to obtain

Presente	Pretérito Indefinido	Pretérito Imperfecto	Futuro
yo consigo	yo conseguí	yo conseguía	yo conseguiré
tú consigues	tú conseguiste	tú conseguías	tú conseguirás
él consigue	él consiguió	él conseguía	él conseguirá
nosotros conseguimos	nosotros conseguimos	nosotros conseguíamos	nosotros conseguiremos

vosotros conseguís	vosotros conseguisteis	vosotros conseguíais	vosotros conseguiréis
ellos consiguen	ellos consiguieron	ellos conseguían	ellos conseguirán

COMENZAR - to begin / to start

Presente	Pretérito Indefinido	Pretérito Imperfecto	Futuro
yo comienzo	yo comencé	yo comenzaba	yo comenzaré
tú comienzas	tú comenzaste	tú comenzabas	tú comenzarás
él comienza	él comenzó	él comenzaba	él comenzará
nosotros comenzamos	nosotros comenzamos	nosotros comenzábamos	nosotros comenzaremos
vosotros comenzáis	vosotros comenzasteis	vosotros comenzabais	vosotros comenzaréis
ellos comienzan	ellos comenzaron	ellos comenzaban	ellos comenzarán

SERVIR - to serve

Presente	Pretérito Indefinido	Pretérito Imperfecto	Futuro
yo sirvo	yo serví	yo servía	yo serviré
tú sirves	tú serviste	tú servías	tú servirás
él sirve	él sirvió	él servía	él servirá
nosotros servimos	nosotros servimos	nosotros servíamos	nosotros serviremos
vosotros servís	vosotros servisteis	vosotros servíais	vosotros serviréis
ellos sirven	ellos sirvieron	ellos servían	ellos servirán

SACAR - to take out

Presente	Pretérito Indefinido	Pretérito Imperfecto	Futuro
yo saco	yo saqué	yo sacaba	yo sacaré
tú sacas	tú sacaste	tú sacabas	tú sacarás
él saca	él sacó	él sacaba	él sacará

nosotros sacamos	nosotros sacamos	nosotros sacábamos	nosotros sacaremos
vosotros sacáis	vosotros sacasteis	vosotros sacabais	vosotros sacaréis
ellos sacan	ellos sacaron	ellos sacaban	ellos sacarán

MANTENER = to maintain

Presente	**Pretérito Indefinido**	**Pretérito Imperfecto**	**Futuro**
yo mantengo	yo mantuve	yo mantenía	yo mantendré
tú mantienes	tú mantuviste	tú mantenías	tú mantendrás
él mantiene	él mantuvo	él mantenía	él mantendrá
nosotros mantenemos	nosotros mantuvimos	nosotros manteníamos	nosotros mantendremos
vosotros mantenéis	vosotros mantuvisteis	vosotros manteníais	vosotros mantendréis
ellos mantienen	ellos mantuvieron	ellos mantenían	ellos mantendrán

LEER - to read

Presente	**Pretérito Indefinido**	**Pretérito Imperfecto**	**Futuro**
yo leo	yo leí	yo leía	yo leeré
tú lees	tú leíste	tú leías	tú leerás
él lee	él leyó	él leía	él leerá
nosotros leemos	nosotros leímos	nosotros leíamos	nosotros leeremos
vosotros leéis	vosotros leísteis	vosotros leíais	vosotros leeréis
ellos leen	ellos leyeron	ellos leían	ellos leerán

CAER - to fall

Presente	**Pretérito Indefinido**	**Pretérito Imperfecto**	**Futuro**
yo caigo	yo caí	yo caía	yo caeré
tú caes	tú caíste	tú caías	tú caerás
él cae	él cayó	él caía	él caerá
nosotros caemos	nosotros caímos	nosotros caíamos	nosotros caeremos
vosotros caéis	vosotros caísteis	vosotros caíais	vosotros caeréis
ellos caen	ellos cayeron	ellos caían	ellos caerán

ABRIR - to open

Presente	Pretérito Indefinido	Pretérito Imperfecto	Futuro
yo abro	yo abrí	yo abría	yo abriré
tú abres	tú abriste	tú abrías	tú abrirás
él abre	él abrió	él abría	él abrirá
nosotros abrimos	nosotros abrimos	nosotros abríamos	nosotros abriremos
vosotros abrís	vosotros abristeis	vosotros abríais	vosotros abriréis
ellos abren	ellos abrieron	ellos abrían	ellos abrirán

OIR - to hear

Presente	Pretérito Indefinido	Pretérito Imperfecto	Futuro
yo oigo	yo oí	yo oía	yo oiré
tú oyes	tú oíste	tú oías	tú oirás
él oye	él oyó	él oía	él oirá
nosotros oímos	nosotros oímos	nosotros oíamos	nosotros oiremos
vosotros oís	vosotros oísteis	vosotros oíais	vosotros oiréis
ellos oyen	ellos oyeron	ellos oían	ellos oirán

CONVERTIR - to convert

Presente	Pretérito Indefinido	Pretérito Imperfecto	Futuro
yo convierto	yo convertí	yo convertía	yo convertiré
tú conviertes	tú convertiste	tú convertías	tú convertirás
él convierte	él convirtió	él convertía	él convertirá
nosotros convertimos	nosotros convertimos	nosotros convertíamos	nosotros convertiremos
vosotros convertís	vosotros convertisteis	vosotros convertíais	vosotros convertiréis
ellos convierten	ellos convirtieron	ellos convertían	ellos convertirán

TRAER - to bring

Presente	Pretérito Indefinido	Pretérito Imperfecto	Futuro

Presente	Pretérito Indefinido	Pretérito Imperfecto	Futuro
yo traigo	yo traje	yo traía	yo traeré
tú traes	tú trajiste	tú traías	tú traerás
él trae	él trajo	él traía	él traerá
nosotros traemos	nosotros trajimos	nosotros traíamos	nosotros traeremos
vosotros traéis	vosotros trajisteis	vosotros traíais	vosotros traeréis
ellos traen	ellos trajeron	ellos traían	ellos traerán

MORIR - to die

Presente	Pretérito Indefinido	Pretérito Imperfecto	Futuro
yo muero	yo morí	yo moría	yo moriré
tú mueres	tú moriste	tú morías	tú morirás
él muere	él murió	él moría	él morirá
nosotros morimos	nosotros morimos	nosotros moríamos	nosotros moriremos
vosotros morís	vosotros moristeis	vosotros moríais	vosotros moriréis
ellos mueren	ellos murieron	ellos morían	ellos morirán

REALIZAR - to accomplish / to achieve

Presente	Pretérito Indefinido	Pretérito Imperfecto	Futuro
yo realizo	yo realicé	yo realizaba	yo realizaré
tú realizas	tú realizaste	tú realizabas	tú realizarás
él realiza	él realizó	él realizaba	él realizará
nosotros realizamos	nosotros realizamos	nosotros realizábamos	nosotros realizaremos
vosotros realizáis	vosotros realizasteis	vosotros realizabais	vosotros realizaréis
ellos realizan	ellos realizaron	ellos realizaban	ellos realizarán

SUPONER - to suppose

Presente	Pretérito Indefinido	Pretérito Imperfecto	Futuro
yo supongo	yo supuse	yo suponía	yo supondré
tú supones	tú supusiste	tú suponías	tú supondrás
él supone	él supuso	él suponía	él supondrá
nosotros suponemos	nosotros supusimos	nosotros suponíamos	nosotros supondremos
vosotros suponéis	vosotros supusisteis	vosotros suponíais	vosotros supondréis
ellos suponen	ellos supusieron	ellos suponían	ellos supondrán

EXPLICAR - to explain

Presente	Pretérito Indefinido	Pretérito Imperfecto	Futuro
yo explico	yo expliqué	yo explicaba	yo explicaré
tú explicas	tú explicaste	tú explicabas	tú explicarás
él explica	él explicó	él explicaba	él explicará
nosotros explicamos	nosotros explicamos	nosotros explicábamos	nosotros explicaremos
vosotros explicáis	vosotros explicasteis	vosotros explicabais	vosotros explicaréis
ellos explican	ellos explicaron	ellos explicaban	ellos explicarán

TOCAR - to touch

Presente	Pretérito Indefinido	Pretérito Imperfecto	Futuro
yo toco	yo toqué	yo tocaba	yo tocaré
tú tocas	tú tocaste	tú tocabas	tú tocarás
él toca	él tocó	él tocaba	él tocará
nosotros tocamos	nosotros tocamos	nosotros tocábamos	nosotros tocaremos
vosotros tocáis	vosotros tocasteis	vosotros tocabais	vosotros tocaréis
ellos tocan	ellos tocaron	ellos tocaban	ellos tocarán

FIFTH CHAPTER: Subjunctive, conditional and Imperative

As we have mentioned before, the **SUBJUNCTIVE** mode is used for expressing desires, doubts, the unknown, the abstract, and emotions. The subjunctive mode has many of the same verb tenses as the indicative mode, including the present, the preterit, and the future. Although the future is rarely used in modern Spanish, but it's good to know it for reading literature.

Some examples:

Es posible que **hable** español (It's possible he speaks Spanish): We don't know if he speaks Spanish.

Ojalá **apruebe** el examen (Hopefully I will pass the exam): This is a desire. The Spanish word "Ojalá" it's like to say "hopefully" or "if only" in English.

¡Que **tengas** un buen viaje! (Have a Good trip!): expressing a wish.

No creo que **venga** a la fiesta (I don't think he's coming to the party): Something that we think, but we aren't sure.

Dudo que **llegue** a tiempo (I doubt he's on time): clear, expressing a doubt.

The subjunctive usually needs a word, verb or expression as introduction such as:

Quizá, tal vez *(maybe, perhaps...)*: Quizá **cante** en el concierto del domingo (Maybe I'm singing at Sunday's concert)
Es posible, es probable *(It's possible...)*: Es posible que **comamos** en el restaurant de Pedro (It's possible we're eating at Pedro's restaurant)
Quiero que... *(I want...)*: Quiero que **vengas** a mi boda (I want you to come to my wedding)
Me gustaría que... *(I would like that...)*: Me gustaría que **leyeras** más durante la semana (I would like you to read more during the week)

Ojalá (Hopefully): Ojalá el avión **salga** puntual (Hopefully the plane will depart on time)

Now that we have seen some examples and some introductions when using the subjunctive, let's see how to form the subjunctive present tense for regular verbs.
As in the indicative mood, we have to separate the ending AR, ER or IR, and change it for the correspondent ending for each person.

First conjugation: **HABLAR** (to speak)
Yo habl + e = **hable**
Tú habl + es = **hables**
Él o **ella** habl + e = **hable**
Nosotros o **nosotras** habl + emos = **hablemos**
Vosotros o **vosotras** habl + éis = **habléis**
Ellos o **ellas** habl + en = **hablen**

Second conjugation: **COMER** (to eat)
Yo com + a = **coma**
Tú com + as = **comas**
Él o **ella** com + a = **coma**
Nosotros o **nosotras** com + amos = **comamos**
Vosotros o **vosotras** com + áis = **comáis**
Ellos o **ellas** com + an = **coman**

Third conjugation: **VIVIR** (to live)
Yo viv + a = **viva**
Tú viv + as = **vivas**
Él o **ella** viv + a = **viva**
Nosotros o **nosotras** viv + amos = **vivamos**
Vosotros o **vosotras** viv + áis = **viváis**
Ellos o **ellas** viv + an = **vivan**

Here you'll find some **irregular verbs** conjugated in present of subjunctive:

HABER	**SER**	**VER**
yo haya	yo sea	yo vea

tú hayas	tú seas	tú veas
él/ella haya	él/ella sea	él/ella vea
nosotros/as hayamos	nosotros/as seamos	nosotros/as veamos
vosotros/as hayáis	vosotros/as seáis	vosotros/as veáis
ellos/as hayan	ellos/as sean	ellos/as vean

IR	**SABER**	**ESTAR**	**HACER**
yo vaya	yo sepa	yo esté	yo hag-a
tú vayas	tú sepas	tú estés	tú hag-as
él vaya	él/ella sepa	él/ella esté	él/ella hag-a
nosotros/as vayamos	nosotros/as sepamos	nosotros/as estemos	nosotros/as hag-amos
vosotros/as vayáis	vosotros/as sepáis	vosotros/as estéis	vosotros/as hag-áis
ellos/as vayan	ellos/as sepan	ellos/as estén	ellos/as hag-an

VENIR	**SENTIR**
yo veng-a	yo sienta
tú veng-as	tú sientas
él/ella veng-a	él/ella sienta
nosotros/as veng-amos	nosotros/as sintamos
vosotros/as veng-áis	vosotros/as sintáis
ellos/as veng-an	ellos/as sientan

PREFERIR	**REÍR**	**PEDIR**
yo prefiera	yo ría	yo pida
tú prefieras	tú rías	tú pidas
él/ella prefiera	él/ella ría	él/ella pida
nosotros/as prefiramos	nosotros/as riamos	nosotros/as pidamos
vosotros/as prefiráis	vosotros/as riáis	vosotros/as pidáis
ellos/as prefieran	ellos/as rían	ellos/as pidan

QUERER	PODER	VOLAR	JUGAR
yo qu**ie**ra	yo p**ue**da	yo v**ue**le	yo j**ue**gue
tú qu**ie**ras	tú p**ue**das	tú v**ue**les	tú j**ue**gues
él/ella qu**ie**ra	él/ella p**ue**da	él/ella v**ue**le	él/ella j**ue**gue
nosotros/as queramos	nosotros/as podamos	nosotros/as volemos	nosotros/as juguemos
vosotros/as queráis	vosotros/as podáis	vosotros/as voléis	vosotros/as juguéis
ellos/as qu**ie**ran	ellos/as p**ue**dan	ellos/as v**ue**len	ellos/as j**ue**guen

Let's practice now with more examples. Can you identify the verb in subjunctive tense?

¿Quieres que te **ayude** a hacer la mudanza? (Do you want us to help you with the moving to a new house?)

¿Te apetece que **salgamos** a bailar esta noche? (Fancy to go out dancing tonight?)

No quiero que **seas** tan exigente con tus compañeros de trabajo (I don't want you to be so exigent with your work's partners)

No creo que Ramon **sea** sincero (I don't believe Ramon is being honest)

Espero que **canten** tan bien como siempre (I hope they will sing as good as always)

Quiero que **celebres** tu cumpleaños con una gran fiesta (I want you to celebrate your birthday party with a big party)

¿Quieres que **cenemos** tortilla de patatas? (Do you want Spanish omelette for dinner?)

¡Qué maravilloso que **cocinéis** para nosotros! (How wonderful is you are cooking for us!)

Es imposible que Manuela **llegue** puntual a su trabajo (It's impossible for Manuela to arrive on time at work)

And let's talk now about the **CONDITIONAL** and learn how to form the simple conditional.

The conditional tense in Spanish is used in a similar way to how we would express conditional ideas in English.

Language	Simple Conditional
English	I would do
Spanish	Yo haría

In Spanish, the simple conditional is used in the following cases:

1. To ask for something from someone in a polite way

    ¿Podrías bajarme ese plato? (Could you get that plate down for me?)

    ¿Te importaría venir conmigo? (Would you mind coming with me?)

2. To give advice

    Deberías cortarte el pelo (You should cut your hair)

    Podrías ponerte el vestido azul (You could wear the blue dress)

3. In the past, when you say or think some event will happen in the future but that doesn´t end up happening and you refer back to that same event.

    Pensé que suspenderías el examen (I thought you would fail the exam)

    Me prometiste que recogerías tu habitación (You promised you would tidy up your room)

4. For past assumptions. When you're not sure of something that happened but you take a guess.

    ¿Quién te arregló ayer la bicicleta? (Who fixed your bike yesterday?)
    No sé, sería David (I don´t know, it might have been David)

Let's see now how to form the simple conditional. And we have some good news about the Spanish conditional tense: it is one of the easiest Spanish verb tenses to conjugate! Why? Because the conjugations for the regular verbs ending in AR, ER and IR, are all the same. And there are only a small number of irregular verbs.

Here we have the simple conditional for regular verbs:

hablar	comer	vivir
hablaría	comería	viviría
hablarías	comerías	vivirías
hablaría	comería	viviría
hablaríamos	comeríamos	viviríamos
hablaríais	comeríais	viviríais
hablarían	comerían	vivirían

Let's look at these examples:

El estudiante dijo que estudiaría un día más (The student said that he would study one more day)
¿Qué hora sería? (What time could it has been?)
Dijo que estaría en su casa (He said he would stay at home)
Estaríamos en el cine cuando llamaste (We were probably at the cinema when you called)

Irregular verbs in the conditional only change the beginning and then follow the rule of the endings, like the regular verbs. For conditional tense, these are the irregular verbs:

IRREGULAR VERB	IRREGULAR BEGINNING
Poner (to put)	pondr-
Salir (to go out)	saldr-
Tener (to have)	tendr-
Valer (to cost)	valdr-
Venir (to come)	vendr-
Caber (to fit in)	cabr-
Poder (to can)	podr-
Saber (to know)	sabr-
Decir (to say)	dir-
Hacer (to do)	har-
Querer (to want, to love)	querr-

	ENDING
yo	-ía
tú	-ías
él, ella, usted	-ía
nosotros/as	-íamos
vosotros/as	-íais
ellos, ellas, ustedes	-ían

Poner:
Yo pondría, tu pondrías, él o ella pondría, nosotros o nosotras pondríamos, vosotros o vosotras pondríais, ellos o ellas pondrían.

Salir:
Yo saldría, tu saldrías, él o ella saldría, nosotros o nosotras saldríamos, vosotros o vosotras saldríais, ellos o ellas saldrían.

Tener:
Yo tendría, tu tendrías, él o ella tendría, nosotros o nosotras tendríamos, vosotros o vosotras tendrías, ellos o ellas tendrían.

Valer:
Yo valdría, tu valdrías, él o ella valdría, nosotros o nosotras valdríamos, vosotros o vosotras valdríais, ellos o ellas valdrían.

Venir:
Yo vendría, tu vendrías, él o ella vendría, nosotros o nosotras vendríamos, vosotros o vosotras vendríais, ellos o ellas vendrían.

Now is your turn! Form the conditional tense for the following irregular verbs:

Venir (to come)	vendr-
Caber (to fit in)	cabr-
Poder (to can)	podr-
Saber (to know)	sabr-
Decir (to say)	dir-
Hacer (to do)	har-
Querer (to want; to love)	querr-

The conditional can also be used to make requests, that way some statements sound less blunt.

- *Me **gustaría** salir (I would like to go out):* This sounds gentler than *"Quiero salir"* (I want to go out)
- *¿**Podría** tener un coche de cortesía mientras arreglan el mío?* (Would it be possible to have a courtesy car meanwhile you fix mine?**)**

Note that *"querer"* is used in subjunctive sometimes for requests as well (while in English we would use 'like' instead of 'want'):

Quisiera un café, por favor (I would like a coffee, please)

Practice time!

Regular verbs

Antes de ir a tu casa, Raúl y yo **deberíamos** pasear al perro (Before going to your house, Raul and me must go to walk the dog)

Mis padres **serían** más felices viviendo en Cuba (My parents would be happier living in Cuba)

Te advertí que Dani no te **devolvería** el dinero (I told you Dani wouldn't give your money back)

Yo **iría** contigo hasta el fin del mundo (I would go with you to the end of the world)

Nos **gustaría** ir a esquiar en invierno (We would like to go to sky in winter)

Irregular verbs

Creí que vosotros **vendríais** hoy (I thought you would come today)

La primera vez que fui a Perú **tendría** 19 años (The first time I went to Peru I would be 19 years old)

¿**Podrías** venir a recogerme? (Could you come to pick me up?)

¿Crees que no **cabría** otra silla de despacho aquí? (Do you think it wouldn't fit another chair here?)

Los alumnos **querrían** tener más tiempo para estudiar (Students would like to have more time to study)

Now it's time for the **IMPERATIVE**.

The Imperative (imperativo) expresses demands, orders and requests addressed to one or more people directly.

The imperative exists for the first person plural (nosotros/-as), the second person singular and plural (tú, vosotros/-as) and the polite form 'usted' in singular and plural (ustedes), but it's always conjugated without the personal pronoun

When we use the imperative?

- Making suggestions: Paremos un taxi (Let's stop a taxi)
- Giving orders: ¡Llévanos a la estación! (Bring us to the station!)
- Giving advice: Si tienes prisa, pide un taxi. (If you are in a hurry, ask for a taxi)
- Making requests: Dame la dirección (Give me the address)

Conjugation:

2nd person singular (tú)

To conjugate the imperative in the 2nd person singular (tú) we use the 3rd person singular form of the present indicative. However, to form a negative imperative, we use the 2nd person singular form of the present subjunctive. And remember that the personal pronoun is not used.

	positive form	negative form
hablar	¡Habla!	¡No hables!
aprender	¡Aprende!	¡No aprendas!
escribir	¡Escribe!	¡No escribas!

Irregular forms for the 2nd person singular:

infinitive	imperative	translation
decir	di	Say!
hacer	haz	Do/Make!
ir	ve	Go!
poner	pon	Put!
salir	sal	Go out!
ser	sé	Be!
tener	ten	Take!
venir	ven	Come!

2nd person plural (vosotros/as)

To conjugate the positive imperative for the 2nd person plural *(vosotros/as)* we take the infinitive and replace the *-r* with a *-d*.
In the negative form, we take the 2nd person plural of the present subjunctive, omitting the personal pronoun.

	positive form	**negative form**
	replace infinitive-r with d	subjunctive (2nd person plural)
hablar	¡Habla<u>d</u>!	¡No habléis!
aprender	¡Aprende<u>d</u>!	¡No aprendáis!
escribir	¡Escribid!	¡No escribáis!

Polite form singular (usted)

	positive form	negative form
	subjunctive (3rd person singular)	subjunctive (3rd person singular)
hablar	¡Hable!	¡No hable!
aprender	¡Aprenda!	¡No aprenda!

escribir	¡Escriba!	¡No escriba!

Polite form plural (ustedes)

	positive form subjunctive (3rd person plural)	negative form subjunctive (3rd person plural)
hablar	¡Hablen!	¡No hablen!
aprender	¡Aprendan!	¡No aprendan!
escribir	¡Escriban!	¡No escriban!

1st person plural (nosotros/as)

	positive form subjunctive (1st person plural)	negative form subjunctive (1st person plural)
hablar	¡Hablemos!	¡No hablemos!
aprender	¡Aprendamos!	¡No aprendamos!
escribir	¡Escribamos!	¡No escribamos!

Let's see some examples for affirmative and negative imperative forms:

Positive imperative:

- Por favor, ¡prestad atencion! (Please, pay attention!)
- ¡Trae tus deberes! (Bring your homework!)
- ¡Por lo menos, alegrémonos un poco! (At least, be a little bit happy!)
- ¡Cámbiate de ropa! (Change your clothes!)
- ¡Ven aquí! (Come here!)

Negative imperative:

- ¡No pagues tú la cuenta! (Don't pay the bill!)
- ¡Por favor, no vayamos a ese restaurante! (Please, don't go to that restaurant!)

- o ¡No juguéis con la pelota dentro de casa! (Don't play with the ball inside the house!)
- o ¡No hablen todos al mismo tiempo! (Don't talk all at the same time!)
- o ¡No te creas tan importante! (Don't belief you are so important!)

BONUS CHAPTER: Tips & Tricks to improve faster our Intermediate Spanish

It's been a dense book, but we have learnt a lot.
When learning Spanish or other foreigner language, do you know what level learners is more common to give up at? Intermediate.
Why? Because when starting from zero is easy to feel you are learning and improving because at the end of each chapter you know something else. But when you are in intermediate, how would you know you are improving? You are starting to be able to understand and communicate in Spanish through a less basic level, however at the very beginning jump from box 1 to 2 implied double your level, but when at intermediate the same absolute improvement means a minor relative improvement (10% if we jump, let's say, from box 10 to 11).
It's, therefore, a misleading feeling because your speed on learning is not slowing down! Besides that, at the beginning the sensation of being learning fast is such clear that you can end up thinking that achieving an expert level is doable in a relative short time.
And not, unfortunately that's not true. What it's true is that listening, reading and speaking Spanish (or another language) will be the only path that will take you to your goal!

Once you can communicate and understand Spanish speakers, you can focus in grammar, and how to speak, write and read properly, not just in an understandable way.

As we have mentioned before, Spanish must be part of your life. If you have a work partner, a neighbour, a friend who speaks Spanish, try to practise with them. If not, some meetups are organized in many locations with the aim to exchange languages (Spanish-English, etc.). You can find out online choices in the location you are living but, before that, remember switch your smartphone into Spanish, including the assistant that can be also very useful to check your pronunciation: if your requests aren't understood then you need to practise more!

And, of course, when heading to the meetup, if the address is unknown, turn your GPS indications into Spanish as well.
All are small details but added can make a real difference!

It's also time to focus on improving your writing skills. Reading in Spanish will help you a lot on that.
And if your laptop has an English keyboard, you can install a new one in Spanish format (e.g. with accents and the letter 'ñ') or you can use ALT shortcuts that will allow you to type anything in Spanish from your English keypad.

Better than anyone else, you know, when using a foreigner language, what skill is more challenging for you. Focus on that. Don't leave it to the end. Don't put it off.
Don't give up.

There are a lot of resources to keep you entertained and improve your Spanish at the same time: newspapers, magazines, eBooks, podcasts… try different ones because each type of resources helps you to develop and improve different skills (listening, writing, speaking and understanding).

The satisfaction of being able to talk more or less fluently in another language is very big. Sometimes the path to get there is very steep, but when the peak is reached the feeling is amazing!!

CONCLUSIONS

Well, now that you have finished this third book, you can sit back, relax and say you have been learning a lot of vocabulary, grammar and examples.

You have seen a lot of verbs and so many different verb tenses. It can be overwhelming but as always, the secret to memorise and to remember when use one or another is practice.
Now is your turn to put together all you have learnt during this all time. Use the verbs, make sentences, practice different tenses writing about the past, the present and the future.
You can also try now to write sentences longer. Confidence is your best friend to speak Spanish without fear. You will likely make mistakes, but mistakes are essential when learning!

Try to summarise all the info in your mind because that summary will be completed, little by little, with examples and your experiences when using the language.
It's essential understand when different verbal moods must be used: indicative, subjunctive, conditional and imperative. In some cases, English can be helpful because some meanings are identical on both languages; pay more attention on the examples when English can't replicate some Spanish verb moods/tenses.
Focus first on the indicative mood. Not only it's the easier one (since English works in a similar way on that context), but it's the most used one as well. Most of verb tenses commonly used in Spain are within the indicative group.

And don't forget about the 3 different Spanish conjugations depending on the verb ending (AR, ER, IR). And either on how to identify if a verb is regular or irregular.

A lot of times the examples will be more helpful for understanding than grammar explanations.

Because examples and practise are everything. If you ask a perfect Spanish speaker about, for instance, when the subjunctive mood needs to be used their answer will be 'I don't know' in 9 out of 10 times. Because, as you have likely done with English too, grammar was essential to lay the foundation at the very beginning, but to build up the building the necessary materials are the regular use, i.e. speaking-listening, writing-reading.

And if you got here, there is only one way left now: forward!!

Thank you for making it through to the end of "Learn Spanish in your car – Level 3", let's hope it was informative and able to provide you with all of the tools you need to achieve your goals whatever they may be.

We really hope you enjoyed this guide, customer satisfaction for us is very important.
If you found this book useful in any way, a review on Amazon is always appreciated! ☺

LEARN SPANISH IN YOUR CAR
for Beginners

The Ultimate Easy Spanish Learning Guide: How to Learn Spanish Language Vocabulary like crazy with 20 SHORT STORIES for beginners + Questions & Exercises.

Final Lesson
VOL. 4

CONTENTS

EN LA FIESTA DE ROSA
  AT ROSA'S PARTY (translation)

UNA CENA EN EL RESTAURANTE EL CASTILLO
  DINNER AT EL CASTILLO RESTAURANT (translation)

UNA NUEVA MASCOTA
  A NEW PET (translation)

PERDIDO EN LA CIUDAD
  LOST IN THE CITY (translation)

EL PRIMER DÍA DE CLASE
  FIRST DAY OF CLASSROOM (translation)

ENCUENTROS EN EL METRO
  ENCONUNTERS IN THE METRO (translation)

UNA CENA CON AMIGOS
  DINNER WITH FRIENDS (translation)

VIAJE A ROMA
  TRIP TO ROME (translation)

EN LA GRANJA
  AT THE FARM (translation)

RESTAURANTE EL VELERO
  EL VELERO RESTAURANT (translation)

LA FAMILIA DE PASCUAL
  PASCUAL'S FAMILY (translation)

MARC Y GINA
  MARC AND GINA (translation)

EN EL AEROPUERTO
  IN THE AIRPORT (translation)

RESACA
   HANGOVER (translation)

EL ULTIMO VERANO
   THE LAST SUMMER (translation)

VACACIONES EN ESPAÑA
   HOLIDAYS IN SPAIN (translation)

UN LAGO Y MILLONES DE ESTRELLAS
   A LAKE AND MILLIONS OF STARS (translation)

EMPEZAR DE NUEVO
   START AGAIN (translation)

UN CACHORRITO LLAMADO KEN
   A PUPPY CALLED KEN

PADRE E HIJO
   FATHER AND SON (translation)

EN LA FIESTA DE ROSA

- Hola! ¿Cómo te llamas?
- Me llamo Ernesto. ¿Y tú?
- Soy Clara, la prima de Rosa. ¿De qué conoces a Rosa?
- Somos **compañeros** de trabajo.
- ¡Ah! ¿Y hace mucho tiempo que os conocéis?
- Hace seis meses. Yo empecé a trabajar en la empresa entonces.
- Ya veo. Voy a buscar una bebida. ¿Quieres algo?
- Sí, gracias. Pero mejor te acompaño y así me cuentas mas sobre ti. **¿A qué te dedicas**?
- Soy profesora de español. Enseño español en una academia de idiomas para extranjeros.
- ¡Qué interesante! ¿Y **de dónde son** tus estudiantes?
- Pues la verdad es que son de todas partes. Pero de donde mas vienen es de Inglaterra, de Francia y de Alemania. También hay algún estadounidense. Son todos muy majos y simpáticos. Nos lo pasamos muy bien en clase.
- ¿Hace mucho tiempo que eres profesora?
- Empecé a enseñar español hace diez años.
  Dime tú ahora, **¿qué haces en la empresa** de mi prima Rosa?
- Soy diseñador gráfico. Básicamente me dedico a diseñar los logotipos de nuestros clientes.
- ¿Te gusta lo que haces?
- Sí. Desde pequeño siempre me ha gustado dibujar. Además, **se me da bien**. Así que me decidí a estudiar diseño gráfico. Estoy contento. Estoy muy bien en esa empresa. Hay un ambiente de trabajo muy agradable.
- Eso es muy importante. ¿Te puedo preguntar de dónde eres? Te noto cierto acento al hablar español.
- Soy de Holanda, pero mi madre es española, por eso hablo español. En casa siempre hemos hablado español y holandés. Pero uso más el español desde que

vivo aquí. Vine a España a estudiar el último año de la **carrera universitaria** y ya me quedé.
- ¡Qué suerte! A mí también me hubiera gustado ir a estudiar a otro país, pero no pude. ¿Qué es lo que más te gusta de España?
- Me gusta esta ciudad, Barcelona. Me gusta que tenga playa y que haya gente de todo el mundo. Me gusta también la manera de tomarse las cosas aquí, es más relajada, ¡aunque a veces demasiado! **La gente es muy abierta**.
- Barcelona es una ciudad muy bella. Además, tienes muchos sitios cerca de Barcelona que son muy bonitos para visitar.
- Rosa me comentó algo de un pueblo llamado Sitges.
- ¡Sí! Se puede ir en tren, no está lejos. Y la verdad es que es un pueblo muy bonito. Es un sitio ideal para ir a pasar un día fuera.
- Igual podríamos ir los tres algún fin de semana...
- ¡Me parece bien! Vamos a buscar a Rosa para proponérselo. Seguro que a ella también le gusta la idea.

AT ROSA'S PARTY (translation)

- Hi! What is your name?
- My name is Ernesto. And you?
- I'm Clara, Rosa's cousin. Where do you know Rosa from?
- We are co-workers.
- Ah! And have you known each other for a long time?
- Six months ago. I started working at the company then.
- I see. I'm going to get a drink. Do you want something?
- Yes, thanks. But I better come with you so you can tell me more about yourself. What do you do?
- I am a Spanish teacher. I teach Spanish in a language school for foreigners.
- Interesting! And where are your students from?
- Well, the truth is that they are from everywhere. But where else they come from is from England, from France, and Germany. There is also some American. They are all very nice and friendly. We had a great time in class.
- Have you been a teacher for a long time?
- I started teaching Spanish ten years ago.
  Tell me now, what are you doing in my cousin's company Rosa?
- I am a graphic designer. Basically, I design the logos of our clients.
- Do you like what you do?

- Yes. Since childhood, I have always liked to draw. Besides, I'm good at it. So, I decided to study graphic design. I am happy. I am very well in that company. There is a very pleasant work environment.
- This is very important. May I ask where you are from? I notice a certain accent when speaking Spanish.
- I'm from Holland, but my mother is Spanish, that's why I speak Spanish. At home, we have always spoken Spanish and Dutch. But I use Spanish more since I live here. I came to Spain to study the last year of the university degree and I already stayed.
- Lucky! I would also have liked to go to study in another country, but I couldn't. What do you like most about Spain?
- I like this city, Barcelona. I like that it has a beach and that there are people from all over the world. I also like the way things are taken here, it is more relaxed, although sometimes too much! The people are very open.
- Barcelona is a very beautiful city. Besides, you have many places near Barcelona that are very beautiful to visit.
- Rosa told me something about a town called Sitges.
- Yes! You can go by train, it's not far. And the truth is that it is a very pretty town. It is an ideal place to go to spend a day out.
- We could go all three some weekend ...
- Seem right! Let's go find Rosa to propose. Surely, she also likes the idea.

Some notes from the text:

Compañeros: this word can have different meanings such as partners, colleagues, companions depending on the context. In this text means work colleagues.
¿A qué te dedicas? This question is used in Spanish to ask about the job, the profession.
¿De dónde son? This question is used to ask where someone is from. We usually ask telling the country or the nationality.
¿Qué haces en la empresa? This question is used in this text to ask about the duties in the company.
Se me da bien: We use this expression to say that we are good at something.
Carrera universitaria: In Spanish "carrera univesritaria" refers to the university studies, the degree.
La gente es muy abierta: this expression means people there are friendly.

Questions about the text:

What is Clara's cousin name?
1. Rosa
2. Clara
3. Ana
4. Emma

What is Rosa's partner name?
1. Eduardo
2. Ernesto
3. Miguel
4. Francisco

Where is Ernesto from?
1. De Alemania
2. De Francia
3. De Holanda
4. De Inglaterra

¿What does Clara do for work?
1. Es profesora de ingles
2. Es profesora de alemán
3. Es profesora de español
4. Es profesora de francés

UNA CENA EN EL RESTAURANTE EL CASTILLO

- Julia: Vamos Paco, acaba de vestirte que vamos a llegar tarde. Tenemos la reserva a las nueve.
- Paco: Casi estoy. Me pongo la chaqueta, cojo las llaves y ya podemos salir.
- Julia: **¡Por fin!**

Ya en el restaurante...
- Camarero: Buenas noches. ¿Tienen mesa reservada?
- Julia: Hola, buenas noches. Sí, tenemos una reserva a nombre de Julia Gutiérrez.
- Camarero: Aquí está. Pasen por aquí. Les acompaño a su mesa.
- Julia: Gracias.
- Camarero: Aquí es. ¿Desean beber algo mientras miran la carta?
- Paco: Para mí una copa de vino tinto, por favor.
- Julia: Para mí una copa de vino blanco, por favor.
- Camarero: **Enseguida**.
- Julia: ¿Ya sabes lo que vas a pedir?
- Paco: Pues la verdad es que no. ¿Y tú?
- Julia: Creo que hoy voy a pedirme los raviolis con ricotta y espinacas.
- Paco: Hum... me apetece algo de pescado a mí. Creo que pediré el bacalao al pil-pil.
  ¿Quieres que compartamos algún entrante? ¿Qué tal una ensalada de tomate y atún?
- Julia: Sí, perfecto.

El camarero trae las bebidas.
- Camarero: Aquí tienen sus bebidas. ¿Saben ya lo que van a pedir?

- Julia: Si, compartiremos una ensalada de tomate y atún como entrante y después yo quiero los raviolis con ricotta y espinaca.
- Camarero: Perfecto. ¿Y para usted?
- Paco: **Para mi el bacalao al pil-pil.**
- Camarero: Muy bien. ¿Desean un poco de pan?
- Julia: Sí, gracias.
- Camarero: Y de beber, ¿qué les traigo?
- Paco: Una botella de vino rosado, por favor. **El de la casa** está bien.
- Camarero: Enseguida.

Julia y Paco están esperando la cena.
- Julia: Este restaurante me encanta. Siempre comemos muy bien y el lugar es muy acogedor.
- Paco: Sí, tienes razón. Aunque algún día podríamos probar algún restaurante nuevo.
- Julia: Está bien. La próxima vez tú te encargas de buscar el restaurante.

Ya en los postres...
- Camarero: ¿Han terminado? ¿Les puedo retirar los platos?
- Julia: Sí, por favor.
- Camarero: ¿Quieren tomar algún postre?
- Paco: ¿Tienen hoy el brownie de la casa?
- Camarero: Sí. ¿Les apetece con nata y helado de vainilla o solo el brownie?
- Julia: ¡Con todo, por favor!
- Camarero: Muy bien. Enseguida se lo traigo.
- Julia y Paco: ¡Gracias!
- Paco: ¡Es uno de los mejores brownies que he comido nunca!
- Julia: ¡Eres un **goloso**! ¡Bueno, somos unos golosos porque nos encanta la comida dulce!
- Camarero: Aquí tienen el postre. ¿Desean tomar café?
- Julia y Paco: No gracias.

- Camarero: ¿Les ha gustado el postre? ¿Han disfrutado de la cena?
- Julia: Sí, todo estaba delicioso. ¿Nos puede traer la cuenta, por favor?
- Camarero: Sí claro, ahora mismo se la traigo. ¿Van a **pagar en efectivo** o con tarjeta?
- Julia: Con tarjeta, gracias.

DINNER AT EL CASTILLO RESTAURANT (translation)

- Julia: Come on Paco, just get dressed that we're going to be late. We have the reservation at nine.
- Paco: I'm almost there. I put on my jacket, take the keys and we can leave.
- Julia: Finally!

  Already in the restaurant ...
- Waiter: Good evening. Do you have a booking?
- Julia: Hello, goodnight. Yes, we have a booking in the name of Julia Gutiérrez.
- Waiter: Here it is. This way. I guide you to your table.
- Julia: Thank you.
- Waiter: Here it is. Do you want to drink something while looking at the menu?
- Paco: For me a glass of red wine, please.
- Julia: For me a glass of white wine, please.
- Waiter: Right away.
- Julia: Do you know what you're going to have today?
- Paco: Well, I'm not sure. And you?
- Julia: I think I'm going to order ravioli with ricotta and spinach today.
- Paco: Hum ... I feel like some fish to me. I think I'll order the Pil-pil cod.

  Do you want us to share a starter? How about a tomato and tuna salad?
- Julia: Yes, perfect.

  The waiter brings the drinks.
- Waiter: Here you have your drinks. Do you already know what you are going to order?
- Julia: Yes. We will share a tomato and tuna salad as a starter and then I want the ravioli with ricotta and spinach.
- Waiter: Perfect. And for you?
- Paco: For me the Pil-Pil cod.
- Waiter: Very good. Do you want some bread?
- Julia: Yes, thanks.
- Waiter: And what about drinking?
- Paco: A bottle of rose wine, please. The restaurant's one is fine.
- Waiter: Right away.

  Julia and Paco are waiting for dinner.
- Julia: I love this restaurant. We always eat very well and the place is very cozy.
- Paco: Yes, you're right. Although one day we could try some new restaurant.
- Julia: It's fine. Next time you look for the restaurant.

Already in desserts ...
- Waiter: Are you done? Can I remove the dishes?
- Julia: Yes, please.
- Waiter: Do you want to have a dessert?
- Paco: Do you have the restaurant's special brownie today?
- Waiter: Yes. Do you fancy with cream and vanilla ice cream or just the brownie?
- Julia: With everything, please!
- Waiter: Very good. I'll bring it to you right away.
- Julia and Paco: Thank you!
- Paco: It's one of the best brownies I've ever had!
- Julia: You're a sweet tooth! Well, we are sweet tooth because we love sugary food!
- Waiter: Here you have dessert. Do you want to drink coffee?
- Julia and Paco: No thanks.

- Waiter: Did you like dessert? Have you enjoyed dinner?
- Julia: Yes, everything was delicious. Can you bring us the bill, please?
- Waiter: Yes, of course, I'll bring it to you right now. Will you pay in cash or by card?
- Julia: Card, thanks.

Notes:

¡Por fin! This expression is used to express relief after being waiting for some time. It's like in English the expression "finally"
Enseguida means "right away"
Para mí el bacalao al Pil-Pil: when we are ordering food and drinks in a restaurant, we use the sentence "para mi" (for me) and then the food or drink we want.
El de la casa: 'el vino de la casa' or 'el postre de la casa' reffers to the resturant's wine or dessert. These will be their special products.
Goloso: we say someone is "goloso" when he likes to eat a lot of sweet food as pastries, cakes, pies...
Pagar en efectivo: means to pay in cash

Questions about the text:

What is the restaurant name?
1. El Palacio
2. El Castillo
3. La Playa
4. El Monasterio

What Julia and Paco are going to share?
1. Ensalada de tomate y queso
2. Ensalada de tomate y cebolla
3. Ensalada de tomate y atún
4. Ensalada de tomate y pepino

What does Julia order?
1. Raviolis con ricota y espinacas
2. Risotto de gambas
3. Raviolis de calabacín
4. Risotto de verduras

Who is going to choose restaurant next time?
1. Julia
2. Paco
3. El camarero
4. El hermano de Paco

UNA NUEVA MASCOTA

Es el cumpleaños de Ricardo. Ricardo va a cumplir nueve años. Sus padres le dijeron que cuando cumpliera nueve años, tendrían una mascota, así que hoy van a ir a una tienda de animales.
Ricardo no sabe qué mascota elegir. Le **gustan** todo tipo de animales: perros, gatos, conejos, hámsteres, conejillos de Indias... Esta tarde, cuando salga del colegio, irán juntos a una tienda de animales a informarse de los cuidados que necesita cada mascota para poder escoger la mejor opción.
Son las tres. La madre de Ricardo va a buscarlo al colegio y de allí, se van a la tienda de animales. El padre de Ricardo irá directamente para allá.
Una vez en la tienda **echan un vistazo**. En la tienda solo tienen mascotas pequeñas, como conejos, ratones, ardillas, conejillos de Indias; pero tienen mucha información sobre el cuidado de cualquier mascota.
Estando allí conocen a Andrea. Andrea trabaja allí y les puede asesorar. Lo primero que les pregunta Andrea es quien va a cuidar de la mascota y Ricardo responde muy excitado que él. Andrea le explica que cualquier mascota requiere tiempo y muchos cuidados, pero Ricardo está entusiasmado con la idea.
Andrea les explica con detalle todas las opciones que tienen para adquirir una mascota y todo lo relacionado con el cuidado. También les explica los **utensilios** que tendrían que comprar para tenerla en casa. Después de la visita a la tienda, disponen de mucha información, pero Ricardo tiene que pensar muy bien qué mascota escoger antes de tomar la decisión.
Él quiere un perro, pero viven en un piso y pasan muchas horas fuera y a los perros les gusta mucho la compañía, así que no sería una buena opción.

En la tienda Ricardo se fijó en un par de **conejillos de Indias**. Andrea les dijo que estos animales tienen que vivir en parejas porque son muy sociables, y que pueden compartir **hábitat**. Además, les gusta que interactúen con ellos. En el balcón tienen suficiente espacio para poner la jaula de madera que necesitarían. La jaula tendría que limpiarla una vez a la semana y mirar que los conejillos tengan agua, comida seca y heno cada día. Además, les encantan los vegetales frescos, así que tendría que darles una vez al día lechuga o col, o pepino, o pimiento o zanahoria.

Ricardo ha decidido que quiere los dos conejillos de Indias que vio en la tienda. Uno era marrón claro y otro era **marrón** oscuro. Les va a llamar "Caramelo" y "Chocolate" por sus colores.

Es el día siguiente. Hoy al salir del colegio, Ricardo ira con su madre y padre a buscar sus nuevas mascotas.

A NEW PET (translation)

It's Ricardo's birthday. Ricardo will be nine years old. His parents told him that when he turned nine, they would have a pet, so today they will go to an animal shop.

Ricardo does not know which pet to choose. He likes all kinds of animals: dogs, cats, rabbits, hamsters, guinea pigs ... This afternoon, when he finishes school, they will go to an animal shop together to learn about the care each pet needs to be able to choose the best option.

It's three o'clock. Ricardo's mother goes to pick him up at school and from there, they go to the animal shop. Ricardo's father will go straight there.

Once in the store, they look around. In the store they only have small pets, such as rabbits, mice, squirrels, guinea pigs; but they have a lot of information about caring for any pet.

While there, they meet Andrea. Andrea works there and can advise them. The first thing Andrea asks them is who will take care of the pet and Ricardo replies that he is, and he's very excited about that. Andrea explains that any pet requires time and a lot of care, but Ricardo is happy about the idea.

Andrea explains in detail all the options they have for acquiring a pet and everything related to care. It also explains the items that they would have to buy to have it at home. After visiting the store, they have a lot of information, but Ricardo has to think very well which pet to choose before making the decision.

He wants a dog, but they live in an apartment and spend many hours out and dogs really like the company, so it wouldn't be a good option.

At the store, Ricardo saw a pair of guinea pigs. Andrea told them that these animals must live in pairs because they are very sociable, and that they can share habitat. In addition, they like to interact with people. On the balcony they have enough space to put the hutch they would need. The cage would have to be cleaned once a week and see that the rabbits have water, dry food and hay every day. In addition, they love fresh vegetables, so you should give them lettuce or cabbage, or cucumber, or pepper or carrot once a day.

Ricardo has decided, he wants the two guinea pigs he saw in the store. One was light brown, and another was dark brown. He will call them "Caramel" and "Chocolate" for their colours.

It is the next day. Today after finishing school, Ricardo will go with his mother and father to get their new pets.

Notes from the text:

Gustan: The verb "gustar" (to like) works differently when we talk about likes and dislikes. This verb only has two forms: gusta and gustan depending on if we are talking about like a single thing or an activity such as "Me gusta cocinar" or " Me gusta el libro que estoy leyendo", and "gustan" when we like more than one thing like "Me gustan las películas de miedo y las comedias.

Echan un vistazo: This expression means to take a look

Utensilios: this word means items

Conejillos de Indias: Guinea Pigs

Hábitat: habitat.

Marrón: This is the colour brown. In the text you can find marrón claro (light brown) and marrón oscuro (dark brown).

Questions about the text:
How old is Ricardo?
1. Nueve
2. Diez
3. Ocho
4. Diecinueve

Who is going to pick up Ricardo at school?
1. Su padre
2. Su madre
3. Su abuela
4. Su tía

What store is going Ricardo with his parents?
1. A una tienda de deportes
2. A una tienda de ropa
3. A una tienda de animales
4. A una tienda de informática

What pet does Ricardo choose?
1. Un conejo
2. Un par de conejillos de India
3. Un perro
4. Ninguna

PERDIDO EN LA CIUDAD

Juan está de vacaciones en Madrid. Va a pasar dos semanas visitando la ciudad y sus alrededores. Hoy va a visitar el centro de la ciudad, pero no es muy bueno **leyendo mapas**, así que tiene que pedir indicaciones.

- Perdone, ¿podría indicarme cómo ir al centro?
- ¡Ui! Estás muy lejos para ir andando. Va a ser mejor que cojas el metro. La parada de metro está en la siguiente esquina. Coge la línea verde con dirección a Casa de Campo y bájate en la parada de Gran Vía. Allí ya estarás en el centro y podrás pasear por las calles.
- Perfecto, muchas gracias.

Juan ahora está en el centro de la ciudad. Quiere visitar la Puerta del Sol, la plaza Mayor y la Catedral de la Almudena. Es un paseo bastante largo y hace calor, así que en su mochila lleva algo de beber y un poco de fruta. Empieza a caminar dirección a la Puerta del Sol.

El centro de Madrid está lleno de gente. La Puerta del Sol es famosa en España porque se celebra una gran fiesta en fin de año. El reloj de la plaza da las **campanadas** cuando son las 12 de la noche. En España es típico comer uvas en fin de año. Se comen 12 uvas a la medianoche, una uva por cada campanada. Dicen que trae buena suerte para el año que empieza.

Después de visitar la Puerta del Sol, sigue andando hacia la Plaza Mayor. Una vez allí, Juan decide parar para comer y beber algo.

- ¡Hola, buenas! **¿Qué te pongo?**
- Querría un bocadillo de queso y una cerveza, por favor.
- ¡Claro! ¡Marchando!

Juan ya tiene el **estómago lleno** y ha descansado un poco, así que ya puede seguir su **paseo** hacia la Catedral.

- Perdona, ¿cómo llego a la Catedral de la Almudena?
- Sigue todo recto por la Calle Mayor y donde se acaba la calle, verás indicaciones de la Catedral porque está al lado. No tiene pérdida.
- Muchas gracias.
- No hay de qué.

La Catedral de la Almudena es muy grande. Hay muchos turistas haciendo fotos y admirando el edificio. Parece que hay alguna celebración porque se oye música en el interior.

Juan está cansado y decide volver al hotel. Va a coger el metro, pero la parada más cercana es de la línea azul. Tendrá que fijarse en qué estación puede hacer transbordo para coger la verde, que es la línea de metro que lo lleva al hotel.

LOST IN THE CITY (translation)

Juan is on holidays in Madrid. He will spend 2 weeks visiting the city and its surroundings. Today he will visit the city centre, but he is not very good at reading maps, so he has to ask for directions.

- Excuse me, could you tell me how to go to the centre?
- Oops! You are too far to walk. It's going to be better if you take the subway. The subway stop is in the next corner. Take the green line towards Casa de Campo and get off at the Gran Vía stop. There you will be in the centre and you can walk down from there.
- Perfect, thank you very much.

Juan is now in the centre of the city. He wants to visit the Puerta del Sol, the Plaza Mayor, and the Almudena Cathedral. It is a fairly long walk and it is hot, so in his backpack, he has something to drink and some fruit. He starts walking towards the Puerta del Sol.

The centre of Madrid is full of people. The Puerta del Sol is famous in Spain because a great party is celebrated at the end of the year, for New Year's Eve. The clock in the square gives the bells when it is midnight. In Spain, it is typical to eat grapes at the end of the year. 12 grapes at midnight, one grape for each chime. They say it brings good luck for the beginning year.

After visiting the Puerta del Sol, continue walking towards the Plaza Mayor. Once there, Juan decides to stop to eat and drink something.

- Hello! What do you want?
- I would like a cheese sandwich and a beer, please.
- Sure! Right away!

Juan already has his stomach full and has rested a little, so he can continue his walk to the Cathedral.

- Excuse me, how do I get to the Almudena Cathedral?
- Go straight ahead on Calle Mayor and where the street ends, you will see directions to the Cathedral because it is nearby. You'll find it.
- Thank you.
- You're welcome.

The Almudena Cathedral is very large. There are many tourists taking pictures and admiring the building. There seems to be some celebration because music is heard inside.

Juan is tired and decides to return to the hotel. He will take the underground, but the closest stop is the blue line. He will have to look at which station can change to catch the green, which is the underground line that takes him to the hotel.

Notes from the text:

Leyendo mapas: if we translate literally these words is "reading maps" and we are referring to manage with a map.
Campanadas: Is the chimes that a clock sound on o'clock hours
¿Qué te pongo? the verb "poner" can be literally translated as "to put", but on this question the waiter is asking Juan what he wants to drink and or eat.
Estómago lleno: when we have eaten enough, and we are feeling full we say we have our stomach full.
Paseo: to go for a walk.

Questions about the text:

For how long is Juan visiting Madrid ?
    1. Diez días
    2. Dos meses
    3. Dos semanas
    4. Dos días

What underground line does Juan take to go to the centre?
    1. La línea azul
    2. La línea verde
    3. La línea roja
    4. La línea amarilla

Where does Juan eat a sandwich?
    1. En la plaza Mayor
    2. En la plaza del Sol
    3. En la Almudena
    4. En el metro

What sandwich does Juan eat?
    1. De jamón
    2. De jamón y queso
    3. De queso
    4. De chorizo

EL PRIMER DÍA DE CLASE

- Profesora: Buenos días a todos y bienvenidos a este curso de español. Me llamo Araceli y soy de Bilbao. **Tengo treinta y nueve años** y soy profesora de español desde hace diez años.
Ahora es vuestro turno. Presentaros en español al resto de compañeros.
- Estudiante 1: Hola, **yo soy John**, **soy de Alemania**. Tengo veintidós años. Estudio arte en la universidad y hace un año que estudio español.
- Estudiante 2: Hola, ¿qué tal? **Me llamo Anna**. Tengo treinta y dos años. **Soy singapurense**. Este es mi segundo curso de español. Trabajo en una oficina.
- Estudiante 3: Encantado de conoceros a todos. Mi nombre es Paul. **Vengo de Inglaterra**. Tengo treinta años. Trabajo en un hospital, soy enfermero. Estudio español porque me gusta vivir en España.
- Estudiante 4: ¡Buenas! Yo me llamo Esther y también soy inglesa. Tengo veintiséis años. Soy profesora de inglés. Estoy aprendiendo español porque quiero viajar por Sudamérica.
- Estudiante 5: Hola, yo soy Nathan. Soy de Malasia, pero no recuerdo como decir mi nacionalidad...
- Profesora: Es malayo.
- Estudiante 5: Ah, sí, gracias. Soy malayo. Llevo tres años en España. Tengo

veinticuatro años y trabajo en una tienda de deportes.
- Estudiante 6: Hola a todos. Yo me llamo Gina y soy irlandesa. Tengo veintinueve años. Soy relaciones públicas. Es mi segundo curso de español.

- Profesora: Gracias a todos por vuestras presentaciones. Buen trabajo. ¿Qué es lo que más os **cuesta** del español?
- Estudiante 1: Para mí lo más difícil es la pronunciación.
- Estudiante 2: A mí me cuesta mucho pronunciar la "r" y recordar los verbos.
- Estudiante 3: Yo creo que la gramática es lo más difícil. Hay muchas reglas.
- Estudiante 4: Para mí, la pronunciación y el pasado. Nunca sé cuándo usar un pasado u otro.
- Estudiante 5: ¡A mí me cuesta todo! Es que practico muy poco durante la semana.
- Estudiante 6: A mí me cuesta hablar con gente. No tengo confianza.
- Profesora: ¿Qué es lo que más os gusta hacer en clase?
- Estudiante 1: A mí me gusta ver videos en español y escuchar canciones.
- Estudiante 2: A mí me gusta hacer ejercicios escritos.
- Estudiante 3: Me encanta leer textos y comentarlos.
- Estudiante 4: Yo quiero hacer ejercicios de gramática.
- Estudiante 5: A mí me gustan las actividades en grupo.
- Estudiante 6: A mí también me gustan las actividades en grupo.

FIRST DAY OF CLASSROOM (translation)

- Teacher: Good morning everyone and welcome to this Spanish course. My name is Araceli and I am from Bilbao. I am thirty-nine years old and I have been a Spanish teacher for ten years.
  Now it is your turn. Introduce yourself to the rest of your classmates in Spanish.
- Student 1: Hi, I'm John, I'm from Germany. I am twenty-two years old. I study art at the university, and I have been studying Spanish for a year.
- Student 2: Hello, how are you? My name is Anna. I'm thirty-two years old. I am Singaporean. This is my second Spanish course. I work in an office.
- Student 3: Nice to meet you all. My name is Paul. I come from England. I am thirty years old. I work in a hospital, I'm a nurse. I study Spanish because I like to live in Spain.
- Student 4: Hi! My name is Esther and I'm also English. I am twenty-six years old. I'm an English teacher. I am learning Spanish because I want to travel to South America.

- Student 5: Hi, I'm Nathan. I'm from Malaysia, but I don't remember how to say my nationality ...
- Teacher: It's Malaysian.
- Student 5: Ah, yes, thanks. I'm Malaysian, I've been in Spain for three years. I am twenty-four years old and work in a sports store.
- Student 6: Hello everyone. My name is Gina and I'm Irish. I am twenty-nine years old. I am a public relations. It is my second Spanish course.
- Teacher: Thank you all for your presentations. Nice job. What is most difficult for you about Spanish?
- Student 1: The most difficult thing for me is pronunciation.
- Student 2: It is very difficult for me to pronounce the "r" and remember the verbs.
- Student 3: I think grammar is the most difficult. There are many rules.
- Student 4: For me, pronunciation and the past. I never know when to use one past or another.
- Student 5: Everything is hard to me! I practice very little during the week.
- Student 6: It is hard for me to talk to people. I have no confidence.
- Teacher: What do you like to do in class?
- Student 1: I like to watch videos in Spanish and listen to songs.
- Student 2: I like to do written exercises.
- Student 3: I love reading texts and commenting on them.
- Student 4: I want to do grammar exercises
- Student 5: I like group activities.
- Student 6: I also like group activities.

Notes from the text:

As you have seen in this text, there are people introducing themselves and giving personal information such as name, age, nationality and work.
Remember, when saying your name you can say "me llamo (name)" or "Yo soy (name)". To say how old we are in Spanish we use the verb "tener" (to have): Yo tengo (number) años.
When we are saying where we are from, we can use the country or the nationality. If we use the country, we have to say "Yo soy de (country)". If we say the nationality, we then say "Yo soy "nationality".
The verb "costar" is "to cost" but when in this context we are referring about the amount of effort it takes to do something.

Questions about the text:

How old is the teacher?
1. Treinta y ocho
2. Treinta y siete
3. Treinta y nueve
4. Treinta y seis

How many students are in the group?
1. Cinco
2. Seis
3. Siete
4. Ocho

Where is Nathan from?
1. De Singapur
2. De Holanda
3. De Malasia
4. De España

What is Singapore nationality?
1. Singapurense
2. Singapuro
3. Singapurado
4. Singapuriso

ENCUENTROS EN EL METRO

Volvía a ser lunes y como cada lunes yo **estaba de mal humor**. Además, estaba lloviendo y hacía frío, así que lo último que me apetecía era ir a trabajar.
Como siempre cogí el metro a las ocho y media. A esa hora el metro siempre va lleno y no hay sitio para sentarse. **Vamos como en una lata de sardinas**.
Mientras escuchaba música, miraba a mi alrededor. Al fondo del vagón le vi. Era bastante alto, pues su cabeza **sobresalía** de entre la multitud. Llevaba el pelo recogido en una cola y por su cara, diría que estaba de tan mal humor como yo. Ya sé que es descarado quedarse mirando a alguien fijamente, pero es que no podía evitarlo. Había algo en él que me atrapaba.
Mientras yo le miraba, él no se había dado cuenta de que le estaba mirando, él seguía atento a su móvil. **Llevaba los auriculares puestos**, así que imagino que estaría escuchando música y parecía leer algo a la vez. De repente su expresión cambió, como si alguien le hubiera contado un **chiste**.
Dejé de mirarle unos segundos, mientras dejaba salir a una pareja de ancianos que bajaba en esa estación, y cuando le busqué otra vez, ya no estaba. ¿Se habría bajado también?
Me quedé un poco deprimida y seguí mi viaje de metro hasta el trabajo.

Los martes me gustan algo más que los lunes, pero tampoco estaba de muy buen humor hoy porque cada martes me toca ir a comer con mi prima Clara y siempre **me pone la cabeza como un bombo** con sus problemas de amoríos.

283

Cogí el metro a las 8:30. Estaba más vacío de lo habitual. Noté que alguien intentaba entrar detrás de mí. Al girarme para **mirarle con cara de pocos amigos** para que se diera cuenta de que sus empujones no eran bienvenidos, me encontré con él. No pude más que poner cara de pez... mirarle fijamente y abrir la boca. Esta vez él si se dio cuenta de que le miraba. Más que nada porque estaba a menos de un metro. Me sonrió y yo le devolví la sonrisa. Me preguntó que música escuchaba, pero en vez de contestarle, le pregunté lo que ayer le hizo cambiar de cara. Se quedó sorprendido por la pregunta. Me explicó que su hermana le estaba contando por WhatsApp que acaba de conocer a un chico muy majo en el autobús y que habían quedado esa misma tarde para tomar algo, y eso a él le pareció una locura. Pero se alegraba por su hermana.

Me hizo gracia la historia y sin rodeos le invité a comer un helado esa tarde. Con los ojos como platos y con una media sonrisa me dijo que los helados eran su **merienda** favorita y que le encantaría quedar luego. Así que quedamos a las siete para comer helado.

ENCONUNTERS IN THE METRO (translation)

It was Monday again and like every Monday I was in a bad mood. Besides, it was raining, and it was cold, so the last thing I wanted was to go to work.

As always, I took the underground at half-past eight. At that time the train is always full and there is no place to sit. We are like sardines in a can.

While listening to music, I looked around. At the bottom of the car, I saw him. He was quite tall, as his head stood out from the crowd. He wore his hair in a tail and for his face, I would say he was in a bad mood like me. I know it's brazen to stare at someone, but I couldn't help it. There was something about him that caught me.

While I looked at him, he had not realized that I was looking at him, he was still attentive to his mobile. He was wearing headphones, so I imagine he would be listening to music and seemed to read something at once. Suddenly his expression changed as if someone had told him a joke.

I stopped looking at him for a few seconds, while letting out an elderly couple coming down at that station, and when I looked for him again, he was gone. Would he have gone down too?

I was a little down and continued my underground trip to work.

On Tuesdays, that I like a bit more than Mondays, but I was not in a very good mood today because every Tuesday I have to go to eat with my cousin Clara and she always gives me a headache telling me her love affairs problems.

I took the underground at 8:30. It was more empty than usual. I noticed that someone was trying to enter behind me. As I turned to look at him with an unfriendly face, for him trealize that his shoves were not welcome, I met him. I could only put on a fish face ... stare at him and open my mouth. This time he did realize he was looking at him. Especially because he was less than a meter away. He smiled at me and I smiled back. He asked me what music he was listening to, but instead of answering, I asked him what made him change his face yesterday. He was surprised by the question. He explained that his sister was telling him on WhatsApp that she had just met a very nice guy on the bus and that they had agreed to meet on that afternoon to have a drink, and he thought it was crazy. But he was glad for his sister.

I liked the story and bluntly invited him to eat ice cream that afternoon. With eyes wide and with a half-smile he told me that ice cream was his favourite snack and he would love to meet later. So we meet at seven to eat an ice cream.

Notes from the text:

Estar de mal humor: to be in a bad mood.
Vamos como en una lata de sardinas: this expression is used when there are a lot of people at same time and same place and you can't move at all.
Sobresalía: He was standing out from the crowd
Llevaba los auriculares puestos: He was wearing his headphones
Chiste: a joke
Me pone la cabeza como un bombo: this typical expression means when someone is always talking a lot about something and we feel our head is going to pop.
Mirarle con cara de pocos amigos: another typical expresión. This means to look to someone with a unfriendly face.
Merienda: to have snack between lunch and dinner.

Questions about the text:

What time does she take the underground?
1. A las 8
2. A las 7:30
3. A las 8:30
4. A las 7

What was she doing meanwhile looking around?
1. Escuchaba música
2. Leia las noticias
3. Leia un libro
4. Miraba su Facebook

What day of the week is she having lunch with her cousin Clara?
1. Los jueves
2. Los viernes
3. Los martes
4. Los lunes

What are they having for snack?
1. Helado
2. Pastel
3. Pizza
4. Chocolate caliente

UNA CENA CON AMIGOS

Ring, ring. Ring, ring...
- ¿Sí?
- Hola Mireia, soy **Asun**. Te llamo para recordarte que hemos quedado a las 8 en mi casa esta noche para cenar. Vendrás, ¿no?
- Hola Asun. Sí, sí, iré, pero seguramente llegaré un poco más tarde porque hoy salgo de trabajar a las 7:30.
- Vale, no hay problema. Te esperaremos para cenar.
- ¿Quieres que traiga algo?
- Si quieres puedes traer algo de postre.
- ¡Genial! Postre entonces. Nos vemos luego.
- ¡Hasta luego!

A las 8 en casa de Asun ya están Juanma, Nuria, Nacho. Mireia todavía no ha llegado y están haciendo tiempo para esperarla para cenar. Todos se conocen desde hace años, desde que estudiaron juntos en el **instituto**. Cada mes organizan una cena y cada mes toca en casa de uno. Asun es un año mayor que todos porque repitió un curso. Mireia llega a las 8:15 con un postre. Mireia ha traído una tarta de chocolate porque sabe que a todos les gusta el chocolate.
Después de charlar durante un rato se sientan en la mesa. La mesa está llena de platos con **comida para picar**: aceitunas, longaniza, pan con tomate, tacos de queso y chorizo. Todos beben vino tinto excepto Juanma que bebe cerveza. Después del

aperitivo Asun saca una ensalada de patata con atún y cebolla y un pollo rustido. A Asun le gusta mucho cocinar y ser la anfitriona. Siempre cuida todos los detalles.

Cuando están acabando de cenar y todos se quejan de que **están llenos**, Mireia les recuerda que ha traído postre, una gran tarta de chocolate, y les dice que tienen que **guardar espacio** para comérsela. Todos se miran y se ríen. Nadie puede decir que no a un trozo de tarta.

Cuando acaban el postre, se toman el café sentados en el sofá. Han decidido que el próximo año, por semana santa, se van a ir de acampada a algún sitio, pero todavía no saben dónde.

Nuria propone ir a Asturias. Ninguno de los cinco ha estado antes, así que sería una novedad para todos. Mientras hablan de Asturias, Asun acerca su **portátil** a la **mesilla** de café para que puedan buscar información sobre Asturias. Entre todos van mirando todas las recomendaciones sobre Asturias: sitios para visitar, lugares donde se puede acampar, platos tipicos... después de estar un rato mirando y leyendo artículos y opiniones, todos **están de acuerdo** en que Asturias es una buena opción.

Son las doce de la noche y todos empiezan a estar cansados y **somnolientos**, así que se despiden y se van. Asun decide acabar de recoger antes de acostarse y así mañana ya estará todo hecho.

DINNER WITH FRIENDS (translation)

Ring Ring. Ring Ring...
- Yes?
- Hi Mireia, I'm Asun. I call you to remind you that we meet at 8 at my house tonight for dinner. You will come, right?
- Hi Asun. Yes, yes, I will come, but I will surely arrive a little late because today I leave work at 7:30.
- Ok, there's no problem. We will wait for you for dinner.
- Do you want me to bring anything?
- If you want you can bring some dessert.
- Great! Dessert then. See you later.
- Bye!

At 8 in Asun's house, Juanma, Nuria, Nacho are there. Mireia has not yet arrived and they are making time to wait for her for dinner. Everyone has known each other for years since they studied together at the institute.

Each month they organize a dinner and every month they choose one's home. Asun is a year older than all because he repeated a course. Mireia arrives at 8:15 with a dessert. Mireia has brought a chocolate cake because she knows everyone likes chocolate. After chatting for a while, they sit at the table. The table is full of dishes with food to snack: olives, sausage, bread with tomato, cheese tacos and chorizo. Everyone drinks red wine except Juanma who drinks beer. After the appetizer, Asun takes out a potato salad with tuna and onion and a roasted chicken. Asun likes to cook and be the hostess. Always take care of all the details.

When they are finishing dinner and everyone complains that they are full, Mireia reminds them that she has brought dessert, a large chocolate cake, and tells them that they have to save space to eat it. Everyone looks at each other and laughs. No one can say no to a piece of cake. When they finish dessert, they drink coffee sitting on the couch. They have decided that next year, for Easter, they will go camping somewhere, but they still don't know where.

Nuria proposes to go to Asturias. None of the five have been before, so it would be a novelty for everyone. While talking about Asturias, Asun brings his laptop to the coffee table so they can look for information about Asturias. Together they look at all the recommendations about Asturias: places to visit, places where you can camp, dishes to eat … after spending a while looking at and reading articles and opinions, everyone agrees that Asturias is a good option.

It's midnight and everyone starts to get tired and sleepy, so they say goodbye and leave. Asun decides to finish picking up before bedtime and so tomorrow everything will be done.

Notes from the text:

Asun: is the short name for Asuncion
Instituto: is the secondary school
Comida para picar: food for sharing
Están llenos: they are plenty of food
Guardar espacio : in this context means that they have to keep some space for the dessert
Portátil: it's a short name for "ordenador portatil" a laptop
Mesilla: it's a small table
Están de acuerdo: They agree
Somnolientos: sleepy

Questions about the text:
Which house is the dinner?
1. Asun
2. Nuria
3. Nacho
4. Mireia

At what time Mireia is finishing work?
1. A las 6:30
2. A las 7:30
3. A las 8:30
4. A las 5:30

Since when they know each other?
1. Desde la universidad
2. Desde la guardería
3. Desde el instituto
4. Desde la escuela primaria

Where are they going for camping?
1. A Alicante
2. A Asturias
3. Al Pirineo
4. A Sierra Nevada

VIAJE A ROMA

Raquel y Marta **están pasando** unos días en Barcelona. Su amiga Ester está en Roma y les ha invitado a pasar el fin de semana con ella, **aprovechando** que, desde Barcelona, Roma no está lejos para ir en avión.

Raquel prepara su equipaje. En Roma hace buen tiempo, hace calor y no se espera que llueva. Decide llevarse unos tejanos y unos pantalones cortos por si acaso, un par de camisetas y un jersey para las noches.
Marta **es un poco desastre** para hacer equipajes. Nunca sabe qué llevarse y acaba **metiendo** casi todo lo que tiene en la maleta. Como Raquel ya la conoce, le ha dado algunos consejos sobre lo que **no hace falta** que se lleve.

Raquel y Marta están **alojadas** en el barrio del Born. Es viernes y van al aeropuerto de Barcelona en autobús. Tienen que coger el autobús en la Plaza Cataluña. Una vez en el autobús compran el billete de **ida y vuelta**, pues el domingo, cuando vuelvan por la noche, cogerán el autobús para volver al hotel.

Les **hace mucha ilusión** ver a Ester, pues hace tres años que no se ven. Las tres estudiaron juntas en la universidad de Salamanca, pero cuando acabaron la carrera se separaron.

Marta está viviendo en Madrid.
Raquel está viviendo en Toledo y Ester se fue a Italia y ahora vive en Roma.

Marta y Raquel han llegado al aeropuerto. Como viajan con equipaje de mano, no tienen que facturar, y las tarjetas de embarque ya las tienen impresas, así que se dirigen directamente al control de seguridad. Una vez han pasado el control de seguridad, buscan en los **paneles de información** sobre el vuelo. Todavía no pone la puerta de embarque, así que deciden ir a tomar un café mientras esperan. Están atentas a las pantallas que hay en la cafetería para ver si anuncian algo sobre su vuelo. Acaban de anunciar su puerta de embarque, así que recogen sus cosas y se dirigen para allá. Ya hay bastante gente esperando en una cola. Parece que el vuelo va en hora.
Ya han embarcado y ya están situadas en sus asientos. Le envían un mensaje a Ester para informarle de que ya están a punto de salir. Ester va a ir a buscarlas al aeropuerto de Roma.
El vuelo sale a la hora **prevista**, con lo que llegan a Roma en hora. El desembarque es bastante rápido y en diez minutos ya están saliendo de la terminal donde Ester las esta esperando. Las tres se abrazan **efusivamente**. Ester ha venido en coche. Las tres se dirigen al parking, pagan el tique y se montan en el coche y se van dirección Roma.

TRIP TO ROME (translation)

Raquel and Marta are spending a few days in Barcelona. Her friend Esther is in Rome and has invited them to spend the weekend with her, taking advantage that, from Barcelona, Rome is not far to go by plane.
Raquel prepares her luggage. In Rome it is good weather, it's hot, and it is not expected to rain. She decides to pack a pair of jeans and shorts just in case, a pair of t-shirts and a sweater to wear at night.
Marta is not good at packing luggage. She never knows what to pack and ends up putting almost everything she has in her suitcase. As Raquel already knows her, she has given him some advice on what she doesn't need to take.
Raquel and Marta are staying in the Born neighbourhood. It's Friday and they go to Barcelona airport by bus. They have to take the bus at Plaza Cataluña. Once on the bus,

they buy the return trip ticket, because on Sunday, when they return at night, they will take the bus to go back to the hostel.

It makes them very excited to see Esther, since they haven't seen each other for three years. They studied together at the University of Salamanca, but when they finished the studies, they split up.

Marta is living in Madrid.

Raquel is living in Toledo and Ester went to Italy and now lives in Rome.

Marta and Raquel have arrived at the airport. As they travel with hand luggage, they do not have to check-in, and they have printed their boarding passes, so they go straight to the security checkpoint. Once they have passed the security check, they look at the flight information panels. There is not boarding gate information yet, so they decide to go for a coffee while they wait. They pay attention to the screens in the cafeteria to see if they announce something about their flight. They have just announced their boarding gate, so they pick up their things and go there. There are already enough people waiting in a queue. It seems that the flight is on time.

They have already embarked and are already located in their seats. They send a message to Ester to let her know that they are about to leave. Esther is going to pick them up at the airport in Rome.

The flight leaves at the scheduled time, so they arrive in Rome on time. The landing is quite fast and in ten minutes they are already leaving the terminal where Ester is waiting for them. The three hugs effusively. Esther has come by car. The three go to the parking lot, pay the ticket and get in the car and go to Rome.

Notes from the text:

Están pasando: in this context means they are spending time in Barcelona
Aprovechando: comes from the verb "aprovechar" that means to take advantage of.
Es un poco desastre: we say that someone is a disaster doing something when is really bad at doing that.
Metiendo: is the gerund form from "meter" (to put, to insert, to place).
No hace falta: means it is not necessary.
Alojadas: to stay in a hotel. Hostel. Bed and breakfast…
Ida y Vuelta: is a ticket to go and return
Les hace mucha ilusión: It makes them very excited
Paneles de información : information panels, boards
Hora prevista: scheduled time
Efusivamente: effusively

Questions about the text:

At what university have they studied?
1. En la universidad de Barcelona
2. En la universidad de Roma
3. En la universidad de Salamanca
4. En la universidad de Toledo

How are they getting to the Barcelona's airport?
1. En autobús
2. En metro
3. En tren
4. En taxi

How they get from the Rome's airport to the city?
1. En tren
2. En autobús
3. En el coche de Ester
4. En metro

Who is not good at packing luggage?
1. Raquel
2. Ester
3. Marta
4. Sara

EN LA GRANJA

Pedro trabaja en la granja de su familia. La granja **pertenece** a su familia desde hace más de cien años. Sus **bisabuelos** compraron la finca y la convirtieron en una granja. Al principio solo tenían vacas y cerdos, pero actualmente tienen también caballos, gallinas, conejos y ovejas.

En la granja trabajan **una docena** de personas. Pedro es el **encargado** de los caballos y Julián, **le echa un cable** siempre que puede. A Pedro siempre le han gustado los caballos. Además, Pedro aprendió a montar a caballo cuando tenía siete años. Julián es su vecino de toda la vida y aprendió a montar con Pedro a la misma edad. Ahora esta estudiando veterinaria en la universidad, pero siempre que tiene tiempo, se pasa por la granja para ayudar.

La mujer de Pedro ahora también trabaja con el en la granja, ella es la que se encarga de las gallinas y de los conejos. Antes trabajaba en una **pastelería**, pero cuando se casó con Pedro, decidió dejar la pastelería e ir a trabajar con él. Además, ahora viven cerca de la granja, en una pequeña casa situada a un kilometro de la granja.

Los padres de Pedro son mayores, así que ahora solo se dedican a dar largos paseos por los **terrenos**.

Su tía Matilda es la encargada de la cocina. Cada día prepara desayuno, comida y cena para todos los que trabajan en la granja. A Matilda le encanta cocinar y además se le **da muy bien**. Tienen un huerto de donde usa todos los vegetales para comer.

Su primo Juanjo se encarga de las vacas y las ovejas. Tienen un **perro pastor** llamado Jack. Jack es muy bueno guiando a las ovejas cuando las tienen que cambiar de **prado**. Juanjo fue un poco **bala perdida** cuando fue adolescente, pero empezar a trabajar en la granja le ayudó a centrarse.

La familia está planeando en acondicionar un establo como **casa de colonias**, pues hay muchas escuelas que vienen de visita que les preguntan si tienen sitio para pasar unos días. El edificio es lo suficientemente grande como para **albergar** a unas 30 personas. Podrían hacer tres habitaciones con diez camas y cuatro baños para compartir. Ya han presentado el proyecto y los planos del arquitecto al ayuntamiento y ahora están esperando que les concedan el permiso de obras.

En teoría tendrían que saber algo en no más de una semana.

Toda la familia esta muy excitada, pues les gusta cuando tienen alumnos **echando una mano** a la vez que aprenden.

AT THE FARM (translation)

Pedro works on his family's farm. The farm belongs to his family for over a hundred years. His great-grandparents bought the property and turned it into a farm. At the beginning, they only had cows and pigs, but currently they also have horses, chickens, rabbits and sheep.

A dozen people work on the farm. Pedro is in charge of the horses and Julian helps him whenever he can. Pedro has always liked horses. Besides, Pedro learned to ride a horse when he was seven years old. Julian is his long-time neighbour and he learned to ride with Pedro at the same age. Now he is studying veterinary medicine at the university, but whenever he has time, he goes to the farm to help.

Pedro's wife now also works with him on the farm. She is the one who takes care of the chickens and the rabbits. Before, he worked in a cake shop, but when he married Pedro, he decided to leave the cake shop and go to work with him. Also, they now live near the farm, in a small house located one kilometre from the farm.

Pedro's parents are older, so now they only take long walks through the land.

His aunt Matilda is in charge of the kitchen. Every day she prepares breakfast, lunch and dinner for everyone who works on the farm. Matilda loves to cook and also cooks very well. They have an allotment where she uses all the vegetables to eat.

His cousin Juanjo takes care of the cows and the sheep. They have a sheepdog named Jack. Jack is very good at guiding the sheep when they have to change the meadow. Juanjo was a little silly when he was a teenager, but starting to work on the farm helped him focus.

The family is planning to set up a stable as a house for schools, as there are many schools that come to visit asking if they have room for people to spend a few days. The building is large enough to accommodate about 30 people. They could make three rooms with ten beds and four bathrooms to share. They have already presented the project and the plans of the architect to the town hall and are now waiting to be granted the building permit.

In theory they would have to know something in no more than a week.

The whole family is very excited, because they like it when they have students helping out while they learn.

Notes from the text:

Pertenece: is from the verb "pertenecer" (to belong).
Bisabuelos: Great-grandparents.
Una docena: twelve of something.

Encargado: been in charge.
Echa un cable: is an expression that means to help with anything.
Pastelería: cake shop
Terrenos: terrain, land
Se le da muy bien: He or she is very Good at something
Perro pastor: shepherd dog
Prado: meadow
Ser un bala perdida: person that does not follow any (expected) rule or path.
Casa de colonias: a house where schools can organise school trips and sleepover
Albergar: to shelter, to harbor
Echando una mano: to give a hand with something, to help.

Questions about the text:
What is the dog name?
1. John
2. Jack
3. Tom
4. Sam

Who is in charge for the horses?
1. Pedro
2. Pablo
3. Paco
4. Patricia

Who helps with the horses?
1. Juan
2. Jorge
3. Julián
4. Juanma

Who cooks for everyone who work at the farm?
1. La tía Matilda
2. La prima Matilda
3. La abuela Matilda
4. La sobrina Matilda

RESTAURANTE EL VELERO

Me llamo Silvia y trabajo como chef en el restaurante El Velero.
El Velero es un restaurante donde no hay una carta fija. Cada día yo, como chef, creo un **menú degustación** que es el que se va a servir esa noche, y **para todo el mundo va a ser igual**. El menú **consta** de dos aperitivos, dos entrantes, un plato principal y dos postres. Además, cada plato se sirve con un determinado tipo de vino que ha escogido un **enólogo**, para que combinen a la perfección. El restaurante casi nunca tiene mesas libres, y la única sala de la que disponen, tienen una lista de espera de meses.

Hoy es una noche de trabajo especial para nosotros porque tenemos a un **invitado famoso**.
El cantautor Francisco Fernández ha alquilado una de nuestras salas para celebrar una fiesta privada y estamos todos muy excitados.

Francesca es la encargada del restaurante y está instruyendo a los camareros. Hoy no puede haber errores y hay que estar bien organizados.
Lo tenemos todo a punto, ahora ya solo queda esperar a que **llegue la hora**.

Son las ocho y media y el restaurante abre para recibir a los **comensales**. Francisco y sus invitados llegan los primeros.
- Francesca: Buenas noches y bienvenidos al restaurante El Velero. Su sala está ya

preparada así que, si lo desean, los acompaño para que puedan sentarse en su mesa.
- Francisco: Perfecto. Sí por favor, vamos para allá.

Francisco y sus invitados están en la sala. En la sala hay una gran **mesa ovalada** con sillas para veinte personas. Una vez están todos sentados, Esteban, el camarero de la sala, entra para presentarse y preguntar por las bebidas.

- Esteban: Buenas noches. Soy Esteban y voy a ser su camarero esta noche. ¿Desean algo para beber antes de servir la cena? Como ya sabrán, en el Restaurante El Velero cada noche servimos un menú degustación diferente. El menú de esta noche va a constar de dos aperitivos, dos entrantes, un plato principal y dos postres. Cada plato se servirá con un vino escogido especialmente por nuestro enólogo.
- Francisco: Gracias, Esteban. Estamos **ansiosos** por probar el menú de hoy. Silvia siempre nos sorprende con sus platos.
- Esteban: Gracias. Esperamos que les guste.

La noche va pasando y Francisco y sus invitados van **degustando** cada plato que se les sirve. Parece que les ha gustado porque al final de la cena preguntan por Silvia, la chef, para poder hablar con ella. Silvia se acerca a la sala y les saluda. Todos la felicitan y halagan lo buena que estaba la comida y lo acertada que ha estado la selección de vinos.

EL VELERO RESTAURANT (translation)

My name is Silvia and I work as a chef at the restaurant El Velero. El Velero is a restaurant where there is no fixed menu. Every day, as a chef, I create a tasting menu that is the one that is going to be served that night, and for everyone it will be the same. The menu consists of two appetizers, two starters, a main course and two desserts. In addition, each dish is served with a certain type of wine that a wine specialist has chosen, so that they combine perfectly. The restaurant almost never has free tables, and the only room they have, they have a waiting list of months.

Today is a special work night for us because we have a famous guest.
The singer-songwriter Francisco Fernández has rented one of our rooms to celebrate a private party and we are all very excited.

Francesca is in charge of the restaurant and is instructing the waiters. Today there can

be no mistakes and we have to be well organized.
We have everything ready, now we just have to wait for the time to come.

It's half past eight and the restaurant opens to receive the guests. Francisco and his guests arrive first.
- Francesca: Good evening and welcome to the restaurant El Velero. Your room is already prepared so, if you wish, I accompany you so you can sit at your table.
- Francisco: Perfect. Yes please, let's go there.

Francisco and his guests are in the room. In the room there is a large oval table with chairs for twenty people. Once they are all seated, Esteban, the waiter in that room, comes in to introduce himself and ask about drinks.

- Esteban: Good evening. I'm Esteban and I'm going to be your waiter tonight. Do you want something to drink before serving dinner? As you know, at El Velero Restaurant every night we serve a different tasting menu. Tonight's menu will consist of two appetizers, two starters, a main course and two desserts. Each dish will be served with a wine specially chosen by our wine specialist.
- Francisco: Thank you, Esteban. We are looking forward to taste today's menu. Silvia always surprises us with her dishes.
- Esteban: Thank you. We hope you like it.

The night is passing, and Francisco and his guests are tasting every dish that is served. They seem to have liked it because at the end of the dinner they ask for Silvia, the chef, so they can talk to her. Silvia approaches to the room and greets everyone. The guests congratulate her and flatter how good the food was and how successful the wine selection has been.

Notes from the text:

Menú degustación: tasting menu
Para todo el mundo va a ser igua: It Will be the same for everyone.
Consta: from the verb "constar" that has different meanings depending on the context: to feature, to be known, to be on record...
Enólogo: oenologist, specialist in wines
Invitado famoso: famous guest
Llegue la hora: the time arrives
Comensales: guests who come to eat

Mesa ovalada: oval table
Ansiosos: anxious
Degustando: gerund form for "gegustar" to taste

Questions about the text:

Who is in charge at the restaurant?
1. Silvia
2. Sonia
3. Francesca
4. Francisco

How many desserts are serving with the menu?
1. Uno
2. Dos
3. Tres
4. Cuatro

What shape is the table?
1. Cuadrada
2. Redonda
3. Ovalada
4. Rectangular

What is the famous guest name?
1. Francisco
2. Francesca
3. Madonna
4. George

LA FAMILIA DE PASCUAL

La familia de Pascual es una familia **peculiar**, no solo por el número de miembros, que, si contamos desde los inicios, son cientos, porque hay muchos gemelos en la familia, sino porque les gusta mucho apostar a todos y jugarse las cosas al azar.

Pascual es el menor de seis hermanos. Bueno, mejor dicho, son tres parejas de gemelos y Pascual fue el último en nacer.
Entre cada par de gemelos solo se llevan dos años y siempre han estado bastante **bien avenidos**.

Los padres de Pascual son los dos profesores. Ahora ya están jubilados y se han ido a vivir a la Manga del Mar Menor.
Todos los gemelos son profesores también, pero cada uno de una especialidad diferente.
Arturo, el mayor de todos, es profesor de geografía.
Andrés da clases de matemáticas en una escuela de secundaria.
Vicente es profesor de música en el **conservatorio**.
Víctor es profesor de alemán en la universidad.
Pedro es profesor de educación física en una escuela primaria.
Y Pascual da clases de cocina en una **academia de restauración**.

Lo de ser profesor les viene a todos por una apuesta con sus padres. Una noche de **semana santa**, después de cenar, su madre les preguntó si ya sabían que querrían ser cuando fueran mayores. Ellos siempre bromeaban con que nunca trabajarían ni se irían de casa sus padres, pues allí estaban bien y tenían de todo. Su madre entonces les dijo, que si acertaba el grupo musical o cantante de la primera canción que iba a sonar en la radio en cuanto la encendiera, ella decidiría por ellos en lo que iban a trabajar. Ellos no duraron ni un momento en aceptar la apuesta pues pensaban que era imposible que acertara. Se lo pensó un par de minutos y dijo que iba a sonar una canción de Abba. **Encendió** la radio y así fue. Nadie se lo podía creer. Ellos se quedaron **boquiabiertos**. Y entonces les dijo que deberían dedicarse a la enseñanza pues ella creía que todos disponían de cualidades para ser buenos profesores, pero que cada uno tendría que escoger la especialidad que más le gustase.

Al principio se quejaron, pero al poco tiempo cada uno tenía claro lo que quería enseñar. Así es como en la familia de Pascual han acabado todos siendo profesores. ¡**Menos mal** que a la madre no se le ocurrió decirles que fueran astronautas!

PASCUAL'S FAMILY (translation)

Pascual's family is a peculiar family, not only because of the number of members, which, if we count from the beginning, are hundreds because there are many twins in the family, but because they like to bet on everything and play things randomly .

Pascual is the youngest of six brothers. Well, rather, there are three pairs of twins and Pascual was the last to be born.
Between each pair of twins they only take two years and have always been quite well avenues.

Pascual's parents are the two teachers. Now they are retired and have gone to live in the Manga del Mar Menor.
All twins are teachers too, but each of a different specialty.
Arturo, the eldest of all, is a geography teacher.
Andrés teaches math in a high school.
Vicente is a music teacher at the conservatory.
Victor is a professor of German at the university.
Pedro is a physical education teacher in an elementary school.

And Pascual teaches cooking at a catering academy.

Being a teacher comes to everyone for a bet with their parents. One night of Holy Week, after dinner, their mother asked if they already knew what they wanted to be when they were older. They always joked that their parents would never work or leave home, because they were well there and had everything. Her mother then told them that if the musical group or singer of the first song that was going to play on the radio was right as soon as she turned it on, she would decide for them what they were going to work on. They did not last a moment to accept the bet because they thought it was impossible for him to succeed. He thought about it for a couple of minutes and said that a song by Abba was going to play. He turned on the radio and it was. No one could believe it. They were speechless. And then he told them that they should dedicate themselves to teaching because she believed that everyone had the qualities to be good teachers, but that each one would have to choose the specialty they liked best.
At first they complained, but soon everyone was clear about what they wanted to teach. This is how everyone in Pascual's family has ended up being teachers. Luckily, it didn't occur to the mother to tell them they were astronauts!

Notes from the text:

Peculiar: quirky
Bien avenidos: to get along
Conservatorio: it's a music school
Academia de restauración: Cooking academy
Semana santa: Easter holidays
Encendió: from the verb "encender", to turn on.
Boquiabiertos: speechless
Menos mal: thank goodness

Questions about the text:

How many pairs of twins are in Pascual's family?
1. 6
2. 3
3. 2
4. 1

Where is teaching Pascual?
1. En una escuela primaria
2. En una escuela secundaria
3. En un instituto
4. En la universidad

What band sounds on the radio?
1. Tina Turner
2. Bruce Springsteen
3. Abba
4. The Beach Boys

Who wins the bet?
1. La madre
2. DaEl padred
3. Pascual
4. El hermano mayor

MARC Y GINA

La historia de Marc y Gina parece **sacada de una película**.
Era un jueves de invierno y estaba nevando en Berlín. Marc, como cada mañana, se dirigía a coger el metro para ir a trabajar. Gina **se había dormido** e iba tarde. Estaba yendo deprisa para coger el metro también.
En la puerta de la estación **chocaron** el uno contra el otro. Gina en ese momento iba a **reprochar** a Marc que fuera con más cuidado y Marc iba a reprochar a Gina que mirara por donde iba, pero una vez se **cruzaron sus miradas**, se enamoraron el uno del otro y se olvidaron de lo que acababa de pasar. Se quedaron mirándose por unos minutos, sin decir nada y al final Marc le dijo:
"Creo que ya no puedo vivir sin ti".

Gina sonrió nerviosa y le dijo a Marc que **estaba loco**, pero ella estaba sintiendo lo mismo, ya no quería separarse de él. La química entre ambos era tan **intensa**, que ninguno de los dos se daba cuenta de que nevaba más fuerte ni de que se habían quedado parados en medio del acceso y había decenas de personas esperando.
- Podríais apartaros para que podamos pasar! - les vociferó un señor que llevaba rato esperando.
Marc y Gina se **sonrojaron** y se situaron a un lado. Gina le dio su teléfono y su dirección de correo electrónico y se fue corriendo, sin darse cuenta de que había perdido su bufanda.
Marc se guardó el papel que le había dado Gina en el bolsillo y recogió la bufanda del suelo.
Nada más llegar al trabajo, Marc encendió el ordenador para escribir a Gina.

"¿Has llegado bien al trabajo? Tengo tu bufanda, por si te preguntas dónde está. ¿Te apetece quedar esta tarde para tomar un café y te la devuelvo? Me muero de ganas de volver a verte"

Marc envió el mail y se dirigió a la sala de reuniones donde le estaban esperando. Cuando acabó la reunión lo primero que hizo fue chequear si había respuesta de Gina, pero nada.
Gina no paraba de pensar en Marc, pero esa misma noche se iba a Múnich una semana por trabajo.
"Hola Marc, gracias por guardarme la bufanda. Me temo que si quieras devolvérmela

hoy tendremos que tomar el café en Múnich, pues en unas horas me voy para allá. Estaré una semana, si quieres podemos quedar cuando vuelva."

Marc leyó el email y se quedó pensativo. No podía esperar una semana para volver a ver a Gina. Hoy era jueves y todavía tenía días de vacaciones. No lo dudó, pidió el viernes libre.

"Hola Gina, me parece bien devolverte la bufanda en Múnich. Igual puedes enseñarme la ciudad pues pasaré el fin de semana allí. No podía esperar una semana para volver a verte"

Gina leyó el email y sonrió. Ella sentía lo mismo. La idea de pasar el fin de semana con Marc en Múnich le hacía muchísima ilusión.

Gina y Marc se encontraron en el aeropuerto de Múnich y desde entonces comparten su vida el uno con el otro.

MARC AND GINA (translation)

Marc and Gina's story seems to be out of a movie.
It was a winter Thursday and it was snowing in Berlin. Marc, like every morning, went to take the subway to go to work. Gina had fallen asleep and was running late. I was rushing to catch the subway too.
At the station gate, they crashed into each other. Gina at the time was going to reproach Marc for going more carefully and Marc was going to reproach Gina for looking where she was going, but once their eyes met, they fell in love with each other and forgot what had just happened. They stared at each other for a few minutes without saying anything and at the end Marc said:
I don't think I can live without you anymore.
Gina smiled nervously and told Marc she was crazy, but she was feeling the same, she didn't want to be separated from him anymore. The chemistry between the two was so intense that neither of them realized that it was snowing stronger or that they had stood in the middle of the access and there were dozens of people waiting.
- You could step aside so that we can pass! - shouted a man who had been waiting for a while.
Marc and Gina blushed and stood aside. Gina gave him her phone number and her

email address and ran away, not realizing she'd lost her scarf.

Marc kept the paper Gina had given him in his pocket and picked up the scarf from the floor.

As soon as we got to work, Marc turned on the computer to write to Gina.

You got to work okay? I have your scarf, if you're wondering where it is. Would you like to stay for coffee this afternoon and I'll pay you back? I can't wait to see you again

Marc sent the e-mail and went to the meeting room where they were waiting for him. When the meeting was over, the first thing he did was check if there was any response from Gina, but nothing.

Gina kept thinking about Marc, but that same night she was going to Munich for a week for work.

Hi Marc, thank you for saving my scarf. I'm afraid, but if you want to give it back to me today, we'll have to have coffee in Munich, because in a few hours I'll be there. I'll stay a week, if you want, we can meet when I get back.

Marc read the email and became pensive. I couldn't wait a week to see Gina again. Today was Thursday and I still had vacation days. He didn't hesitate, he asked for Friday off.

Hello Gina, I'm happy to return your scarf in Munich. You can still show me around the city as I will spend the weekend there. I couldn't wait a week to see you again

Gina read the email and smiled. She felt the same way. She was very excited about spending the weekend with Marc in Munich.

Gina and Marc met at the airport in Munich and have since shared their lives with each other.

Notes from the text:

Sacada de una película: something that seems to come from a movie.
Se había dormido: she overslept
Chocaron: from the verb "chocar" that means to crash, but in this context means to bump into each other.
Reprochar: to blame
Cruzaron sus miradas: to have eye contact intentionally

Estaba loco: he was crazy
Intensa: intense
Sonrojaron: they blushed

Questions from the text:

Where are they?
1. Munich
2. Zurich
3. Berlin
4. Paris

How is the weather?
1. Esta nevando
2. Hace sol
3. Hace viento
4. Hace calor

For how long Gina is going to be in Munich?
1. Una semana
2. Un día
3. Un mes
4. Una hora

What Gina has lost during the encounter?
1. El gorro
2. Los guantes
3. La bufanda
4. La chaqueta

EN EL AEROPUERTO

Silvia está **haciendo cola** en el aeropuerto. Es su turno y camina hacia el **mostrador**. La mujer del mostrador le pide su pasaporte y **verifica** sus datos personales y los detalles de su vuelo. Sí, ella tiene la plaza confirmada en el vuelo 2233 desde Barcelona hacia Budapest a las 11:35 de la mañana. Silvia no tiene maletas para **facturar**, pero lleva una maleta de mano pequeña que subirá consigo en el avión, además de un bolso pequeño. El asistente de vuelo imprime su tarjeta de embarque.
Los oficiales de seguridad del aeropuerto pasan junto a ella con un perro grande y color oscuro. El perro está **olfateando** alrededor del equipaje de las personas de las colas, tratando de **detectar** drogas o explosivos. Silvia se siente aliviada cuando ve que el perro pasa junto a ella sin detenerse. De repente, el perro se **da la vuelta** y empieza a olfatear una maleta que esta justo al lado de la suya. El oficial de seguridad la mira y le pregunta si esa maleta es suya. Silvia contesta rápidamente que no, pero el oficial se la mira **dubitativo**, pues la maleta esta justo al lado de su equipaje de mano y no hay nadie más cerca. Silvia les explica nerviosa que recuerda que había una mujer delante suyo. Solo recuerda que era más alta que ella y que vestía un abrigo de color azul. Preguntan a los demás pasajeros que están cerca de la zona, pero nadie ha visto nada **sospechoso** ni saben nada de una mujer alta con un abrigo azul. Los oficiales siguen sin creérsela, les parece extraño que nadie más haya visto a esa mujer. De repente, a lo lejos, Silvia cree distinguir un abrigo azul como el que recuerda que llevaba la mujer y les hace una señal a los oficiales para que miren en esa

dirección. Los oficiales se giran rápidamente y ven a una persona con un abrigo azul correr al fondo de la terminal. Dan el aviso por radio a sus compañeros. Ellos, por mucho que corran no van a llegar, y cerca de donde estaba la sospechosa había otra unidad. Enseguida recibieron un comunicado por radio de que había detenido a la mujer del abrigo azul y que se dirigían a la sala para interrogarla. Silvia pudo seguir su camino y coger a tiempo su vuelo a Budapest.

IN THE AIRPORT (translation)

Silvia is queuing at the airport. It is her turn and she walk to the counter. The woman at the counter asks for her passport and verifies her personal data and the details of your flight. Yes, she has a confirmed seat on flight 2233 from Barcelona to Budapest at 11:35 in the morning. Silvia has no luggage to check in, but she has a small handbag that she will carry with her on the plane, plus a small bag. The flight attendant prints her boarding pass. The airport security officers pass near by her with a big dark dog. The dog is sniffing around the luggage of people in the queues, trying to detect drugs or explosives. Silvia is relieved when she sees the dog pass by her without stopping. Suddenly, the dog turns around and starts sniffing a suitcase that is right next to hers. The security officer looks at her and asks if that suitcase is hers. Silvia answers quickly no, but the officer looks at her doubtfully, because the suitcase is right next to her carry-on luggage and there is no one else closer. Silvia explains nervously that she remembers that there was a woman in front of her. Just remember that she was taller than her and that she wore a blue coat. They ask the other passengers who are close to the area, but nobody has seen anything suspicious or know anything about a tall woman in a blue coat. The officers still don't believe Silvia, it seems strange that no one else has seen that woman. Suddenly, in the distance, Silvia thinks she distinguishes a blue coat like the one she remembers the woman was wearing and make a signal to the officers to look in that direction. Officers turn quickly and see a person in a blue coat run to the bottom of the terminal. They give the radio notice to their partners. They are too far and no matter how much they run, they will not arrive, and near where the suspect was, there was another unit. They immediately received a radio statement that the woman in the blue coat has been arrested and that they were going to the room to interrogate her. Silvia was able to continue her way and could catch her flight to Budapest on time.

Notes from the text:

Haciendo cola: queuing
Mostrador: counter
Verifica: from the verb "verificar", to verify
Facturar: to check in
Olfateando: sniffing
Detectar: to detect
Da la vuelta: turn around
Dubitativo: hesitant
Sospechoso: suspect

Questions from the text:

Where is Silvia flying to?
1. Londres
2. Budapest
3. Berlin
4. Paris

What colour was the dog?
1. Claro
2. Oscuro
3. Blanco
4. Dorado

How many suitcases is Silvia carrying with her?
1. Una maleta grande
2. Una maleta de mano
3. Una maleta de mano y un bolso pequeño
4. Una mochila grande

What colour was the suspect woman's coat?
1. Negro
2. Rojo
3. Azul
4. Verde

RESACA

Yvette no se siente bien. Estuvo en una fiesta anoche y llegó a casa a las 2 am. Tiene **dolor de cabeza** y está un poco **mareada**. Bebió bastante y comió poco. Se levanta de la cama y se da cuenta que ha dormido vestida y con los zapatos puestos.

Mira alrededor pero no reconoce donde está. Yvette oye voces. Sale del dormitorio, baja por las escaleras y entra a la cocina. Hay gente hablando y riéndose en la cocina. No consigue **reconocer** a nadie de esas personas y empieza a **preocuparse**. No está en su casa y no conoce a nadie.

Yvette, por fin -oye de una voz familiar que se acerca por su espalda. Yvette se gira y ve a su prima Emma. Recuerda que fueron juntas a la fiesta.

Emma, ¿dónde estamos? -pregunta nerviosa Yvette.

Estamos en casa de Roger. ¿No te acuerdas de que vinimos anoche? ¿Tanto bebiste que no lo puedes recordar? -Emma empezaba a preocuparse por el estado de Yvette.

Recuerdo que vinimos sí, pero **no me suena** nada de esta habitación.

Eso es porque estamos en el otro lado de la casa. Entramos por la cocina anoche y ahora estamos en el salón principal. ¿Te encuentras bien?

La verdad es que no, me duele mucho la cabeza y estoy muy mareada. Creo que tengo una gran resaca.

¡Bueno, no te preocupes! Te acompaño a casa y así puedes descansar. ¡Además, aquí la fiesta ya se ha acabado!

Emma e Yvette van en taxi a casa de Yvette. Yvette casi nunca sale y cuando bebe algo, por poco que sea, enseguida se le sube a la cabeza. Emma la acompaña hasta arriba y la ayuda a sacarse los zapatos. Cuando Yvette cae dormida en el sofá, la cubre con una manta para que no se enfríe. En la mesilla de café le deja un vaso de agua y un paracetamol para cuando se despierte.

HANGOVER (translation)

Yvette doesn't feel well. She was at a party last night and came home at 2 am. She has a headache and she is feeling a little dizzy. She drank too much and she ate little. She gets out of bed and realizes that she has slept dressed and with her shoes on. She looks around but she doesn't recognize where she is. Yvette hears voices. She leaves the bedroom, goes down the stairs and enters the kitchen. There are people talking and laughing in the kitchen. She fails to recognize anyone of those people and begins to worry. She is not at home and does not recognize anyone.

Yvette, finally -hears a familiar voice approaching from behind. Yvette turns and sees her cousin Emma. Remember that they went to the party together.

Emma, where are we? -asks Yvette nervously.

We are at Roger's house. Don't you remember we came last night? Did you drink so much that you can't remember it? -Emma began to worry about Yvette's condition.

I remember that we came but can't remember this room.

That is because we are on the other side of the house. We entered the kitchen last night and now we are in the main hall. Are you okay?

The truth is that I'm not, I have a terrible headache and I am very dizzy. I think I'm having a big hangover!

Okay, do not worry! I you accompany home and so you can rest. Also, here the party is over!

Emma and Yvette go by taxi to Yvette's house. Yvette almost never goes out and when she drinks something, however little it may be, she immediately goes drunk. Emma walks her to her door and helps her take off her shoes. When Yvette falls asleep on the couch, she covers her with a blanket, so she doesn't get cold. On the coffee table he leaves a glass of water and a paracetamol for when she wakes up.

Notes from the text:

Dolor de cabeza: headache

Mareada: dizzy
Reconocer to recognise
Preocuparse: to worry
No me suena: it doesn't ring the bell to me

Questions about the text:

Where Yveete has waken up?
1. En su casa
2. En la casa de Roger
3. En la casa de Emma
4. En la casa de su abuela

With whom did Yvette come to the party?
1. Con su prima Emma
2. Con su prima Georgia
3. Con su primo David
4. Con su primo Roger

Who was with Yvette when she got home?
1. Emma
2. Roger
3. David
4. Anna

What did Emma leave on the Yvette's coffee table?
1. Un vaso de zumo de naranja
2. Un vaso de agua y un paracetamol
3. Una coca cola
4. Una limonada

EL ULTIMO VERANO

El último verano fui a la Costa Brava. Estuve en Cadaqués una semana. Cadaqués es un **pueblo pescador** muy bonito situado al norte, muy cerca de Francia.
Cada mañana me levantaba e iba a desayunar a la cafetería de la esquina. Paquita, que es la **dueña** de la cafetería, ya me conocía y me tenía preparado el desayuno antes de que fuera: zumo de naranja y tostadas con pan con tomate y embutido. Después de desayunar aprovechaba para ir a comprar algo de fruta fresca para llevarme a la playa. Los martes, además, había **mercadillo** y allí podías comprar además de fruta y hortalizas, ropa, complementos, bisutería.... ¡De todo!
En la paya me encontraba con Frank y Pamela. Frank y Pamela eran dos italianos que había conocido allí. **Nos llevamos bien** desde el primer día. Frank Y Pamela eran muy majos y divertidos. No era la primera vez que pasaban el verano en Cadaqués. ¡Eran unos enamorados del pueblo! Venían cada dos años.
Después de la playa. Me iba para casa a darme una ducha y comer. Hacia tanto calor que no me apetecía estar por la calle. Después de leer un rato y descansar, cuando el sol empezaba a esconderse, salía a pasear por el pueblo. A esa hora las calles estaban llenas de gente y en el pueblo había mucho ambiente.
No solía salir por las noches, porque, aunque estaba de vacaciones, tenía que preparar mi proyecto de final de carrera.
Un fin de semana me fui desde Cadaqués con Frank y Pamela a Colliure. Colliure es otro pueblo pescador situado al sur de Francia. Es un pueblo muy bonito. Allí vimos la

tumba del famoso escritor español Antonio Machado. La gente que la visitaba dejaba todo tipo de obsequios.

Otro fin de semana llevé a Frank y Pamela al pueblo de Empúries. Empúries es un pueblo medieval donde puedes visitar también unas ruinas romanas. Comimos un arroz caldoso de bogavante exquisito.

Y sin darme cuenta el verano pasó.

THE LAST SUMMER (translation)

Last summer I went to the Costa Brava. I was in Cadaqués for a week. Cadaqués is a very pretty fishing village located to the north, very close to France.

Every morning I got up and went to breakfast at the cafeteria around the corner.

Paquita, who is the owner of the cafeteria, already knew me and she had prepared my breakfast: orange juice and bread toast with tomato and ham. After having breakfast, I went to buy some fresh fruit to take it to the beach.

On Tuesdays, there was also a market where you could buy fruit and vegetables, clothes, accessories, jewellery... A bit of everything!

On the beach I usually met with Frank and Pamela. Frank and Pamela were two Italians I had met there. We get along from day one. Frank and Pamela were very nice and funny. It was not the first time they spent the summer in Cadaqués. They were in love with that village! They came every two years.

After the beach. I went home to take a shower and have lunch. It was so hot that I didn't feel like being in the street. After reading for a while and resting, when the sun began to hide, I went for a walk. At that time the streets were full of people and in the village there was a lot of ambient.

I didn't usually go out at night, because, although I was on vacation, I had to prepare my final year project.

One weekend I went with Frank and Pamela to Colliure. Colliure is another fishing village located in the south of France. It is a very pretty town. There we saw the grave of the famous Spanish writer Antonio Machado. The people who visited the grave left all kinds of gifts.

Another weekend I took Frank and Pamela to the town of Empúries. Empúries is a medieval town where you can also visit some Roman ruins. We ate an exquisite lobster rice.

And without noticing the summer was gone.

Notes from the text:

Pueblo pescador: it is fishermen village
Mercadillo: it's an itinerant market
Nos llevamos bien: to get along
Tumba: grave

Questions from the text:

Where do I went my last summer?
   1. Barcelona
   2. Figueres
   3. Cadaqués
   4. Girona

Where are Frank and Pamela from?
   1. Alemania
   2. Francia
   3. Holanda
   4. Italia

Where do we eat lobster rice?
   1. Empuries
   2. Cadaques
   3. Colliure
   4. Girona

Who was the famous Spanish writer?
   1. Antonio Machado
   2. Javier Bardem
   3. Antonio Banderas
   4. Pedro Almodóvar

VACACIONES EN ESPAÑA

Andrea estaba muy contenta. Había acabado el curso y hoy era su primer día de vacaciones de verano.
Tenía 2 meses por delante e iba a **aprovecharlos** al máximo.
Su mejor amiga, Lisa, y ella habían decidido pasar **la mayor parte** de sus vacaciones en España. Los abuelos de Andrea tenían una casa en la costa de Málaga, al sur de España, y estaban muy contentos de que Andrea y Lisa pasaran varias semanas con ellos. Andrea y Lisa, además, habían estudiado español durante todo el año y el profesor les había **aconsejado** que para perfeccionar el idioma no había nada mejor que pasar un tiempo viviendo en un país de habla hispana.
¡El plan era perfecto!
Y un plan perfecto para Andrea debía incluir playa. ¡Practicar español con, por ejemplo, el instructor de windsurf era la mejor manera de practicar y divertirse a la vez!
Y aunque todavía quedaban 3 días para el viaje, Andrea ya había empezado a preparar su equipaje. Empezando, por supuesto, por lo imprescindible: bañadores, toallas, chanclas, gafas de sol, revistas y protector solar. No debía olvidar incluir sandalias y vestidos menos informales por si surgía la ocasión propicia -pensó Andrea con una **pícara sonrisa** dibujada en su cara-.

Lisa y ella habían quedado por la tarde para seguir practicando el idioma de la mejor manera posible: viendo una película romántica en español. Aunque en los últimos meses habían mejorado mucho su nivel de comprensión auditiva, todavía tenían problemas para entender ciertas palabras o expresiones. Lo bueno de las películas es que podías rellenar esas lagunas de interpretación a través del contexto y del lenguaje corporal de los actores.

Cuando Lisa llegó a casa de Andrea, no podía **disimular** su emoción por las excitantes semanas que tenían por delante. El final de curso, con los exámenes finales, había sido duro para ambas. Apenas habían tenido tiempo para nada más que estudiar. Pero ahora sentían que el esfuerzo tenía su recompensa: habían aprobado todas las asignaturas y podían disfrutar de las vacaciones sin pensar en nada más que disfrutar.

¿Qué vamos a ver hoy? -preguntó Lisa mientras se tiraba en el sofá.

He descargado una película de uno de tus actores favoritos, Antonio Banderas - respondió Andrea con una radiante sonrisa.

¡Guay! -exclamó Lisa sin poder contenerse-.

¿Sabías que Antonio Banderas es de la misma zona a la que vamos de vacaciones, Málaga? -preguntó Andrea-.

¡Por supuesto que lo sabía! -contestó Lisa antes de que Andrea acabara su pregunta-.

¡De hecho, esa es la razón por la que te acompaño estas vacaciones! -añadió mientras guiñaba un ojo-.

¡Igual nos lo encontramos en la playa! -exclamó Andrea riéndose-.

Estaba claro que ambas estaban de muy buen humor. En septiembre volverían las rutinas académicas, los madrugones, los viajes a la universidad en metros y trenes atestados de gente, los exámenes... pero septiembre estaba ahora muy lejos. Muy, muy lejos.

Habían cambiado la mochila escolar por un capazo playero y eso podía significar solo una cosa: ¡es tiempo de vacaciones!

HOLIDAYS IN SPAIN (translation)

Andrea was very happy. He had finished the course and today was her first day of summer vacations.

She was having 2 months ahead and she was going to make the most of them.

Her best friend, Lisa, and she had decided to spend most of their holidays in Spain. Andrea's grandparents had a house on the coast of Malaga, in southern Spain, and they were very happy that Andrea and Lisa spent several weeks with them. Andrea and Lisa, in addition, had studied Spanish throughout the year and the professor had advised them that to improve the language there was nothing better than spending time living in a Spanish-speaking country.

The plan was perfect!

And a perfect plan for Andrea should include a beach. Practicing Spanish with, for example, the windsurf instructor was the best way to practice and have fun at the same time!

And although there were still 3 days left for the trip, Andrea had already started preparing her luggage. Starting, of course, for the essentials: swimsuits, towels, flip flops, sunglasses, magazines and sunscreen. She shouldn't forget to include sandals and less casual dresses just in case an occasion was worth, thought Andrea with a naughty smile drawn on her face.

She and Lisa were going to meet in the afternoon to continue practicing the language in the best possible way: watching a romantic movie in Spanish. Although in recent months they had greatly improved their level of listening comprehension, they still had trouble understanding certain words or expressions. The good thing about movies is that you could fill in those gaps in interpretation through the context and body language of the actors.

When Lisa arrived at Andrea's house, she couldn't hide her excitement for the weeks ahead. The end of the course, with the final exams, had been hard for both. They had barely had time for anything else to study. But now they felt that the effort had its reward: they had passed all the subjects and could enjoy the holidays without thinking about anything else to enjoy.

What are we going to see today? asked Lisa while sitting on the couch.

I've downloaded a movie from one of your favourite actors, Antonio Banderas - Andrea replied with a radiant smile.

Cool! Lisa exclaimed, unable to contain herself.

Did you know that Antonio Banderas is from the same area where we are going on holiday, Málaga? asked Andrea.

Of course I knew it! Lisa replied before Andrea finished her question. In fact, that's the reason I make you company on this holiday season! She added as she winked.

We can still find him on the beach! Andrea cried laughing.

It was clear that both were in a very good mood. In September the academic routines, the early risers, the trips to the university in crowded undergrounds and trains, the exams would return ... but September was now far away. Very far.

They had changed the school backpack for a beach bag and that could mean only one thing: it's holidays time!

Notes from the text:

Tenía 2 meses por delante: she had two months ahead of her
Aprovecharlos: to take advantage of them
La mayor parte: the most part of it
Aconsejado: from the verb "aconsejar" (to advise → advised)
¡El plan era perfecto!: The plan was perfect
Pícara sonrisa: naughty smile
Disimular: to disguise

Questions about the text:

Where are they going to spend their holidays?
1. España
2. Francia
3. Alemania
4. Inglaterra

Where are they going to be accommodated?
1. En casa de los abuelos de Lisa
2. En casa de los abuelos de Andrea
3. En casa de los primos de Andrea
4. En casa de la hermana de Lisa

Who is one of Lisa's' favourite actor?
1. Javier Bardem
2. Antonio Banderas
3. Pedro Almodovar
4. Paco Millas

What kind of film are they going to watch?
1. Un drama
2. Una comedia
3. Una película romántica
4. Un musical

UN LAGO Y MILLONES DE ESTRELLAS

Amanda no creía que pasar cuatro días en aquella **cabaña** fuera a ser un gran plan.
Un lugar apartado de la civilización sin nada que hacer en todo el día.
Amanda había pasado toda su vida en la gran ciudad y no podía imaginar mejor manera de pasar el fin de semana que yendo de tiendas y pasando la noche bailando y bebiendo con sus amigos en el club.
Se sentía muy **urbanita** y, por tanto, fuera de lugar cuando se alejaba de la urbe.
Pero sus amigos habían organizado una **escapada** a un apartado lugar en la orilla de un aislado lago y ella tuvo que apuntarse para no quedarse sola en la ciudad durante todos aquellos días.
Fue a **regañadientes** y no paró de quejarse durante todo el viaje: que si el calor, que si los mosquitos, que si el aburrimiento...
Y **para colmo de males**, cuando deshacía el equipaje se dio cuenta de que había olvidado su móvil en casa.
¡Cuatro días en una cabaña sin televisión, internet ni móvil! Esa iba a ser una prueba muy dura de superar.
Se tumbó en la cama **fastidiada** y pasada casi una hora se dio cuenta que no había nadie en casa. Todos sus amigos habían salido así que se puso unas sandalias y salió en su busca.

No fue difícil encontrarlos porque las voces y risas de todos ellos se podían escuchar desde el porche de la casa. Giró a la izquierda y rodeando la cabaña pudo verlos en el lago, jugando en el agua, nadando y saltando desde el **embarcadero**.

Amanda no pudo evitar sonreír porque no era habitual ver a sus amigos disfrutar de aquella manera. Se acercó lentamente hacia el embarcadero y se detuvo a unos pocos metros para observar como el sol se reflejaba en el agua, cuya superficie emitía unos preciosos destellos dorados. Hacía tiempo que no veía algo tan objetivamente bello y no pudo evitar estremecerse.

¡Corre, ven aquí Amanda! ¡El agua está deliciosa! – gritaron sus amigos cuando se percataron de su presencia.

Amanda sonrió, se deshizo de las sandalias de una patada, dejó caer el vestido por sus hombros y corrió hacia el final del embarcadero. ¡Allá voy! -exclamó mientras saltaba y se **zambullía** en medio de todo el grupo.

El agua estaba inesperadamente fría, pero esa sensación tan refrescante la invadió de energía y optimismo.

Por primera vez en muchos años, volvió a sentirse una niña sin más preocupaciones que disfrutar del momento.

Cuando más tarde, todos se secaban alrededor de una hoguera, ella tuvo que admitir lo equivocada que estaba. ¡Estar en medio de aquel paraje era fantástico!

¡Mirad, mirad el cielo! – exclamó Amanda señalando por encima de sus cabezas.

Todos callaron y observaron cómo millones de estrellas refulgían en aquel infinito tapiz que era el cielo nocturno.

Tras unos minutos de asombrado silencio, Rebecca, que estaba sentada a su lado, preguntó: ¿Verdad que este espectáculo no puedes contemplarlo en la ciudad, Amanda?

Amanda la miró, sonrió tímidamente, y dijo:

No hay nada comparable en el mundo. ¡La naturaleza es increíble!

A LAKE AND MILLIONS OF STARS (translation)

Amanda didn't think that spending four days in that cabin would be a great plan.
A place away from civilization with nothing to do throughout the day.
Amanda had spent her entire life in the big city and could not imagine a better way to spend the weekend than going shopping and spending the night dancing and drinking with her friends at the club.
She felt very urban and, therefore, out of place when she moved away from the city.
But her friends had organized a getaway to a isolated place on the shore of a lake and she had to sign up not to be alone in the city for all those days.

He was reluctantly and did not stop complaining during the whole trip: if the heat, if the mosquitoes, if the boredom ...
And to make matters worse, when she unpacked her luggage she realized that had forgotten her mobile phone at home.
4 days in a cabin without television, internet or mobile! That was going to be a very hard test to overcome.
She laid in bed annoyed and after almost an hour she realized that there was no one at home. All her friends had left so she put on some sandals and went looking for them.
It was not difficult to find them because the voices and laughter of all of them could be heard from the porch of the house. She turned left and went around the cabin from where she could see them in the lake, playing in the water, swimming and jumping from the pier.
Amanda couldn't help smiling because it wasn't usual to see her friends enjoy that way. She approached slowly towards the pier and stopped a few meters to observe how the sun was reflected in the water, whose surface emitted precious golden sparkles. She had not seen something so objectively beautiful in a while and could not help but shudder.
Run, come here Amanda! The water is delicious! -her friends shouted when they noticed her presence.
Amanda smiled, got rid of the sandals with a kick, dropped the dress down her shoulders and ran towards the end of the pier. I'm going there! -she exclaimed as she jumped and dived in the middle of the whole group.
The water was unexpectedly cold, but that refreshing sensation invaded her with energy and optimism.
For the first time in many years, she felt again a little girl with no more worries than enjoying the moment.
When everyone later dried around a bonfire, she had to admit how wrong she was.
Being in the middle of that place was fantastic!
Look, look at the sky! - Amanda exclaimed pointing over their heads.
Everyone was silent and watched as millions of stars glowed in that infinite tapestry that was the night sky.
After a few minutes of astonished silence, Rebecca, who was sitting next to her, asked: truth that this spectacle cannot be seen in the city, Amanda?
Amanda looked at her, smiled shyly, and said:
There is nothing comparable in the world. Nature is amazing!

Notes from the text:

Cabaña: cabin
Un lugar apartado: a remote place
Urbanita: urban
Escapada: getaway
Regañadientes: grudging
Para colmo de males: it's an expresión to say that is the worst of the worst
Fastidiada: annoyed
Embarcadero: pier
Zambullía: from "zambullirse" (to dive)

Questions about the text:

Who is complaining about everything?
1. Araceli
2. Rebecca
3. Amanda
4. Astrid

What has Amanda forgotten?
1. El ordenador portátil
2. El teléfono móvil
3. El cargador
4. El cepillo de dientes

Where were they swimming?
1. En una playa
2. En un rio
3. En un lago
4. En una cala

Where were they allocated?
1. En una cabaña
2. En un camping
3. En un hotel
4. En un refugio

EMPEZAR DE NUEVO

Jen se sentó en la única silla vacía de la sala y observó al resto de **candidatos** que, como ella, venían a la entrevista de trabajo.
Algunos repasaban sus notas mientras otros se limitaban a esperar **con la mirada perdida en el infinito**, probablemente repasando mentalmente los detalles de sus currículums.
Al cabo de unos pocos minutos, vino a buscarla una mujer de **mediana edad** y la acompañó a una sala contigua.
La sala estaba ocupada en su mayoría por una gran mesa alargada. La señora, que dijo llamarse Olga, la invitó a sentarse a la vez que ella ocupaba el asiento de enfrente.
Jen empezó a sentir un creciente nerviosismo mientras su **interlocutora** repasaba los documentos que Jen le había entregado. Básicamente el resumen de toda su carrera profesional y académica.
- ¿**Puedo tutearte**, Jen? -empezó preguntando la señora con una sonrisa-.
- Por supuesto señora -contestó Jen intentando emular la sonrisa de Olga-.
- Gracias y, por favor, tutéame tú también. Veamos… veo que no tienes demasiada experiencia en este sector -empezó diciendo Olga-.
- No, la verdad es que no la tengo. He invertido muchos años en una carrera profesional que no me satisfacía y ahora he decidido intentar empezar de cero en un trabajo que me apasiona, como el que vosotros ofrecéis -respondió Jen con toda sinceridad-.
- ¿Y por qué crees que debería considerarte como opción si varios de los candidatos que he entrevistado hoy tienen una vasta experiencia en este trabajo? -inquirió Olga-.

- Porque creo que el mayor valor de un trabajador es el interés genuino que el trabajo le suscita. Y eso es indiscutible en mi caso. He dejado un puesto muy bien pagado porque no me motivaba. Prefiero empezar de nuevo si ello conlleva volver a levantarme feliz por las mañanas. El dinero es secundario.
- Entiendo lo que dices, Jen. Suena muy razonable, pero si te contrato a ti pierdo la experiencia que otros pueden aportar... -replicó Olga-.
- Sí, lo sé. Yo puedo intentar suplir esa carencia a través de mi **involucración**, pero, sinceramente, no hay mucho más que pueda ofrecer en este momento -dijo Jen bajando la mirada hacia sus manos-.
- Recuerdo que cuando era joven como tú, fui **rechazada** por alguien que creía que la pasión era inútil en el trabajo -empezó a decir Olga mientras se recostaba informalmente en la silla-.
- Vaya -acertó a decir Jen desconcertada por la franqueza de su interlocutora-.
- Pero, en realidad, aprendí algo de esa experiencia negativa.
- ¿El qué? -preguntó Jen.
- En no cometer los mismos errores que otros habían cometido conmigo -respondió Olga irguiéndose sobre la silla-. He entrevistado a varias personas hoy, pero tú has sido la primera que has mostrado interés por el trabajo de por sí antes que por las **condiciones económicas**.
- Me halaga que pienses eso -le interrumpió Jen mientras se sonrojaba levemente-.
- Creo que voy a apostar por ti, Jen -dijo Olga poniéndose en pie-. Todavía tengo que hacer un par de entrevistas, pero si nada cambia, y apuesto que no, mañana tendrás una llamada mía.

Olga se despidió rápidamente y, cuando desapareció de la sala, Jen no pudo evitar soltar una exclamación de alegría.

Salió al vestíbulo y se despidió ruborizada de la recepcionista que, sin ninguna, duda habría oído su grito.

START AGAIN (translation)

Jen sat in the only empty chair in the room and watched the rest of the candidates who, like her, came to the job interview.
Some of them reviewed their notes while others simply waited with their eyes lost in the infinite, probably mentally reviewing the details of their resume.
After a few minutes, a middle-aged woman came looking for her and accompanied her to an adjoining room.
The room was mostly occupied by a large table. The lady, who said her name was Olga,

invited her to sit down while she sat down in the front seat.

Jen began to feel a growing nervousness while her interlocutor reviewed the documents Jen had given her. Basically, the summary of her entire professional and academic career.

- Can I call you just Jen? She began asking with a smile.

"Of course, madam, -Jen replied, trying to emulate Olga's smile.

- Thank you and please you can too. Let's see... I see you don't have much experience in this sector -Olga began.

- No, truth is that I don't have it. I have invested many years in a professional career that did not satisfy me and now I have decided to start from scratch in a job that I am passionate about, like the one you offer -Jen answered sincerely.

- And why do you think I should consider you as an option if several of the candidates I have interviewed today have a lot of experience in this job? -asked Olga.

- Because I believe that the greatest value of a worker is the genuine interest that work arouses. And that is indisputable in my case. I've left a very well-paid position because it didn't motivate me. I prefer to start over if that means getting up happy again in the morning. The money is secondary.

- I understand what you say, Jen. Sounds very reasonable. But if I hire you I lose the experience that others can bring... -Olga replied.

- Yes I know. I can try to make up for that lack through my involvement, but, honestly, there isn't much else I can offer right now -Jen said, looking down at her hands.

I remember when I was young like you, I was rejected by someone who believed that passion was useless at work -Olga began as she reclined informally in her chair.

Oh -Jen said, puzzled by the frankness of her interlocutor.

- But actually I learned something from that negative experience.

- What? -asked Jen.

In not making the same mistakes others had made with me -Olga replied, standing up on the chair. I have interviewed several people today, but you have been the first to show interest in the work itself rather than the economic conditions.

I'm flattered that you think that -Jen interrupted as she blushed slightly.

I think I'm going to bet on you, Jen -Olga said, standing up. I still have to do a couple of interviews, but if nothing changes, and I bet not, tomorrow you will have a call from me.

Olga said goodbye quickly and, when she disappeared from the meeting room, Jen couldn't help but let out an exclamation of joy.

She went out into the lobby and said blushed goodbye to the receptionist, who, without any doubt, would have heard her scream.

Notes from the text:

Candidatos: candidates
Con la mirada perdida en el infinito: This expresión means that someone is looking at no specific point.
Mediana edad: middle age
Interlocutora: interlocutor
Puedo tutearte: "Tutear" is the verb that in Spanish we use to ask permission to use the pronoun "tú" instead of the formal pronoun "usted".
Involucración: involvement
Rechazada: rejected
Condiciones económicas: economic conditions

Questions about the text:

What was the interviewer's name?
1. Samantha
2. Olga
3. Rose
4. Emma

What was the interviewee's name?
1. Jane
2. Jen
3. Joe
4. Jace

Did Jen have a lot of experience in that field?
1. No
2. Si, dos años
3. Si, tres años
4. Si, diez años

How is the table where they were talking?
1. Pequeña
2. Redonda
3. Alargada
4. Cuadrada

UN CACHORRITO LLAMADO KEN

Riley no cabía en sí de emoción. Tras su fiesta de cumpleaños con los amigos, volvió a casa con sus padres y estos le dieron su regalo. Una gran caja sin **envoltorio** ni lazo. ¡Una caja que, de hecho, se movía!

Riley retiró la tapa con cuidado y vio los ojitos de un cachorrito de perro que le observaban desde el interior. Era un perrito mezcla de razas y era precioso. Imposible no cogerlo en brazos y **acunarlo**.

¿Qué edad tiene? ¿Cómo se llama? – preguntó Riley a sus padres sin apartar la vista de su nuevo amiguito.

Tiene solo 3 meses y no tiene nombre. **¡Está esperando que tú le pongas uno!** - respondieron sus padres al unísono.

Pero no sé cómo llamarlo -dijo Riley mostrándose preocupado.

Te voy a contar un secreto -dijo su madre-, si sabes escuchar con atención, el **perrito** te dirá su nombre muy pronto.

¡Pero si los perros no hablan! -exclamó el niño.

No hablan nuestro idioma, pero saben comunicarse de otra manera. La clave es estar atento y saber escuchar -añadió el padre **guiñándole** el ojo a su hijo-.

Riley pensó que sus padres le estaban intentando tomar el pelo, pero no se daban cuenta de que él ya no era ningún niño ingenuo. ¡Ya había cumplido 10 años!

Mientras los padres preparaban la cena, Riley estuvo jugando con el perrito. Era muy torpe y divertido. Ambos iban a ser grandes amigos.

¿Por qué me habéis regalado un perrito ahora después de tantos años pidiéndolo? - preguntó Riley a sus padres.

No quisimos hacerlo antes, hijo, porque un perrito no es un juguete. Es un ser vivo que va a formar parte de la familia, como tú o nosotros -contestó la madre-. Criarlo conlleva

una gran responsabilidad y pensamos que ahora que ya eres tan mayor, ya podíamos confiar en ti y en que ibas a cuidarlo como si fuera tu hermanito.
Sí, tiene sentido lo que dices -dijo Riley-, ahora que soy mayor ya puedo asumir grandes responsabilidades. Prometo que velaré siempre por él, le daré de comer, le sacaré de paseo, le lavaré, jugaré con él y le querré siempre.
Mira, Riley, el perrito mueve la colita. Creo que está contento por lo que acabas de decir -dijo el padre mientras **señalaba** al animal con el dedo-.
Riley miró al perrito y sonrió. El animalito le devolvió la mirada y, **súbitamente**, Riley se quedó serio y en silencio. Giró la cara hacia sus padres y les dijo: se llama Ken.
¿Ken? ¿Cómo lo sabes? -preguntó su padre
No sé... pero lo sé -respondió Riley dubitativo-.
De repente abrió mucho los ojos y añadió: ¡teníais razón, de alguna manera me lo ha dicho!
Desde aquel preciso instante, Riley fue consciente del tipo de comunicación que puede establecerse entre una persona y su mascota. Si la relación es muy estrecha, ¡no hacen falta palabras para entenderse!

A PUPPY CALLED KEN

Riley was very excited. After his birthday party with friends, he returned home with his parents and they gave him his gift. A large box without wrapping or bow. A box that, in fact, moved!
Riley carefully removed the lid and saw the eyes of a dog puppy watching from inside. It was a puppy mix of breeds and was beautiful. Impossible not to take it in your arms and cradle it.
How old are you? What is your name? - Riley asked her parents without looking away from her new friend.
He is only 3 months old and has no name. He is waiting for you to put one on him! -their parents answered in unison.
But I don't know how to call him -said Riley, looking worried.
I'm going to tell you a secret -said his mother-, if you can listen carefully, the puppy will tell you his name very soon.
But if dogs don't talk! -exclaimed the boy.
They don't speak our language, but they know how to communicate differently. The key is to be attentive and know how to listen -the father added, winking at his son.
Riley thought his parents were trying to tease him, but they didn't realize that he was no longer a naive child. He had already turned 10!
While the parents prepared dinner, Riley was playing with the puppy. It was very clumsy

and fun. Both were going to be great friends.

Why have you given me a puppy now after so many years asking for it? -Riley asked his parents.

We didn't want to do it before, son, because a puppy is not a toy. It is a living being who is going to be part of the family, like you or us -said the mother-. Raising him carries a great responsibility and we think that now that you are so old, we could already trust you and that you were going to take care of him as if he were your little brother.

Yes, what you say makes sense -Riley said-, now that I am older, I can take on great responsibilities. I promise that I will always watch over him, feed him, take him out for a walk, wash him, play with him and love him forever.

Look, Riley, the puppy moves the tail. I think he is happy for what you just said -said the father, pointing at the animal with his finger-.

Riley looked at the puppy and smiled. The little animal looked back at him and, suddenly, Riley was serious and silent. He turned his face to his parents and said: his name is Ken.

Ken? How do you know? asked his father

I don't know… but I know, "Riley replied hesitantly.

Suddenly he opened his eyes wide and added: you were right, somehow he told me!

From that precise moment, Riley was aware of the type of communication that can be established between a person and his pet. If the relationship is very close, no words are needed to understand each other!

Notes from the text:

Envoltorio: wrapping
Acunarlo: from the verb "acunar" to cradle
¡Está esperando que tú le pongas uno! In this expresión the verb "poner" to put means to get a name for the puppy
Perrito: Little dog
Guiñándole: winking
Señalaba: from the verb "señalar", to point
Súbitamente: suddenly

Questions about the text:
How old is Riley?
1. 8
2. 9
3. 10
4. 11

What is the puppy's name?
1. Arthur
2. Ken
3. Jack
4. Tristan

Where did Riley find the puppy?
1. En una caja
2. En una tienda
3. En la calle
4. En un prado

What was the special occasion?
1. El cumpleaños de la madre
2. El cumpleaños del padre
3. El cumpleaños de Riley
4. El cumpleaños de Ken

PADRE E HIJO

Robert miraba a su padre mientras hablaba, aunque no le oía.

De vez en cuando movía su cabeza en señal de **asentimiento** evitando, así, que su padre **advirtiera** que no estaba escuchando.

Robert no quería ser **maleducado**, pero había escuchado el mismo discurso decenas de veces. Básicamente una sucesión de las virtudes que la carrera de abogacía aportaría al indeciso Robert en su futuro. Su padre era abogado y siempre había deseado que su hijo siguiera sus pasos profesionales. Robert, sin embargo, no sentía el menor interés en un trabajo que implicaba moverse de oficina en oficina enfundado en traje y corbata.

Había pasado los dos últimos veranos trabajando como guarda forestal voluntario en los bosques del norte, y el amor por ellos y por la naturaleza en general habían prendido en él de tal manera que sabía que cualquier cosa que hiciera en el futuro implicaría trabajar en la naturaleza.

Y no, la abogacía no parecía **encajar** bien en ese **anhelo**.

Cuando su padre terminó el discurso preguntando, una vez más, ¿y tú cómo lo ves?, Robert se quedó callado, pero, por una vez, evitó contestar con una evasiva.

¿Recuerdas cuando me decías que una persona debe guiarse siempre por sus pasiones? – preguntó mirando a su padre directamente a los ojos-.

¡Claro que lo recuerdo! Lo decía y lo seguiría diciendo porque es lo que pienso – contestó su padre **sin dudar ni un instante** -.

Lo sé. Por eso escogiste ser abogado -añadió Robert- y, por esa misma razón, yo no puedo escoger esa carrera…

El padre se sentó en una silla enfrente de Robert, entrelazó sus dedos y escuchó con atención las palabras de su hijo. No osó **interrumpirle** porque, como buen abogado, sabía lo importante que era escuchar para extraer las conclusiones apropiadas.

Y no solo escuchar sino, también, observar el lenguaje no verbal del interlocutor, mirarle a los ojos, respetar sus silencios. Porque un buen abogado no solo sabía de leyes. Un buen abogado era un buen psicólogo que sabía leer a las personas. A sus clientes, a los jueces y fiscales, a los jurados.

Y el padre de Robert era un buen abogado.

Y Robert no era un cliente sino la persona más importante en su vida.

Y por eso escuchó con tanta atención. Y por eso se tomó su tiempo antes de replicar.

Y su primera respuesta no fue una palabra. Su primera respuesta fue una sonrisa.

Tímida al principio y radiante después.

Su hijo había hecho un alegato en defensa de sí mismo y su amor a la naturaleza preciso e incontestable.

Puedes llevar corbata o puedes llevar camiseta, no importa, lo único que importa es creer en lo que haces, dejar que sea el amor el que te guíe y no los anhelos de otras personas -pensó el padre para sí-.

¿Por qué sonríes papá? – inquirió Robert extrañado y divertido a la vez-.

Sonrío por un par de razones, hijo. La primera es porque tienes razón y has sabido convencerme con mis propios **argumentos**.

¿Y la segunda, papá? – preguntó Robert.

¡La segunda es que me acabas de dar una lección de cómo un abogado debe defender una causa! -contestó el padre antes de soltar una sonora **carcajada**.

FATHER AND SON (translation)

Robert looked at his father as he spoke, although he did not hear him.
Occasionally he shook his head in assent, to prevent his father from warning that he was not listening.
Robert didn't want to be rude, but he had heard the same speech dozens of times. Basically, a succession of the virtues that the legal profession would bring to the undecided Robert in his future. His father was a lawyer and had always wanted his son to follow his professional steps. Robert, however, had no interest in a job that involved moving from office to office wearing a suit and a tie.
He had spent the last two summers working as a volunteer forest ranger in the northern forests, and the love he feels for them and for nature in general had caught him in such a way that he knew that whatever he did in the future would involve working in nature .

And no, the advocacy did not seem to fit well in that desire.

When his father finished the speech asking, once again, and how do you see it?, Robert was silent, but, for once, he avoided answering with an evasion.

Do you remember when you told me that a person should always be guided by his passions? - He asked looking his father straight in the eye.

Of course I remember! -he said- and I would keep saying it because that is what I think - his father replied without hesitation.

I know. That's why you chose to be a lawyer -Robert added- and, for that very reason, I can't choose that career.

The father sat in a chair in front of Robert, laced his fingers and listened carefully to his son's words. He dared not interrupt him because, as a good lawyer, he knew how important it was to listen to draw the appropriate conclusions.

And not only listen but also observe the nonverbal language of the interlocutor, look into his eyes, respect his silences. Because a good lawyer not only knew about laws. A good lawyer was a good psychologist who could read people. To their clients, to judges and prosecutors, to jurors.

And Robert's father was a good lawyer.

And Robert was not a client but the most important person in his life.

And that's why he listened so carefully. And that's why he took his time before replying. And his first answer was not a word. His first response was a smile. Shy at first and radiant later.

His son had made a precise and incontestable plea in defence of himself and his love for the nature.

You can wear a tie or you can wear a t-shirt, it doesn't matter, all that matters is believing in what you do, letting it be love that guides you and not the desires of other people -thought the father to himself-.

Why do you smile dad? -asked Robert, surprised and amused at the same time.

I smile for a couple of reasons, son. First because you're right and you've managed to convince me with my own arguments.

And the second one, dad? -Robert asked.

The second is that you just gave me a lesson on how a lawyer should defend a case! -the father replied before releasing a loud laugh.

Notes from the text:

Asentimiento: from "asentir" to assent

Advirtiera: from "advertir" to warn
Maleducado: impolite
Encajar: to fit in
Anhelo: desire
Sin dudar ni un instante: with no doubt
Interrumpirle: interrupt him
Argumentos: arguments
Carcajada: laugh

Questions about the text:

What wants Robert's father for him?
1. Ser abogado
2. Ser medico
3. Ser arquitecto
4. Ser maestro

What Roberts desires to work with instead of that?
1. Naturaleza
2. Coches
3. Tecnología
4. Ordenadores

What is Robert's father profession?
1. Abogado
2. Juez
3. Profesor
4. Piloto

Where Robert was volunteering?
1. En los bosques del Sur
2. En America del Norte
3. En los bosques del Norte
4. En Oceania

We really hope you enjoyed this Bundle, customer satisfaction for us is very important.
If you found this book useful in any way, a review on Amazon is always appreciated! ☺

THANK YOU

Copyright © 2022

- Marissa Noble & Juan Mendez -

All rights reserved.

Printed in Great Britain
by Amazon